DECOLONIZING AND INDIGENIZING EDUCATION IN CANADA

DECOLONIZING AND INDIGENIZING EDUCATION IN CANADA

*Edited by Sheila Cote-Meek
and Taima Moeke-Pickering*

Toronto | Vancouver

Decolonizing and Indigenizing Education in Canada
Edited by Sheila Cote-Meek and Taima Moeke-Pickering

First published in 2020 by
Canadian Scholars, an imprint of CSP Books Inc.
425 Adelaide Street West, Suite 200
Toronto, Ontario
M5V 3C1

www.canadianscholars.ca

Copyright © 2020 Sheila Cote-Meek, Taima Moeke-Pickering, the contributing authors, and Canadian Scholars.

All rights reserved. No part of this publication may be reproduced, stored in a retrieval system, or transmitted, in any form or by any means, without the prior written permission of Canadian Scholars, under licence or terms from the appropriate reproduction rights organization, or as expressly permitted by law.

Every reasonable effort has been made to identify copyright holders. Canadian Scholars would be pleased to have any errors or omissions brought to its attention.

Library and Archives Canada Cataloguing in Publication

Title: Decolonizing and indigenizing education in Canada / edited by Sheila Cote-Meek and Taima Moeke-Pickering.
Names: Cote-Meek, Sheila, 1957- editor. | Moeke-Pickering, Taima, 1961- editor.
Description: Includes bibliographical references and index.
Identifiers: Canadiana (print) 20200193759 | Canadiana (ebook) 20200193775 |
    ISBN 9781773381817 (softcover) | ISBN 9781773381831 (PDF) |
    ISBN 9781773381824 (EPUB)
Subjects: LCSH: Indigenous peoples—Education—Canada. | LCSH: Indigenous peoples—Education—Canada—History. | LCSH: Indigenous peoples—Canada—Intellectual life. | LCSH: Culturally relevant pedagogy—Canada. | CSH: Native peoples—Education—Canada. | CSH: Native peoples—Education—Canada—History. | CSH: Native peoples—Canada—Intellectual life.
Classification: LCC E96.2 .D43 2020 | DDC 371.829/97071—dc23

Cover art: Patrick Cheechoo
Cover design: Rafael Chimicatti
Page layout: S4Carlisle Publishing Services

Printed and bound in Ontario, Canada

Canada

ABOUT THE COVER ART

ARTWORK: *KOOKUM'S FLOWERS*

Kookum's Flowers is a tribute to my late Kookum Lottie Bird (Constance Lake First Nation). Kookum was a master beader, and I remain blessed that she generously shared her knowledges with me. Painting flowers is an embodiment of the time we spent together, and I feel strengthened as we (re)visit through this generational enactment of art creation. It is my opinion that the methodology behind art creation travels from generation to generation, through hands-on approaches that are accompanied by storytelling and language teachings. Through the imagery of *Kookum's Flowers*, we are reminded that Indigenous Peoples are connected to all our relations as we embody teachings and traditions. It is through our own worldviews that we generate and hold space within post-secondary institutions for the new generations of Indigenous scholars who bring their collective Indigenous Knowledges and expand the trail for generations to come.

ARTIST: PATRICK CHEECHOO

Patrick Cheechoo and his wife, Dr. Keri Cheechoo, are proud parents of five adult children and Kookum and Mooshum to two wonderful grandchildren. Mr. Cheechoo is Mushkego (James Bay Cree) from Constance Lake First Nation. Patrick loves to sketch, paint, carve, and create unique jewellery from organic materials such as antler, wood, and bark. He is also an avid wildlife photographer and an award-winning graphic design artist.

We honour those Indigenous educators who came before us for laying a strong foundation for Indigenous education. To all the Indigenous educators and allies who currently work in the academic system, we hope that this book supports your scholarly work and provides some assurance that you are not alone. To the Academy: We hope that you pick up your part in transforming the post-secondary education system to provide a rightful place for Indigenous education.

CONTENTS

Preface   *ix*

Introduction: From Colonized Classrooms to Transformative Change in the
Academy: We Can and Must Do Better!   xi
Sheila Cote–Meek

THEME 1: INDIGENOUS EPISTEMOLOGIES: EXPLORING THE PLACE OF INDIGENOUS KNOWLEDGES IN POST-SECONDARY CURRICULUM, INCLUDING INDIGENIZATION OF THE CURRICULUM AND PEDAGOGY

Chapter 1   *Askiy Kiskinwahamākēwina*: Reclaiming Land-Based
Pedagogies in the Academy   3
Angelina Weenie

Chapter 2   Gii Aanikoobijigan Mindimooyehn: Decolonizing Views of
Anishinaabekwe   19
Patricia D. McGuire

Chapter 3   Reconciliation through Métissage   31
Bryanna Rae Scott

Chapter 4   Indigenous Thinkers: Decolonizing and Transforming the
Academy through Indigenous Relationality   51
Candace Kaleimamoowahinekapu Galla and Amanda Holmes

Chapter 5   Thinking with Kihkipiw: Exploring an Indigenous Theory of
Assessment and Evaluation for Teacher Education   73
Dr. Evelyn Steinhauer, Dr. Trudy Cardinal, Dr. Marc Higgins,
Dr. Brooke Madden, Dr. Noella Steinhauer, Dr. Patricia Steinhauer,
Misty Underwood, and Angela Wolfe, with Elder Bob Cardinal

Chapter 6   Centring the Lived Struggle of Indigenous Women in the
Academy: A Performance Autoethnography   91
Celeste Pedri–Spade

viii Contents

THEME 2: DECOLONIZING POST-SECONDARY INSTITUTIONS: BUILDING SPACE IN THE ACADEMY FOR INDIGENOUS PEOPLES, RESISTANCE, AND RECONCILIATION

Chapter 7 Is Decolonization Possible in the Academy?   117
Lynn Lavallee

Chapter 8 The Dynamics of Decolonization and Indigenization in an Era of Academic "Reconciliation"   135
Emily Grafton and Jérôme Melançon

Chapter 9 Urban and Inner-City Studies: Decolonizing Ourselves and the University of Winnipeg   155
Chantal Fiola and Shauna MacKinnon

Chapter 10 Speaking Back to the Institution: Teacher Education Programs as Sites of Possibility   175
Fiona Purton, Sandra Styres, and Arlo Kempf

Chapter 11 "If Not Here, Where?": Making Decolonization a Priority at an Undergraduate University   193
Mary Ellen Donnan, Avril Aitken, and Jean L. Manore

Chapter 12 Reconciliation Rainbows and the Promise of Education: Teaching Truth and Redress in Neocolonial Canada   211
Michelle Coupal

Chapter 13 Decolonizing Non-Indigenous Faculty and Students: Beyond Comfortable Diversity   229
Linda Pardy and Brett Pardy

Chapter 14 Reframing Reconciliation: Turning Our Back or Turning Back?   247
Keri Cheechoo

Chapter 15 The Future for Indigenous Education: How Social Media Is Changing Our Relationships in the Academy   267
Taima Moeke-Pickering

Contributor Biographies   279
Index   285

PREFACE

As co-editors, we have been working in the area of decolonizing education for over 25 years as students, professors, program developers, administrators, and activists. While in life we both took up topics relating to Indigenous education much earlier, which included interrogating the impact of colonization and examining ways to decolonize, as Indigenous educators we have both been committed to bringing about systemic change to educational institutions.

More recently, post-release of the Truth and Reconciliation Commission (TRC) report and 94 Calls to Action (2015), there has been critical attention to how the academy can respond and meet the educational needs of Indigenous communities. There have also been critiques on how to respond to the TRC in a meaningful and sustained way. Integral to this discussion is working through what decolonization and indigenization means in the academy, both theoretically and in more concrete terms, and how the strategic initiatives that have been developed to respond to the TRC can be concrete, meaningful, and sustained.

LAYOUT OF THE BOOK

In total, this edited book features 16 chapters written by a wide range of authors, Indigenous and non-Indigenous, from across 14 Canadian universities, whose positions include Full Professors, Associate Professors, Assistant Professors, PhD candidates, Elders, and Administrative Assistants. Authors share their experiences and provide diverse perspectives on what it means to decolonize and indigenize the academy. The diversity is also reflected in various contributors' approaches to their writing and therefore includes chapters that tackle decolonization and indigenization from a theoretical lens, others that take a case-study approach providing concrete examples of pedagogical and curricular practices, and still others that utilize poetry and storytelling. The chapters in this book underscore how definitions of decolonization and indigenization vary across a spectrum of initiatives and institutions. Broad concepts often have a variety of interpretations and applications depending on situations. The expansive nature of these varying definitions also highlights overlaps. This book therefore offers a range of definitions that assist with understanding the complexities of decolonization and indigenization.

In order to ensure consistency in approach, each author or series of co-authors situates themselves in their work, providing the reader a better understanding of their lens, context, and definitions. The end of each chapter includes additional readings and websites as well as a series of questions designed to enhance a deeper and critical understanding of the chapter and facilitate further thought and discussion. The intent is to reflect and think critically about how we can do education differently. Each chapter also includes a glossary of terms. These terms are bolded within the chapter.

This edited volume will be useful across a range of undergraduate and graduate courses and programs that discuss the complexities of decolonization and indigenization, including Indigenous studies, education, social work, health and social sciences, and humanities. It will also have applications in other fields, including health and justice.

An introductory chapter by Cote-Meek is followed by 15 chapters subdivided into two themes: Indigenous Epistemologies: Exploring the Place of Indigenous Knowledges in Post-Secondary Curriculum, Including Indigenization of the Curriculum and Pedagogy; and Decolonizing Post-Secondary Institutions: Building Space in the Academy for Indigenous Peoples, Resistance, and Reconciliation. The introductory chapter situates the current educational institutional responses to the TRC (2015) within the context about why decolonization and indigenization are important and links these to larger transformative changes that are necessary in the academy. The chapter also contextualizes the chapters that follow.

The final chapter by Moeke-Pickering provides a critical lens on the future of Indigenous education. She emphasizes that decolonizing and Indigenizing strategies must incorporate technology. As co-editors of the book, we situated the opening and closing chapters to serve as bookends.

—Sheila Cote-Meek and Taima Moeke-Pickering

INTRODUCTION

From Colonized Classrooms to Transformative Change in the Academy: We Can and Must Do Better!

Sheila Cote-Meek

> Justice Murray Sinclair statement: "Education is what got us into this mess—the use of education at least in terms of residential schools—but education is the key to reconciliation."
> —*Watters, 2015*

In Canada, most, if not all, post-secondary institutions are in the process of dialogue and engagement on how best to respond to the Truth and Reconciliation Commission of Canada's (TRC) 94 Calls to Action (2015). There is no doubt that the TRC (2015) has been important in terms of mobilizing action. The TRC calls on post-secondary institutions to engage in the reconciliation process and essentially lead change in education that promotes awareness and understanding and importantly integrates Indigenous histories, knowledges, and pedagogies in the classroom. Recognizing that there are long-standing colonial practices that remain deeply entrenched within the educational system, there are significant challenges and complexities in bringing about meaningful change. This introductory chapter explores critical questions about what might constitute an appropriate pedagogical and institutional response within a decolonizing and indigenizing frame of reference in order to conceptualize how we can bring about sustained transformative change to the post-secondary educational system. Like all the authors in this book, it is important to situate myself before going further.

SITUATING SELF

Boozhoo, Kwe kwe Semaa Kwe ndishnikaaz, Mukwa dodem, Tema-Augama Anishnabai. My spirit name is Tobacco woman, I come from the Bear clan and come from the Teme-Augama Anishnabai, the people of the deep water. I introduce myself in my own language so that, as a reader, you know who I am and how I am connected to this land. It also provides clues about my path and purpose in life. I have worked in Indigenous education for 30 years and, over the course of that time, have always been a strong advocate for change at the post-secondary level—to make education more accessible and meaningful for Indigenous learners. My passion is rooted in who I am and life experiences that include confronting racism at an early age and witnessing countless examples of racism directed to my siblings, family, and friends. This introductory chapter draws on some of my experiences, both personal and academic, to provide some strategies to consider in bringing about change. This chapter also builds upon some of my earlier work in my book *Colonized Classrooms: Racism, Trauma and Resistance in Post-Secondary Education* (Cote-Meek, 2014). Both myself and my co-editor hope this book will stimulate critical thought and conversations about what we do in the academy and how this impacts Indigenous Peoples.

TERMINOLOGY

It is also important that I touch briefly on the use of terminology. I use the term *Indigenous Peoples* to reflect the United Nations Permanent Forum on Indigenous Issues working definition:

> there are more than 370 million indigenous peoples spread across 70 countries worldwide. Practicing unique traditions, they retain social, cultural, economic and political characteristics that are distinct from those of the dominant societies in which they live ... [Indigenous Peoples are the] descendants—according to a common definition—of those who inhabited a country or a geographical region at the time when people of different cultures or ethnic origins arrived. The new arrivals became dominant through conquest, occupation, settlement or other means. (Secretariat, Permanent Forum on Indigenous Issues 2009, n.p.)

In Canada, First Nations, Métis, and Inuit are recognized as Indigenous Peoples. It is also important to recognize that there are many Nations of

Indigenous Peoples in Canada, each with their own culture, tradition, and languages. This distinction is important because the stories, languages, cultures, and worldviews held by a Nation are unique.

COLONIZED CLASSROOMS

In reflecting on my work and role in the academy as an academic and as an academic administrator, I often think about what has changed and how far we have or have not moved with respect to inclusion, equity, and diversity, especially where Indigenous Peoples are concerned. I also reflect a lot about reconciliation. What does it mean? And is it even possible? For me, it is difficult to imagine reconciliation without thinking about debwewin, truth. Debwewin is about speaking your truth, from your heart. Have we heard the truth? Have you heard the many truths out there about Canada's history with Indigenous Peoples?

In a paper I co-authored with colleagues Moeke-Pickering, Hardy, Manitowabi, Mawhiney, Faries, Gibson van-Marrewijk, and Taitoko (2006), we discussed the notion of "white amnesia" and defined it as a

> disease rooted in racism [that] is a common strategy used to ignore the historical and ongoing injustices perpetrated on Indigenous peoples. These learned behaviors and associated attitudes stem from a lack of acceptance and continued denial among non-Indigenous academics about their potential roles as anti-colonisers and anti-oppressors. White amnesia allows non-Indigenous peoples to continue in their day to day world without seeing or involving themselves in other worldviews that would challenge their understanding of their oppressive practices. (p. 2)

I have to wonder with all the emphasis on reconciliation (and not truth) whether what is operating is a form of white amnesia, another process to ignore and silence the telling of debwewin. If we do not talk about debwewin, the truth, we will not get to a place of reconciliation. The truth is in the difficult stories, the harder ones to speak out loud. They are the more difficult ones to hear and listen to because they are stories about injustices, abuse, and genocide. They are painful. Importantly, these stories also lay the basis for understanding why we have so much work do and why reconciliation is not a feel-good process or an easy one. They are the stories that easily get forgotten by white amnesia as we barrel on ahead so quickly with reconciliation.

The opening quote from Justice Murray Sinclair, now Senator Murray Sinclair, emphasizes the role that education has played in ongoing colonization and its central role in addressing reconciliation. In order to achieve reconciliation, we also need to understand deeply what colonization is and the impact it has on Indigenous Peoples. Elsewhere, I have defined colonization as having four critical dimensions: "It concerns the land, it requires a specific structure of ideology to proceed, it is violent and it is ongoing" (Cote-Meek, 2014, p. 18). Colonization has always been and continues to be about the land and the resources. See, for example, the Oka crisis of 1990, the more recent dispute in the Wet'suwet'en territory, and in my own territory, Teme Auguama Anishinaabe. Land is still contested.

Briefly, colonization advanced from the East to the West coast of Canada through active appropriation of lands justified through the denigration of Indigenous knowledges and Indigenous Peoples. It is well documented that in order for the colonial project to continue to advance, Indigenous Peoples were reduced as inferior and subordinate. Underlying contestations over land also posit Indigenous Peoples as holding up progress for the benefit of all, which supports the racialized notion of the primitive Other. These racialized constructions include a range of negative attributes that reduce Indigenous Peoples as incapable of taking care of themselves, incapable of taking care of the land, inferior, and ultimately as primitive and standing in the way of progress (Loomba, 1998). The Canadian landscape has often been described as a vast, untouched wilderness (Monet & Skanu'u, 1992), which effectively erased Indigenous Peoples' existence from their lands. These widespread colonial beliefs provided the justification for forced domination and control over the lives of Indigenous Peoples. As a result we are still witnessing government control over the lives of Indigenous Peoples. As Malinda Smith (2013) points out,

> unsettling the durable legacies of settler colonialism will be no easy feat, given the unresolved land claims, chronic under-resourcing of Indigenous health, education, housing; the large numbers of Indigenous children still being removed from homes and placed ineffective child welfare services; the large numbers of Indigenous men and women imprisoned, including for minor infractions; and the violence against women and the growing number of missing and murdered Aboriginal women. (p. 12)

While it is beyond the scope of this introduction to detail the full history of ongoing colonization, suffice it to note that land continues to be highly contested and Indigenous Peoples are always positioned as second-class citizens in their own lands. In order for colonization to continue to advance, the government put in place policies such as the *Indian Act* to take full control of the lives of Indigenous Peoples. Part of taking control also included setting up residential schools where Indigenous culture, languages, and ways of knowing and being were stripped away from the minds of young children under conditions of extreme violence now documented as genocide (Truth and Reconciliation Commission of Canada, 2015). Indigenous knowledges were effectively debased and devalued. This devaluing of Indigenous Peoples and Indigenous knowledges was an intentional act to disrupt our ways of knowing and ways of being and to sever the transmission to the next generation. There is no doubt that educational institutions are still very much colonial institutions with deeply held convictions about what constitutes education, research, and pedagogy. Mihesuah and Wilson (2004) note that one way the academy continues to support ongoing colonization is through maintaining control over access to knowledge and knowledge production. This is done through the devaluing of Indigenous knowledges and Indigenous Peoples.

The academy is also a central site of ongoing colonialism. Goldberg (1993) noted that knowledge is not produced in a vacuum; rather, knowledge producers are situated within a social, political, and economic context that influences and frames mainstream ideologies, values, and beliefs. In this way, knowledge that is produced is reflective of worldviews and epistemologies that often exclude Indigenous worldviews. Research then becomes knowledge produced on and about Indigenous Peoples through a very Westernized, Eurocentric lens. Goldberg (1993) further discussed how "Power is exercised epistemologically in the dual practices of naming and evaluating.... Once defined, order has to be maintained, serviced, extended, operationalized. Naming the racial Other, for all intents and purposes, is the Other" (p. 150). Extending his analysis, Goldberg (1993) noted that "social science of Other established limits of knowledge about the Other, for the Other is just what racialized social science knows. It knows best for the Other ..." (p. 150). Knowledge that is produced through academic research then often not only names the Other but also controls, manages, and directs that research through writing about the Other outside the culture, thus silencing and delegitimizing, in this case, Indigenous voices and worldviews. This is critical to understanding what underlying systemic changes need to be made if we are moving toward decolonizing and indigenizing Western-based institutions.

In addition, we need to document the experiences of Indigenous students and faculty in the academy, which I have done in previous research (Cote-Meek, 2014). Since that research, I have continued to hear countless stories of similar experiences from current Indigenous students and professors. Here are a few examples to make my point. With the introduction of mandatory courses on Indigenous content, there has been a backlash from students who effectively dismiss anything Indigenous, who are disengaged and uninterested in anything that pertains to Indigenous Peoples (Hamilton, 2018). This has created a difficult and challenging learning environment for students who are interested in the content and for Indigenous learners who have to witness and experience inappropriate and often racist commentary about the required course content. In my view, it has only been after these requirements have been instituted that post-secondary institutions have begun to look for ways to mitigate racist commentary in the classrooms and are understanding the critical importance of supports for these initiatives. Another example is witnessing racist graffiti on the office doors of Indigenous colleagues being treated with little action. These examples are indicative of the complexities of initiatives and how these initiatives can further perpetuate the marginalization of Indigenous Peoples in the academy.

Therefore, decolonization is a complex process and will take much time, effort, and systemic changes. Simply defined, it is putting an end to ongoing colonization and addressing the impacts of colonization. It is about returning lands and ending the violence against Indigenous Peoples; this includes addressing racism. It requires a divesting of power back to Indigenous Peoples so that self-determination is fully realized and in a meaningful way. Any transformative change to the academy needs also to address this.

TRANSFORMATIVE CHANGE

What can we do in the academy to engage in debwewin and foster stronger, more respectful communities of learning? What are the possibilities for bringing about a transformative change?

Transformative change is defined in a number of ways. Duffy and Reigeluth (2008) identified six core elements to a transformative systemic change, which include changing the institutional culture, changing the entire institution, change that is intentional and occurs over time, change that creates a system that continually pursues an idealized future for itself, and change that is significant. Similarly, Gass (2010) described transformative change as "profound, fundamental and irreversible. It is a metamorphosis, a radical change from one form to another" (p. 1). Eckel and Kezar (2003) also identified six specific aspects to bring about transformative change to higher education. These include senior administrative support, collaborative leadership, flexible vision, faculty and staff development, and visible action. In another work (Cote-Meek, 2018a), I framed my discussion around a case example of transformative change using the concepts of the Medicine Wheel, which assisted in depicting a change in a more holistic, inclusive, and encompassing manner. Essentially, transformative change is disruptive. It is a change that moves an organization to a drastically different way of being, doing, and working. It is my contention that deep systemic and transformative changes are needed in the post-secondary system if we are ever to achieve reconciliation. Education plays a significant role in shaping the next generation, and it is important that every citizen is aware, has an understanding of, and takes up responsibility for reconciliation. This requires nothing less than transformation of the educational systems and structures. It also begs the question of what might constitute an appropriate pedagogical and institutional response that would move post-secondary institutions toward sustained transformative change.

A critical step in bringing about any change, large or small, is establishing a clear and concrete vision (Cote-Meek, 2018a). We must ask ourselves questions such as: What do we aspire post-secondary institutions to do? What needs to be changed? How do we imagine that change can occur? Are we open to change? What is decolonization? What is indigenization? Will decolonization and indigenization lead to wider systemic change? Wolverton (1998) similarly noted that "leaders and organisations must ask themselves: Do we want this kind of change? Is it necessary? Is our organisation ready for it?" (p. 29). Institutions like universities rely on the development of strategic plans, academic plans, research plans, and departmental/faculty plans. If done well, these plans are integrated and lead to achievable outcomes and have the potential to contribute to change in a big way, depending on how well they are constructed and implemented. If we want transformative change, we need to think big and boldly and imagine what we want in the academy of the future. A critical part of the development of strategic plans is community engagement. Institutions must get better at engaging with First Peoples of this country. Simply put, we as Indigenous Peoples need to be at the table(s) to ensure our voice is heard and included. Indigenous Peoples have not always had a voice in these plans, and if the academy truly wants to take up effort to decolonize and respond to the TRC, they must engage with Indigenous Peoples in concrete ways. The vision can then start including attention to larger systemic issues. For example, explicit strategies to transform the academy have to include: coming to terms with ongoing colonization and racism; increasing access and success for Indigenous Peoples whether they are students, staff, or faculty; addressing the underrepresentation of Indigenous students in particular faculties and disciplines; addressing the underrepresentation of Indigenous faculty and staff across the university, including administration and senior leadership; and addressing ethics in research so they are not barriers for Indigenous students and faculty carrying out research. In fact, many Canadian universities have started initiatives aimed at increasing Indigenous representation in the academy through targeted Indigenous faculty hires, enhancing Indigenous student supports and spaces, increasing Indigenous content in the curriculum, and examining research ethics. Changes such as these require continued supportive actions by many people within the system, from the department, faculty, dean, and senior administration levels. It takes an enormous effort to build support across the system.

Foundational to this process is building relationships. Relationships are vital to creating awareness, building trust, and garnering support in order to mobilize action. Responding to the TRC must be an active and meaningful process that includes concerted visible actions that move us away from further colonization. It is important to understand that relationships take time to build and must be nurtured over time. Trust does not come easy when Indigenous Peoples have been subjugated and denied access to meaningful education, excluded from decision-making structures and processes, and largely alienated in the system. Part of the work here is that settler society needs to take a hard look at the history in this country and the impact that colonial imperial relations have had on Indigenous Peoples, communities, and Nations. This also includes deconstructing existing racialized constructions of Indigenous Peoples.

Finally, there needs to be action. Without movement or meaningful action, responding to the TRC will not amount to change. Any sustained change must attend to, at the very least, the colonial structures, control of knowledge and its production, and decision-making. As noted earlier in this chapter, the academy maintains control over the production of knowledge and what gets acknowledged as legitimate knowledge. This is largely through research. Smith and Webber (2018) contend that Indigenous knowledges do not need to be validated through Westernized views; rather they note that "the prospect of actively applying Indigenous knowledges in ways that disrupt euro-centric knowledge systems is in itself a transformative endeavor" (p. 4). This disruption needs to be supported in the academy, a place where new ideas and ways of understanding the world are supposed to be valued.

Further, post-secondary institutions must consider how they are reproducing conditions whereby Indigenous students are unsuccessful and whereby Indigenous faculty are so over-burdened by seemingly endless requests to sit on committees, provide advice on matters of curriculum and research, provide guest lectures, or be members of teams that are submitting grants under an Indigenous envelope of funding. The increasing expectations placed on Indigenous students and faculty result in a burden of representation. Those in the academy must also take up their responsibility to go out and find the information they need. Having said that, I am not advocating that non-Indigenous people move ahead without consulting with Indigenous Peoples.

Bringing about transformative change is no easy task. Smith and Webber (2018) argue that "multiple interventions, utilizing multiple strategies that respond to multiple issues" are required, highlighting the fact that single-focused projects will not produce any sustained change (p. 3). I would also add that project-based funding will also not result in sustained change because the minute the project funding stops, so will the project. Commitments need to be much larger than specified special funding envelopes. Multiple interventions and strategies also point to working collaboratively across various sectors and institutions versus competing as no one academic institution can be all things.

A comment about leaders. Leaders and leadership are absolutely critical to transforming a system. Within any system, leaders can become key drivers or resistors to change. I like Wolverton's (1998) idea that there are three types of leadership needed to drive change: champions of change, change agents, and collaborators of change. In essence, bringing about change requires leaders who are willing to step up and lead the change. We cannot merely sit back and expect a system to change without people who are actively engaged in making the institution a better place for all. This means that leaders need to figure ways forward when trying to mobilize transformational change.

Wolverton (1998) also notes that change leaders think integratively, in that they understand the importance of involving people in the planning phases so that alignment among goals is increased and resistance is

xx Introduction

decreased. In terms of structure, change leaders also understand that for substantive change to occur, processes must be fully integrated into the way the organization operates. This means that when contemplating transformative change, one needs to reflect on process and structure and ensure there are policies in place that will sustain the changes. In a *University Affairs* column, I recommended that at a minimum leaders should consider the following:

- Commit to the inclusion of Indigenous histories, culture, language, and knowledges in the curriculum and include this in senate policies. This will require laying a solid foundation with the academic faculties to ensure support.
- Include Indigenous representation on the board of governors and senate to ensure access to decision-making bodies.
- Embed Indigenous councils into the governance of the university, rather than leaving them as advisory-only. Indigenous councils also require formal links to the board and senate to ensure cross-representation.
- Negotiate formal retention initiatives with the faculty association and administration to support Indigenous faculty and ensure that they are set up to succeed.
- Re-examine research ethics protocols and ensure that they are not creating undue hardship for Indigenous faculty and students who are also doing research.
- Dedicate and name spaces. While many universities already have cultural spaces, there needs to continue to be physical markers of Indigenous presence on the campus by way of bilingual signage and named spaces that use the Indigenous language of the territory. It is also important to erect signage across campuses that accentuate and acknowledge the presence of Indigenous peoples. (Cote-Meek, 2018b)

These are in addition to those identified earlier in this paper. It will also be important to address the burden imposed on current Indigenous faculty and staff.

In closing, as I reflect back on the academy's response to Indigenous Peoples, I recognize the enormous struggle we have had in mobilizing change. I hope that what we are building today will sustain itself and that further changes will come more quickly than those that have been realized. In the chapters ahead, contributors provide their perspectives on decolonizing and indigenizing the academy under two thematic headings.

Theme 1: Indigenous Epistemologies: Exploring the Place of Indigenous Knowledges in Post-Secondary Curriculum, Including Indigenization of the Curriculum and Pedagogy. In this section, five authors share their experiences and insights about: importance of reclaiming land-based pedagogies (Angela Weenie); the strength of Anishinaabekwe (Anishnaabe women; Patricia McGuire); reconciliation strategies for Métis (Bryanna Scott); Indigenous relational networking (Candace Galla and Amanda Holmes); Indigenous theories of assessment (Evelyn Steinhauer, Tracy Cardinal, Marc Higgins, Brooke Madden, Noella Steinhauer, Patricia Steinhauer, Misty Underwood, Angela Wolfe, and Elder Bob Cardinal); and understanding of the struggle of Indigenous women in the academy (Celeste Pedri-Spade).

Theme 2: Decolonizing Post-Secondary Institutions: Building Space in the Academy for Indigenous Peoples, Resistance, and Reconciliation. The chapters in this section cover topics such as: questioning whether decolonization is actually possible in the academy (Lynn Lavallee); examining the dynamics of decolonization and indigenization (Emily Grafton and Jérôme Melançon); ways of decolonizing ourselves (Chantal Fiola and Shauna MacKinnon); education programs as sites of possibility (Fiona Purton, Sandra Styres, and Arlo Kempf); making decolonization a priority (Mary Ellen Donnan, Avril Aiken, and Jean L. Manore); teaching truth and redress (Michelle Coupal); examining white fragility and learning to work beyond comfortable diversity (Linda Pardy and Brett Pardy); reframing reconciliation (Keri Cheechoo), and engaging social media as indigenizing and decolonizing strategies (Taima Moeke-Pickering).

These chapters contain logistical solutions and strategies for decolonizing and indigenizing the academy. The book covers a wide range of current issues in the academy, providing insight into the layers, depths, and breadths of the systemic changes that are needed.

DISCUSSION QUESTIONS

1. How does the author define colonization?

2. What is the significance of understanding colonization relative to understanding how to respond to the Truth and Reconciliation Commission's calls to action?

3. How might you apply the learnings of how to transform the academy in your work?

xxii Introduction

FURTHER READINGS/WEBSITES

Truth and Reconciliation Commission of Canada (TRC) website: http://www.trc.ca/.

REFERENCES

Cote-Meek, S. (2014). *Colonized classrooms: Racism, trauma and resistance in post-secondary education*. Winnipeg, MB: Fernwood Publishing.

Cote-Meek, S. (2018a). The age of reconciliation: Transforming postsecondary education. In E. McKinley & L. Smith (Eds.), *Handbook of Indigenous education* (pp. 1–10). Singapore: Springer.

Cote-Meek, S. (2018b, November 6). Making a long-term commitment to Indigenous education. *University Affairs*. Retrieved from https://www.universityaffairs.ca/opinion/from-the-admin-chair/making-a-long-term-commitment-to-indigenous-education/

Duffy, F., & Reigeluth, C. (2008). The School System Transformation (SST) Protocol. *Educational Technology, 48*(4), 41–49.

Eckel, P., & Kezar, A. (2003). Key strategies for making new institutional sense: Ingredients to higher education transformation. *High Education Policy, 16*(1), 39–53. doi:10.1057/palgrave.hep.8300001

Gass, R. (2010). What is transformational change? Retrieved from http://hiddenleaf.electricembers.net/wp-content/uploads/2010/06/What-is-Transformational-Change.pdf

Goldberg, D. (1993). *Racist culture: Philosophy and the politics of meaning*. Cambridge, UK: Cambridge University Press.

Hamilton, G. (2018, May 25). As universities "Indigenize," some see a threat to open inquiry. *National Post*. Retrieved from https://nationalpost.com/news/canada/as-universities-indigenize-some-see-a-threat-to-open-inquiry

Loomba, A. (1998). *Colonialism/postcolonialism*. New York, NY: Routledge.

Mihesuah, D., & Wilson, A. C. (Eds.). (2004). *Indigenizing the academy: Transforming scholarship and empowering communities*. Lincoln: University of Nebraska Press.

Moeke-Pickering, T., Hardy, S., Manitowabi, S., Mawhiney, A. M., Faries, E., Gibson van-Marrewijk, K., & Taitoko, M. (2006). Keeping our fire alive: Toward decolonising research in the academic setting. *World Indigenous Nations Higher Education Consortium Journal.*

Monet, D., & Skanu'u. (1992). *Colonialism on trial: Indigenous land rights and the Gitksan and Wet'suwet'en sovereignty case*. Philadelphia, PA: New Society Publishers.

Secretariat, United Nations Permanent Forum on Indigenous Issues. (2009). Indigenous peoples, Indigenous voices factsheet. Retrieved from http://www.un.org/esa/socdev/unpfii/documents/5session_factsheet1.pdf

Smith, G., & Webber, M. (2018). Transforming research and Indigenous education struggle. In E. McKinley & L. Smith (Eds.), *Handbook of Indigenous education*. Singapore: Springer.

Smith, M. (Ed). (2013). *Transforming the academy: Essays on Indigenous education, knowledges and relations*. Edmonton, AB: University of Alberta Press.

Truth and Reconciliation Commission of Canada. (2015). *The survivors speak: A report of the Truth and Reconciliation Commission of Canada*. Retrieved from http://nctr.ca/assets/reports/Final%20Reports/Survivors_Speak_English_Web.pdf

Wolverton, M. (1998). Champions, agents and collaborators: Leadership keys to successful systemic change. *Journal of Higher Education Policy and Management, 20*(1), 19–30. doi:10.1080/1360080980200103

Watters, H. (2015, June 1). Truth and Reconciliation chair urges Canada to adopt the UN declaration on Indigenous Peoples. *CBC News*. Retrieved from https://www.cbc.ca/news/politics/truth-and-reconciliation-chair-urges-canada-to-adopt-un-declaration-on-indigenous-peoples-1.3096225

THEME 1
INDIGENOUS EPISTEMOLOGIES

Exploring the Place of Indigenous Knowledges in
Post-Secondary Curriculum, Including Indigenization
of the Curriculum and Pedagogy

CHAPTER 1

Askiy Kiskinwahamākēwina: Reclaiming Land-Based Pedagogies in the Academy

Angelina Weenie

> I stood there in the stillness, the quietness broken only by the sounds of birds, the sound of the water trickling down the stream, and the gentle wind blowing through the trees. I remain in awe of this place. There is a mystery to this place.
> —*Weenie*

INTRODUCTION

This chapter is a contributing work toward an understanding of the place of Indigenous epistemologies in the academy. The primary focus will be on Indigenous epistemologies as learned from *askiy kiskinwahamākēwina*. *Askiy* is the Cree word for earth or land, and *kiskinwahamākēwina* means teachings. An articulation of Indigenous epistemologies begins by acknowledging and honouring our languages. It is proposed that by using our languages, we can privilege Indigenous knowledges. It is in our languages that we come to know and understand deeply about Indigenous epistemologies. This approach supports knowledge of the spiritual ecology of Indigenous Peoples, which is integral to bringing forth traditional perspectives in the academy. The basis of this work is to draw on insights gained by developing connections to land, language, culture, and community. A foundational knowledge of appropriate processes and protocols in working with community, *kēhtē-ayak*, and knowledge keepers is also required. These elements of Indigenous epistemologies will be elaborated on and discussed as pathways to indigenizing the academy. A personal journey into learning from and on the land and becoming a traditional medicine keeper will be shared. How this type of cultural learning is translated into the academy will be explored.

SITUATING SELF

As an Indigenous academic, my work is premised on acknowledging and privileging Indigenous knowledges. This chapter will explore how land-based pedagogies can teach us what it is to be Indigenous and how we can Indigenize the academy. It is proposed that *askiy kiskinwahamākēwina* can bridge that knowledge between the academy and First Nations epistemology. Land-based education and knowledge of *askiy-maskihkiya*, earth medicines, can provide insight into the place of Indigenous epistemologies in the university setting.

Knowledge and awareness about the impact of land on learning began with early childhood experiences. It then became more formal with facilitating culture camps as an assistant professor at the First Nations University of Canada. I was assigned to teach the First Nations Outdoor Education courses, as they were called, and that was my introduction to this area of teaching. Most recently, my learning has extended to learning to be a traditional medicine keeper. I am sharing insights into these aspects of *kiskinwahamākēwina*.

In Cree, the term for passing on the teachings is *āsōnamekēwin*. I am passing on what I have learned from *kēhtē-ayak* and knowledge keepers and through lived experience, about land-based education. This paper utilizes a reflective methodology based on my cultural identity and cultural positioning to discuss land-based teaching.

In the Cree language, **etah kohkiskeyihtakosihk** is translated as "identity," and it means from the place that one is known. Meyer (2008) writes that "Indigenous people are all about place ... you came from a place. You grew in a place and you had a relationship with that place. *This is an epistemological idea*" (p. 219). The place where I grew up is Sweetgrass First Nation, Saskatchewan, Canada. This is Treaty 6 territory. In Cree, this reserve is called **nakīwacīhk**, at hill's end. I am a **nehiyaw iskwew**, a Cree woman. I introduce myself by acknowledging my connection to land and territory in the manner that *kēhtē-ayak* taught us. It is part of our cultural ways.

LEARNING FROM LAND

I begin by sharing part of a poem I had written in 2008. It was included in my dissertation (Weenie, 2010). I was on a spiritual retreat. At the time of the writing, I needed to find some solace and comfort in my life. I was observing the hillside and the early spring flowers, and I was reminded of home. The prairie lily is the flower for Saskatchewan and it grows on the reserve. The crocus flower grew on the hill beside our house. Seeing the beauty in the universe was truly uplifting.

> I am the wild prairie lily, elusive and wondrous
> I am the purple crocus that brings color and beauty
> I am the rich brown earthy soil from which all things grow
> I am the water, life-giving, healing and sustaining.
> (Weenie, 2010, p. 1)

I am revisiting and sharing this earlier writing as it reflects a process of becoming aware of the restorative aspect of land. I have found that being in the outdoors is healing for my mind and spirit, and I regularly seek out these spaces for my well-being. Having a sense of connectedness to this place through my memories and in my heart was part of a spiritual awakening. Cajete (2015) perceived that "plants, animals, and other natural phenomena and entities are imbued with power ... A guiding creative force in nature affects everything" (p. 51). I felt that power in this moment of insight. Similarly, Elder Archie Weenie from Sweetgrass First Nation has shared that land and plants *e-nihtawemakaki*, they have power and energy (personal communication, June 16, 2018). These understandings describe a form of spiritual energy, one that is transformational. Another dimension to this understanding is that "the animals, plants, waters and the sky participated in teaching the people how to read signs accurately as a means of survival" (Swan, 1998, p. 49). These are time-held knowledges that have led me to become more spiritually attuned to my surroundings and to appreciate the power of land-based education. This form of knowing is supported by Ermine (2018), who writes that "the holistic paradigms that drive this form of education enhance subjectivity where learners experience heightened sensitivities about themselves and their environment" (n.p.).

Knowledge about land was acquired through the stories I heard as a child. We lived on a reserve and people knew the land. It was not a formalized

6 Decolonizing and Indigenizing Education in Canada

learning but part of our everyday livelihood. I listened to my parents and grandparents tell stories about sacred places. We have a legend about a place called Sliding Hill. There is a deep crevice in this hill and it is said that this was where *Wīsahkēcāhk* was last seen. *Wīsahkēcāhk* is the trickster in our culture. He had been sliding down the hill and left a big hole in the side of the hill. The most intriguing story was related to a place called *Manito Kamatweyiket*, Drumming Hill. The story is that people could sometimes hear drumming and singing in the distance. This place is also where the *memekwesisak*, or the Little People, lived. Indigenous epistemologies and ontologies are passed on through these stories. Based on her work with Elders, Wheeler (2010) has suggested that "the land is mnemonic, it has its own set of memories, and when the Old People go out on the land, it nudges or reminds them, and their memories are rekindled" (p. 55). This understanding of place, land, and being is significant as it represents how Indigenous knowledges evolve.

The Naskapi men and women from the subarctic region in Quebec were part of an ethnographic study from 2000 to 2012, and they expressed that "our knowledge is the product of our observation of the environment during thousands of years and of these observations, influenced by our beliefs, customs, values and customs" (Levesque, Geoffrey, & Polese, 2016, p. 65). They are also quoted as saying that they tell stories about their history "in hopes of transmitting the teachings and the memory of that time to the young people of their community" (Levesque et al., 2016, p. 65). The stories of the land that my grandparents and parents shared with me reflect this process. Thus, memories of land and cultural teachings keep me ever cognizant of the rich body of knowledge that constitutes Indigenous identity.

Cultural understandings of *askiy* or land are rooted in me. I would hear my grandparents and parents talk about *okāwīmāwaskiy*, mother earth. To me, it meant that we were dependent on our mother to provide for our needs. I remember how we would go berry-picking with my grandmother. The berries that we did not eat would be stored for winter use as it was important to prepare for the hard winters. My grandmother knew how to snare rabbits. My mother would make rabbit soup and cook deer meat. My mother would send me to go and pick raspberries so that she could make pie. We were taught how to plant and tend to the garden. Our families were self-sufficient, and I was learning how to interact with land-based activities. My mother and grandmothers were sharing cultural practices with me in a significant way. Even though my life journey would take me far from the reserve, what they taught me is still important to me today. My early childhood experiences were empowering and facilitated a cultural grounding and an embodied knowing.

I went home to Sweetgrass First Nation on August 21, 2015, to visit the graves of my deceased relatives, and Drumming Hill is not far from there. This place is etched in my mind as I remember how I stood there in the stillness, the quietness broken only by the sounds of birds, the sound of the water trickling down the stream, and the gentle wind blowing through the trees. I remain in awe of this place. There is a mystery to this place and it holds me and keeps me.

THE CULTURE CAMP APPROACH IN EDUCATION

The First Nations University of Canada was established in 1976 and it exists as an institution to educate others about First Nations culture, language, traditions, values, and worldview. This vision was articulated by our *kēhtē-ayak*, and through time it was held that this type of learning could be best facilitated through culture camps. The *kēhtē-ayak* thought that it was important for Indigenous Education students to be learning on the land and from the land. As future teachers, they needed to learn from community and from *kēhtē-ayak*. Under the guidance of the *kēhtē-ayak*, our Outdoor Education courses were changed to fall and winter culture camp experiences.

Culture camps have become a common approach used by institutions to teach First Nations perspectives. They vary in focus. Land-based learning is referenced in various ways such as environmental education, ecological education, place-based education, and outdoor leadership education (Lewis, 2018). What distinguishes land-based education or culture camps from these other types of programming is the focus on spirituality (Ermine, personal communication, March 27, 2018). The purpose of land-based programs is the advancement of a cultural base for working with communities. Indigenous ways of knowing, protocols, and localized stories become central to this type of learning (Lewis, 2018).

I started teaching at First Nations University of Canada, then known as the Saskatchewan Indian Federated College, Regina, Saskatchewan, in 1997. As a faculty member I took up the opportunities offered to learn more about culture. I attended the monthly pipe ceremonies, I participated in the sweat lodge ceremonies, and I also did the sun dance for four years at Piapot First Nation. This personal learning served to deepen my understanding of traditional knowledge, and I worked to incorporate that knowledge into my teaching. Authentic learning experiences helped me to speak to these ways of knowing. From my perspective, this is what "Indigenizing" really means. The current rhetoric about "Indigenizing and decolonizing" education is not a new phenomenon. As First Nations educators, we have long understood that it is through our lived experiences, culture, and language that we come to know and are able to teach through an Indigenous lens. This pedagogical approach encompasses all our work, our research, and our teaching.

As children, we knew the joy of playing outdoors and we were probably happiest when we were playing outside. As a classroom teacher, I saw my students become more open and engaged when we went outdoors for activities. They had been let out of the confines of a classroom. Likewise, in a university setting, land-based learning in the form of culture camps can have potential to enhance learning. Ermine (2018) writes that "land-based learning is a form of education that connects learners to the land in ways that engage the interconnecting modes of mind, body, spirit into a symphony of elevated awareness" (n.p.). It brings good energy and we can function at a higher level of being.

Goulet and McLeod (2002) wrote about the culture camps that had been developed by Indigenous Education. As faculty members of Indigenous Education, they worked toward providing authentic learning experiences on the land through culture camps (Goulet & McLeod, 2002). They claimed that past colonial practices and the residential schools had caused "the disruption of cultural continuity" (Goulet & McLeod, 2002, p. 355). It was felt that students did not have a strong cultural identity and the culture camp was a place where students could learn their culture from Elders. They felt that the culture camp was a way of doing "uniquely Aboriginal education" (Goulet & McLeod, 2002, p. 358).

As academics, we talk about ideas and theories inside the walls of an institution. These ideas can become more meaningful when presented in cultural settings. I believe that it is important for universities to be in the community and allowing what we learn from community to become a basis for our teaching. As Kovach (2010) states, "our teachers are not really in the academy. Our teachers are in community" (p. 152).

When I taught the culture camp courses, it became apparent that it was important to first establish connections with the surrounding First Nations communities. I was not from this area and I had to learn the protocols and practices of the people in this area. I was primarily working with resource people, *kēhtē-ayak*, and **oskapewisak** (Elders' Helpers) from the communities to organize the cultural activities. I listened and learned from the people who were involved in the culture camps.

Culture camps are not without their challenges. Louv (2008) has theorized that there is a need to save children from nature deficit disorder. He states that "as the young spend less and less of their lives in natural surroundings, their senses narrow, physiologically and psychologically, and this reduces the richness of human experience" (Louv, 2008, p. 3). Students also become accustomed to learning inside the artificial walls of the classroom. To be learning in a culture camp setting is often unfamiliar. Being in a new community or a new territory also presents a new learning process.

Spirituality is central to all that happens at a culture camp. It is understood that spirituality guides a respectful process in all things. Yet spirituality is the least understood form of knowing. Participating in ceremonies is intended to help us connect with our inner spirit and this is new for many. Spirituality is not about religion, nor is it about imposing any specific beliefs. Wilson (2008) states that "when ceremonies take place, everyone who is participating needs to be ready to step beyond the everyday and to accept a raised state of consciousness" (p. 69). In First Nations ways, this epistemological process is aided through song, language, prayer, medicines, and ceremony. Further, Cajete (2015) maintains that "spirituality and a sense of the sacred permeate all aspects of Indigenous knowledge" (p. 28). These aspects call attention to the need to enter cultural and sacred spaces with an open heart and an open mind, and to be receptive to the teachings shared.

The Indigenous Education culture camps include pipe ceremonies, sweat lodge ceremonies, feasts, traditional arts and crafts, storytelling, traditional song and dance, berry-picking, rattle making, beading, traditional food preparation, and medicine walks. Students also have opportunities to listen to Elders about women's knowledge, women's roles, and cultural protocols. These are rich cultural understandings that lend to an Indigenized approach to curriculum development. However, much like Goulet and McLeod (2002), I felt that the learning taking place at the culture camps was not enough. My questions were about how effectively the students would apply their new learning to their teaching. It was a short amount of time to be processing traditional knowledge, and it seemed that what they were learning was superficial knowledge. Much more needed to be learned. I also wondered what the *kēhtē-ayak*, the *oskapewisak* (Elders' Helpers), and the community members thought of the culture camps. Therefore, I did a small research project, titled "Exploring the Culture Camp Approach in Aboriginal Education."

I travelled to Ministikwan First Nation on April 7, 2011. This community is located 302 kilometres from Regina, Saskatchewan, and we have had culture camps in this area. The purpose of my research was to hear the perspectives of those who had been involved in the culture camps. Our day began with the offering of tobacco and cloth, a pipe ceremony, and a feast ceremony. It is understood that spiritual practices take precedence in any undertaking. Then our learning circle session began, with each person having an opportunity to share. The late Elder Harry Blackbird was the lead Elder, and he shared that the work they did at culture camp was to help the children and to let them know, understand, and relearn our ways. He related about how hard it is to relearn our ways and that we should have been teaching the children all along. He said that an offering of tobacco was all that was needed in seeking knowledge from *kēhtē-ayak*. Other participants talked about their own healing journeys and stated that when they were invited to culture camps, they welcomed the opportunity to be able to give back.

This research project reflects in part about how I have worked to learn as much as I can about traditional ways. It was for personal and professional reasons, and my experiences paved the way for me to pass on the teachings. Teaching at the First Nations University of Canada marked the first time that I participated in a sweat lodge ceremony, and I also did my first sun dance under the mentorship of our late Elder, Bea Lavallee. The learning has been life-changing.

Every culture camp that I have attended has revealed new knowledge and insight. I have come to believe that firsthand experience is the best teacher, especially about culture. I feel that I cannot effectively teach my students unless I have experienced these cultural aspects for myself. I cannot speak to them unless I have experienced them. Often it is about going beyond and learning more. What I have taken away from the culture camps is a stronger foundation of self, mentally, emotionally, spiritually, and physically. I am continually on a journey to learn more about *askiy kiskinwahamākēwina* so that I can bring this type of knowledge to my students so that they too will value and use traditional knowledge.

Most recently, the *kēhtē-ayak* from First Nations University of Canada were involved in the production of the video *Waniska: An Awakening of Indigenous Knowledge* (2018). **Waniska** means "wake up" in the Cree language. Footage from the *Askīw-Maskihkiy* Traditional Medicine Camp, which was held at Sturgeon Lake First Nation, is included. In this video production, the *kēhtē–ayak* from First Nations University of Canada convey the urgency for the young people to learn traditional ways and how they need to learn to be keepers of the land. Students share how the camp has a profound impact on them and how their camp experience has motivated them to learn and carry on the culture and language. Margaret Reynolds, a Dene Elder from English River First Nation, speaks about the teachings from her grandmother about medicines. She states that the Elders of the past were "chemists, physicists, and astrologers," and their knowledge was valuable and it is time to awaken that knowledge. Ermine (2018), who is a member of the Elders Council, affirms, "We need this knowledge for the whole world. It is not just a classroom activity."

The culture camp approach is, in part, about addressing, individually and collectively, the way we have been negatively impacted by oppression, marginalization, colonialism, and racism. Although there have been positive changes in how First Nations people are viewed and treated, there is more to be done. Living in a racist society creates woundedness. Therefore, we do need to find ways to counter the racism and colonial practices we are subjected to. I believe that it is through traditional and cultural practices that we can find a renewed sense of self and direction.

Drywater-Whitekiller (2017) did a study on how Native Americans cope with racial microaggressions, and her findings were that "moving on to more positive things reflects the ability to return and re-engage in spite of obstacles, and this is the foundation of cultural resilience" (p. 170). This concept of resilience takes up cultural ways as the basis for positive life adaptation. According to the participants in the study, "the land was also seen as the basis of education for indigenous pathways and thinking" (Drywater-Whitekiller, 2017, p. 165). This viewpoint echoes what the Elders and students shared in the video titled *Waniska* (2018). This video was produced by First Nations University of Canada, Regina, Saskatchewan. Further, these perspectives reflect the importance of ongoing efforts to revitalize our knowledges and to draw on our own epistemologies through land-based education.

NÁTAWIHOWIN ASKĪW-MASKIHKIY TRADITIONAL MEDICINE CAMP

The Health Clinic from Sturgeon Lake First Nation had sent a number of their community members to take part in the medicine camp at Peguis, Manitoba, to learn about ***nátawihowin askīw-maskihkiy***, healing earth medicines. When the fourth year was completed, the medicine camp was passed on to the community of Sturgeon Lake First Nation. Those who had been taught to be medicine keepers took on the responsibility to offer the medicine camp.

I was part of the *Askīw-Maskihkiy* Traditional Medicine Camp at Sturgeon Lake First Nation from 2014–2017. The medicine camp was in a beautiful, idyllic setting by the lake. Being there was like breathing in new life. We were a mixed cultural group of about 40 men and women, with some being from Manitoba, while others were from Alberta and Saskatchewan. Through the four years, friendships and connections with one another were developed. At the end of the fourth year, the ceremonial way of adopting others as a relative, *tāpākōtowin*, was performed. Some were taken as adopted sisters and brothers.

Intention or *itēyihtamowin* begins the process. What were my thoughts and intentions as I engaged in this new type of learning about medicines? Being an academic and, at times, being far removed from community, it was about *nâtawihowin*, being well in a world that is often hard to negotiate. My intention and purpose for starting this camp was also determined by a need to feel connected once more to community. Haig-Brown and Dannenmann (2002) have written that "an Indigenous pedagogy of the land [is] learning through watching and doing" (p. 452). The medicine camp offered some time to step back and learn ancestral knowledge from *kēhtē-ayak*.

Culture camps and land-based education can be part of a process of reclaiming our identities and cultures, where land is the teacher and helps us to feel connected. In my own healing journey, I had experienced the power of sweetgrass as a healing and cleansing medicine. I would often go to *kēhtē-ayak* for spiritual help and they would give me medicines. I believe now that there had been a reason for this. I came to see that it had been the start of my learning about *askīy-maskihkiy* and I needed to be part of the camp. The land as teacher implies that teachings from and on the land can provide insight into traditional values, customs, and practices. *Kēhtē-ayak* model this form of learning at our culture camps. This pedagogy is derived from historical and geographical time and place.

The medicine camp lasted for four days each year. Each day, the *askīy-maskihkiy* (earth medicine) camp began with songs, prayers, and a pipe ceremony. On the first day of the camp, we were instructed on how to make willow bundles. We were to pray and to put tobacco in the bundle and think of all the things that we needed to let go of. Then we let the bundle go in the water. This helps to clear those kinds of things that try to harm us. Being a medicine keeper means that we must work from a good frame of mind. Working with plants and medicines is a sacred undertaking and we need to "spiritually shine" (Ermine, personal communication, August 3, 2017). We were told that there is a responsibility when we pick up the medicine bundle.

Each year we learned about the medicinal qualities of 12 plants. Some of the plants we learned about included sweetgrass, cedar, sage, blueberry, raspberry, chaga, and rat root. We were taught about how to harvest, use, and store them. We were told to learn to identify plants by their aroma. I took careful notes and photos of each plant. We were to say the name of the plant out loud as we were introduced to them. I kept a journal to record what we were being taught. Whenever we went out on the land to harvest, we made sure to bring tobacco as it is important to give back when we take things from mother earth. I listened carefully to the songs and the prayers. I believe that whatever enters my mind and my heart will one day come alive and be useful to a situation that I come across. We must always be open to learning from others. One of the main understandings is that this type of work is a life-long endeavour of learning and walking this path.

As a First Nations academic, I am required to be knowledgeable about Western knowledge, but for me, in my heart and in my soul, I also need to be grounded in the ways of our grandfathers and grandmothers. From the beginning, being an apprentice medicine keeper seemed mysterious and beyond what I would be capable of. However, as I listened to the teachings, I soon realized that we must each do our part to reclaim and restore important knowledge about medicines. It was part of ensuring that our knowledges are not lost and that we all be part of helping our families and communities recover from a colonial and racist legacy. Passing on knowledge of medicines was denied to First Nations people due to residential schools and to other oppressive government policies and it is time to reclaim that knowledge.

DISCUSSION

In this time of highly technological ways of interacting with the world, it is important to take time to explore a human and personal connection with nature. The beauty and bountifulness of nature beckons and feeds our inner spirit. It is the "kindness," from *okāwīmāwaskiy*, mother earth, which we need to draw on (Elder Archie Weenie, personal communication, June 16, 2018). From long ago, Indigenous people studied and knew the land *tānisi esi pimātsīkoyak*, how it gives us life. In Cree, this power is referred to as *e-niytawemakahk*. The land and all within has power. This is the essence of land-based pedagogy. *Kēhtē-ayak* tell us that *e-kiysawēmikosiyahk*, which means that we were gifted with knowledge to help ourselves and we must honour this.

Land represents "a relationship between people and place, a profound feature of the resilience of the Indigenous peoples of the Americas" (Dunbar-Ortiz, 2014, p. 208). Protecting mother earth remains an enduring aspect of Indigenous worldview, one that is needed to preserve our water, land, and ecosystems. This philosophical standpoint is necessary in withstanding the destruction of our land. Climate change and the need for clean water have become critical issues. In these troubled times, the spiritual ecology of Indigenous peoples has much to offer in protecting mother earth, thereby ensuring our survival on this planet.

Based on the ideas that have been discussed, several key considerations for implementing land-based education at other institutions are suggested:

- To be clear on the intent. Spirit and intent create the pathway.
- To personally experience the transformative nature of land-based learning. It is from this place that one can convey the power of this type of learning.
- To become familiar with Indigenous knowledge systems and the differences between cultures.
- To build relations with Indigenous communities and learn about their protocols, language, customs, and traditions.
- To work with Elders and resource people to provide authentic learning experiences that are distinct and unique to the territory.

Most importantly, collaboration and interaction with land, community, *kēhtē-ayak*, the old people, and traditional knowledge keepers are necessary for implementing land-based education effectively. The protocols and processes I have shared are integral to connecting with Indigenous communities. It is important to take these teachings to heart, and in the process, new insight and knowledge can be gained to Indigenize the academy and to advance Indigenous epistemologies.

DISCUSSION QUESTIONS

1. What is the philosophy of land-based education?

2. Discuss the process of implementing land-based education.

3. What are the potential pitfalls and opportunities in land-based education programming?

4. How can land-based education transform the academy?

GLOSSARY

Plains Cree y Dialect

askiy: earth
askiy kiskinwahamākēwina: earth teachings
askīw: a variation of the word *askiy*
āsōnamekēwin: passing on the teachings
e-nihtawemakaki: having power
e-kiysawēmikosiyahk: gifted
etah kohkiskeyihtakosihk: identity
itēyihtamowin: intention
kēhtē-ayak: Elders
Manito Kamatweyiket: Drumming Hill
nakīwacihk: at hill's end
nâtawihowin: wellness
nâtawihowin askīw-maskihkiy: healing earth medicines
nehiyaw iskwew: Cree woman
okāwimāwaskiy: mother earth
oskapewisak: Elders' Helpers
tānisi esi pimātsīkoyak: how it gives us life
tāpākōtowin: adopting another as your relative
waniska: wake up
Wīsahkēcāhk: Cree trickster

FURTHER READINGS/WEBSITES

Simpson, L. B. (2014). Land as pedagogy: Nishnaabeg intelligence and rebellious transformation. *Decolonization: Indigeneity, Education & Society, 3*(3), 1–25.

Tuck, E., McKenzie, M., & McCoy, K. (2014). Land education: Indigenous, post-colonial, and decolonizing perspectives on place and environmental education research. *Environmental Education Research, 20*(1), 1–23.

Wildcat, M., McDonald, M. Irlbacher-Fox, & Coulthard, G. (2014). Learning from the land: Indigenous land-based pedagogy and decolonization. *Decolonization: Indigeneity, Education & Society, 3*(3), i–xv.

Land-Based Learning Websites

Land-Based Learning, Living Sky School Division: https://learning.lskysd.ca/indigenouseducation/land-based-learning/

Cultural Camps: https://www.culturalcamps.com/Cultural_Camps/School_Programs.html

Land-Based Learning for ETEC 501: https://landbasedlearning.wordpress.com/indigenous-land-based-learning-programs/

First Peoples' Cultural Council: http://www.fpcc.ca/language/Programs/Language-Culture-Camp.aspx

Linklater Lodge: http://www.linklaterlodge.com/lll_cody_bear.php

Wanuskewin Heritage Park: https://wanuskewin.com

B Dene Adventures: http://www.bdene.com/camps/cultural-camps

REFERENCES

Cajete, G. (2015). *Indigenous community: Rekindling the teachings of the seventh fire.* St. Paul, MN: Living Justice Press.

Drywater-Whitekiller, V. (2017). We belong to the land: Native Americans experiencing and coping with racial microaggressions. *The Canadian Journal of Native Studies, 37*(1), 153–174.

Dunbar-Ortiz, R. (2014). *An Indigenous Peoples' history of the United States.* Boston, MA: Beacon Press.

Ermine, W. (2018). The philosophy of land-based education: Learning to be an indigenous being. Unpublished manuscript.

First Nations University of Canada. (Producer). (2018). *Waniska: An awakening of indigenous knowledge* [DVD]. Retrieved from www.4SeasonsReconciliation.ca

Goulet, L., & McLeod, Y. (2002). Connections and reconnections: Affirming cultural identity in aboriginal teacher education. *McGill Journal of Education, 37*(3), 355–369.

Haig-Brown, C., & Dannenmann, K. (2002). A pedagogy of the land: Dreams of respectful relations. *McGill Journal of Education, 37*(3), 451–468.

Kovach, M. (2010). *Indigenous methodologies: Characteristics, conversations, and contexts.* Toronto, ON: University of Toronto Press.

Levesque, C., Geoffrey, D., & Polese, G. (2016). Naskapi women: Words, narratives, and knowledge. In N. Kermoal & I. Altamirano-Jimenez (Eds.), *Living on the land: Indigenous women's understanding of place* (pp. 59–84). Edmonton, AB: Athabasca University Press.

Lewis, K. (2018). Land-based programming: A comprehensive study of K-12 and post-secondary land-based education programs. Unpublished manuscript.

Louv, R. (2008). *Last child in the woods: Saving our children from nature-deficit disorder.* New York, NY: Algonquin Books of Chapel Hill.

Meyer, M. A. (2008). Indigenous and authentic: Hawaiian epistemology and the triangulation of meaning. In N. K. Denzin, Y. S. Lincoln, & L. T. Smith (Eds.), *Handbook of critical and indigenous methodologies* (pp. 217–232). London, UK: Sage.

Swan, I. (1998). Modelling: An aboriginal approach. In L. Stiffarm (Ed.), *As we see … Aboriginal pedagogy.* Saskatoon, SK: University Extension Press.

Weenie, A. (2010). Self-study: The inbetween space of an aboriginal academic. Unpublished dissertation. Regina, SK: University of Regina.

Wheeler, W. (2010). Cree intellectual traditions in history. In A. Finkle, S. Carter, & P. Fortna (Eds.), *The West and beyond: New perspectives on an imagined region* (pp. 47–61). Edmonton, AB: Athabasca University Press.

Wilson, S. (2008). *Research is ceremony: Indigenous research methods.* Winnipeg, MB: Fernwood Publishing.

CHAPTER 2

Gii Aanikoobijigan Mindimooyehn: Decolonizing Views of Anishinaabekwe

Patricia D. McGuire

INTRODUCTION AND SITUATING SELF

Nii Kishebakabaykwe, nii Makwa dodem nii bami'aagan Bizhiw, daa-jiibaa Bingwii Neyaashi Anishinaabe, nii intawem Kiashke Zaaging Anishinaabek. There is a personal basis for many Indigenous knowledge(s). My story of knowledge includes how I have come to know who I am, who my ancestors are, and who they will be. Indigenous knowledges invigorate Indigenous women's responsibilities to our knowledges within our societies. These transformative processes are undertaken as multilayered processes in dynamic Indigenous societies. This is decolonizing and Indigenizing work.

Indigenous women's knowledge(s) have imbued Indigenous social thought and practice. While diversity and uniqueness exist within Anishinaabe societies on Turtle Island, foundational aspects are discerned about Anishinaabe knowledge(s), and critical differences exist between Anishinaabe in societal perspectives. Yet most Anishinaabe would agree their worldview and way of life are based on an intimate relationship with land. Land-centred concepts, particularly dealing with Anishinaabekwe, Ojibwe women, are the focus of this writing. There are two main reasons for this discussion. First, knowledge about land has been the basis for the relationships Anishinaabe have with Canada. Missing from these discussions are Anishinaabekwe understandings, although they are an integral part of stories, oral, written, and pictorial histories and teachings of the land. Secondly, focusing on Anishnaabekwe illustrates continuity and shifts in this ongoing dialogue about land.

INDIGENOUS KNOWLEDGE STORIED LANDSCAPES

Some Anishinaabe societies were known by other Indigenous peoples as the people who write. These records, writing, are evident on rocks, trees, birch bark, porcupine quill work, beadwork, clothes, lodging, the land, and so on. Erdrich (2003) argues writing, ozhibii'iwe, was part of who the Ojibwe were. Recitation and reiteration of significant events, stories, were part of this system of records. My parents, Patrick McGuire and Anne McGuire, née LeGarde, provided knowledges to my family about **Gii Aanikoobijigan**, my ancestors; chim dimooyenh, women; and chic akiwenzii, men. My father spoke about stories written on stone and birch bark, and messages on trees, as navigational devices. My mother spoke of birch-bark scrolls considered so vital to Anishinaabe, they were hidden to prevent access. Rock paintings were storied aspects of knowledge(s). My parents knew and told me to find the following stories and records of the storytellers who ensured their continuation. The sources may be dated but the oral history captured enables nuanced views of Anishinaabe thought.

Morrisseau was inspired by the rock paintings around Lake Nipigon and Lake Superior (Sinclair & Pollock, 1979). A birch-bark scroll by Morrisseau is housed within the Indian Affairs Art Gallery in Gatineau, Quebec. This scroll depicts spiritual ceremonies specific to the Anishinaabe and illustrates continued land relationships. Despite being outlawed by Canada, spiritual ceremonies have been conducted on a regular basis to current day. When I first saw this scroll, it acted as a navigational device: Indigenous knowledge(s) are grounded in the geographical landscape of home territories of the Anishinaabe. Dynamic Indigenous peoples on their lands and the waters surrounding them have created, maintained, and continue to create specific knowledge(s) relating to their societies.

Indigenous communities surrounding Lake Nipigon and Lake Superior have Anishinaabe land protocols indicating who can and cannot use the lands and waters. Protocols exist on how to access and other protocols determine shared land and water spaces. These land protocols enable the creation of relationships such as alliances and treaties. Lake Nipigon is a large, spring-fed lake. This lake has experienced many changes, yet this source of ancient water continues. **Animipeegoong** or **Animbiigoo** Zaaga'igan means Lake Nipigon and refers to the deep water of the lake. Lake Nipigon now flows into Lake Superior by way of the Nipigon River by a contemporary diversion. Lake Superior is called Chi Onigaaming. Chi has two meanings: One is large and the other is sacred. In Sinclair and Pollock (1979), Morrisseau shared a story about the creation of Lake

Superior, Aamikwag abinaaniwan, a beaver house, and miskwi onaman, red ochre.

In our past, Chii Aamikwag (sacred beavers) lived together in groups. The Animki Binesiwag, thunderbirds, knew these beavers were in Lake Superior and often tried to hunt them. The beavers had to make sure they were not caught out on the open waters. The beavers would surface and sun themselves when the weather was good. No one knew when the thunderbirds would be out on the water. The Animki Binesiwag could materialize fast, so the beavers had to keep alert. One of these sacred white beavers forgot these teachings and was grabbed by the Animki Binesiwag, who had transformed into the form of an angry cloud. The beaver was carried into the sky and his miskwi, blood, spilled from the wounds made by the claws of the Animki Binesiwag, onto the rocks of the land. The huge red sand blotches, miskwi onamon, came from the blood of this beaver. Morriseau concluded this story by stating Anishinaabe "still tell this story about the Sacred Red Sands" (Sinclair & Pollock, 1979, p. 78).

This story is one of a series describing the creation of the landscape surrounding Lake Nipigon and Lake Superior. Miskwi onaman is often used when recording stories on rock. It is used as paint when it is mixed with the fat. Some Anishinaabe say this red ochre is used with sturgeon oil and other fish oils. Some have said turtle blood, although this may be a metaphor, as turtle blood comes from the earth, Turtle Island. Conway (1993), who worked with Chi Akiwenzii Dan Pine, a friend of my father, described how red ochre is used to make rock paintings, as a medicine and, at one time, was used for burials. Miskwi onaman was used to make stories painted on rock and to renew stories painted on rock.

When the Anishinaabe speak of their storied history, included in these stories are teachings on life, lessons on behaviour, relational understandings, discussions of origin sites and spiritual practices, as well as many other aspects. Rock painting sites are sacred spaces for Indigenous peoples; these are medicine spaces, where spirits reside. Rajnovich (1994) stated rock painting sites are important places on the landscape where cultural stories are recorded for memory; she worked with Chim Dimooyenh and Chic Akiwenzii in the Treaty 3 area. Storied land carries meaning for Indigenous landscapes. They are reminders of the significance of the land for their relational understandings with others and with the land and waters. Rock paintings, for Morton and Gawboy (2000), serve as cultural memories of Anishinaabe being on this land as well as the continuance of Anishinaabe knowledge. In a structured Anishinaabe world, Conway (1993), taught by Chic Akiwenzii Dan Pine, said these sites contain "a richness that included native oral history, associations with historical individuals, delineations of specific family hunting territories, and connections to local" stories, including relationships to land and to shared land with other Anishinaabe peoples (p. 32). Conway, with Chic Elder Pine's teachings, contended these rock painting sites are critical for Anishinaabe cultures as these sites are considered dynamic sacred spaces and places where Manitouwag live. The aasiinwag, rocks, and red ochre paintings help Anishinaabe maintain and renew relationships with one another, with their spirituality, and with their Anishinaabe storied past(s).

WOMEN'S RESPONSIBILITIES TO LAND KNOWLEDGES AND ERASED HISTORIES

Anishinaabekwe's responsibilities regarding land relationships need to be revitalized. Rajnovich (1994) records a story about **Misakamigokwe**, which means the Great Earth Woman, who agrees to remain on her earth lodge, "so that the people could always call upon her for help" (p. 72). Misakamigokwe entrusted into her care all those who seek her help, by observing the protocol of accepting offerings and medicine songs. My parents said that like in Treaty 3 territory, Indigenous knowledge(s) around Lake Superior and Lake Nipigon indicate Anishinaabekwe, women's responsibilities toward natural resources and land. Within Anishinaabe societal knowledge(s), women's responsibility extends to the protection and preservation of Nibi, water. In these understandings, all forms of water are considered. Women generate water, while their child is within their first lodge, within their bodies. Anishinaabekwe have these life responsibilities.

What else does this responsibility for water involve? As an indicator of their authority, women are considered as keepers of the water. My mother related stories of my great-grandmother who was a knowledge holder for the waters, with specific ceremonial responsibilities for water. The last ceremony she knew was conducted sometime between the mid-1930s and mid-1940s, by my great-grandmother, at Anemki Wajiw, by Lake Superior at Fort William First Nation. These responsibilities also encompass water animals and other beings. For example: Anishinaabekwe responsibilities extend to the maple harvest, with women and men sharing responsibility for the care, harvest, and distribution of the ziinzibaakwadwaabo, maple water. The maadoomin, wild-rice harvest, women and men share responsibilities for maintenance of the rice beds with the women, in many cases, being responsible for the care and allocation of the rice beds.

As Anishinaabe, we are spirit first in this world. Anishinaabekwe responsibilities have come from our nurtured land relationships. These reciprocal relationships with land sustain and nourish our societies. It is our first relationship with water and land that feeds our spirit. It determines and informs our relationships with our self and with others in our families and community. This is one of the ways the land is conceptualized within current Anishinaabe thought. Did my ancestors think this way about land? I do not know. Our discussions of these historical stories reflect our current social and political understandings of these relationships between land, spirit, and human beings.

Anishinaabekwe had a powerful influence on the societies in northern Ontario. Stories in Lake Nipigon discuss the responsibilities of women that invoked this authority. Wasaaykejick, a leader in Sandpoint and nii aanikoobijigan, my ancestor, before the signing of the Robinson-Superior treaty in 1850, would not begin a meeting without his granddaughter being present. The French fur-traders recognized this and conveyed their understandings of women by calling her "Queen Anne." Overall, Canada sought to silence these women's responsibilities by developing federal legislation to limit women's influence. Indian agents and missionaries to the area sought to eliminate these impacts at the societal level.

Considerable efforts were taken to erase Indigenous histories in Canada. Targeted were histories based on gender relationships that diverged from European patriarchal understandings of women. Male ascendency became the societal model allowed under the *Indian Act, 1876.* This erosion of a gender equilibrium was and is enforced by Canadian laws. Anishinaabe societies do not have the sharp gender delineation European societies had developed. Spaces on the land are shared spaces of responsibility for collective survival, with various genders contributing to this nurturance. This idea of survival is one focused on preserving the land for future ancestors, gii Aanikoobijigan, while recognizing past ancestors. In this intersection between past and future, current Anishinaabekwe responsibilities focus on continuing the relationships needed for life.

INDIGENOUS KNOWLEDGE PRACTICE OF LAND

As I reflect on September 7, 1850, 168 years ago, I realize gii Aanikoobijigan were thinking about their future generations. Oral history of the Robinson-Superior treaty offers glimpses of the unique responsibilities Anishinaabekwe had in relation to land and community. Mindimooyehn was translated by

Treuer as meaning "those who hold the world together" (Childs, 2012, p. 63). This word usually refers to women within Anishinaabe society, although the word itself does not specify gender. My friend Susan Bebonang, before her untimely death in 2015, talked about Gekaanik and Gchin-shinaabe as meaning wise older peoples. Bebonang said that Gchin-shinaabe-kwe specified a wise original woman. During the signing of the Robinson-Superior treaty in 1850, at Bawatiing by Sault Ste. Marie, Ontario, gii Aanikoobijian, my father's grandmother, Kidgishabun, attended this event with her grandfather. Kidgishabun was about ten years old. She acted as a waabangekwe, a witness to these events. There was a practical reason for her being there: She could speak English, French, and different dialects of Anishinaabemowin. Her remembrances deal with land, resources, and the circumstances surrounding these meetings. My parents discussed these stories as forms of Indigenous knowledge(s) needed in the future.

My mother related a story to me about when my great-great-grandparents were crossing Lake Nipigon in late summer. With them was their grandchild, my mother's mother, who was about five years old. Unexpectedly, my grandfather died on one of the islands. My grandmother buried him. In the fall, the water had gotten too rough to continue to Sandpoint, so she made a birch-bark lodge for her and her granddaughter to live in over the winter months. Niin Aanikoobijigan lived there for several years. This meant my grandmothers hunted, trapped, fished, and gathered resources so they could survive. My grandmother only left this island when she became too old to take care of herself and her granddaughter. She then travelled to the Sandpoint, Bingwii Neyaashi, community with her granddaughter, who was my grandmother.

When I was writing my dissertation in 2013, I reflected on how I was raised by my parents. My family was taken onto the land around July, and sometimes, we did not return to MacDiarmid, Ontario, until late fall, when the snow would fly. While we were on the land, my parents and other family members taught me and my siblings about our relatives from Lake Nipigon and Lake Superior. Through this, I discovered my family had close relationships with other families spanning generations. Our families would camp in the same areas at different times of the year. We practised land-based knowledge(s) in our everyday living practice. My father fished Lake Nipigon and Lake Superior. He and my brothers had trap lines close to MacDiarmid. Sometimes, we were invited to check traps and stay in the trapping cabin. I watched my father and brothers, but mainly my father, skin animals. My parents ensured we were taught the basics of how to survive on the land. We always had a cold space, which was dug by our campsites and in our home, to store our food. As a family, we would leave and go out in the bush, picking blueberries, raspberries, and fall hunting. Crooked Green was where we picked berries and fall camped. Some summers, there was an entire community out on both sides of the river. Each family camped in their own space. Anishinaabe came from Kiashke Zaaging Anishinaabek, Biinjitiwaabik Zaaging Anishinaabek, MacDiarmid, Nipigon, Lake Helen, Red Rock, Geraldton, Jellico, Long Lac, and other communities in the Robinson-Superior treaty and even from the Treaty 3 area.

My father and brothers, usually, killed either moose or caribou or deer, although my sisters, if needed, could kill these animals too. Although other Anishinaabe may have prohibitions, in the Lake Nipigon and Lake Superior region, I am not aware of any prohibition on women hunting, fishing, trapping, or gathering. The spaces on land where these responsibilities occurred were shared. My mother would organize the processing, storage, and distribution of the meat within our family and to others within the community, mostly older people and women with children. Some of my sisters and I were trained in how to take care of, prepare, and store moose meat and other animals, just like my brothers were. Women's responsibility was not restricted to food resources and food allocation. These responsibilities for taking care of the meat were equally shared among Anishinaabe of our territory.

According to stories around the Lake Superior region extending into the United States, Anishinaabekwe had responsibilities relating to assiniikaa, rocks. In earlier European history, of Lake Superior mining, the record of mining activities indicates access to both silver and copper mining resources was enabled by the Anishinaabekwe. This meant if anyone wanted access, they would do so with the consent of Anishinaabe women, who would provide the location and the permission to access. Jesuits, who were the first Europeans to complete surveys of natural resources, detailed natural resources in this area, including rock minerals. The colonial government in Canada in 1850 recognized the importance of Anishinaabe knowledge of rock minerals. Treaty negotiations only began because mining was being conducted without Anishinaabe protocol-based approval. The signing of the Robinson-Superior treaty in the fall of 1850 resulted from this. The significance of Anishinaabe oral history is evident in histories of Canadian colonialism.

Canada attempted to erase Indigenous peoples, by federal laws, Indian agents, enforced education, and forced Christianity. Canada was to be a modern civilized state, no matter what genocidal methods were applied to achieve this policy goal. The settlement of Canada, the development of national transportation systems, particularly the rail system, and the economic development of extractive natural resources enabled the marginalization and devastation of Indigenous societies. Provincial governments supported these federal systems by making Indigenous presence on the land illegal and use of the land for survival untenable.

Using federal legislative measures, Canadian governments divided family and societal relationships by membership provisions in the *Indian Act, 1876* that privileged male-based "Indians" with "Indian Status" while forcing women out of the community. In my family's case, these provisions meant hunting and caring for the meat to enable survival had to be completed fast. We were not allowed to have wild meat in our homes, so our food security consisted of hidden storage so if the Ontario Ministry of Lands and Forests (now called Ministry of Natural Resources) raided our home(s), they could not find our wild food. My family is now considered "status," but at that time, my family was not considered "Indians" under the *Indian Act, 1876*, due to the Canadian government's "Indian Registry." This meant the provincial government enforced restrictions on who could hunt and harvest from our treaty lands. Indigenous women were targeted, and their significance in Indigenous societies is evident by the scope of restrictive membership measures in the *Indian Act, 1876*. Indigenous women taught their children their languages, stories of their land, and relationships with others in their territories, and they held their community together.

Colonial laws, agents, and structures created challenges in Indigenous societies in Canada. Anishinaabe remembrances of their grandmothers and grandfathers were interrupted by genocidal planning, such as Indian residential schools and the wholescale apprehension of Anishinaabe children for provincial child welfare and social services coffers. Indigenous children, today, continue being economic stimulus for provincial governments. Recent reports detail how children within the child welfare system are a pipeline to human sex trafficking. Currently, in Canada there are record numbers of child apprehensions and missing Indigenous women and girls. More class action suits have been launched against the Canadian state, for child welfare, the Sixties Scoop, and more recently, the forced sterilization of Indigenous women.

The Canadian state sought to obliterate the authority of Indigenous women. The active and planned destruction of languages and cultures, the planned destruction of Indigenous families, the forced removal from land, and the active dispossession of Indigenous lands all point to a colonial project made to exclude Indigenous women. Indigenous women bear the weight of the colonial enterprise in their relationships with Canada and with their own societies, particularly in federally approved governance structures. Indigenous peoples' overall knowledges within Indigenous societies are targeted by colonial agents, structures, and processes, but these structural processes continue to enact against Indigenous women. Imposed governance structures were complicit in the marginalization of Indigenous women, the knowledge bundles they safeguard, and the knowledges that enabled their society's survival.

Like Geniusz (2009) discussed as storied Anishinaabe knowledge(s), the stories of my community constitute specific knowledge(s) ignored, fragmented, or made irrelevant by the state. Relational understandings, to yourself, family, and community, and other relationships, including the spiritual world, are fundamental to Anishinaabe knowledge. The basis for truth within Anishinaabe societies is personal. You are an active agent. Early in my academic writing, I made the decision, any creating I did must honour my society and be ingrained with the beauty of the land. This mental processing is necessary as theses, dissertations, and other writings on Indigenous life have a way of ending up in court, especially during land claims proceedings. I reflect on what I am doing, why, and what purposes this writing is serving every time I write.

Writing must be approached with caution. I am not unique in my caution. In this time of external experts, whose narrow historical and legal focus impedes the recognition of the beauty of our knowledge(s). Stories sustaining us at least since the last ice age, possibly longer, if archaeological research is as accurate as our stories of our origin. With the growth of global positioning mapping, treaty land entitlements, community planning processes, etc., Indigenous knowledge(s) are at risk. Indigenous knowledge(s) become considered only in isolation of the parts that are needed for a specific purpose. The conceptualization of Indigenous knowledge(s) as the life blood of our Anishinaabe societies is missing from such a fragmented dialogue.

Some experts external to our communities assume the knowledge(s) of Indigenous peoples and feed it back to us, at high cost. We are taught about Indigenous societies through the lens of this settler deficit and in uncomplicated histories about nomadic, savage wanderers after large game. These narratives are founded upon maintenance of the ideologies of male ascendency and extractive resource capitalism. The narrative structures employed ensure there is no questioning of colonial structures operating in Canada. This narrative is problematic. The continuing impact of foreign enforced **patriarchy** cannot be understated. There are unconscious hegemonic practices in these external narratives simplifying Anishinaabe knowledge(s) and Anishinaabekwe responsibilities into folklore. In these representations, Indigenous knowledge(s) grounded in the lands and waters of specific areas are not considered. Anishinaabekwe stories of waters, resources, and lands remain silenced as external discourses are not grounded in decolonization, but the continuation of the Canadian status quo. Allowing external structures to enforce this will only further oppress and remove what limited lands and resources, including people, remain.

CONCLUSION

My community continues to be a significant influence in the work that I do. This indicates responsibility to ensure preparation of this academic ground for the next generation of Indigenous scholars. In the storytelling processes of my home territory, I search for stories of Anishinaabe understandings of the Anishinaabe world. These records include Anishinaabe Chi Dimooyenh and Chic Akiwenzie telling and recording, in their own words, of their experiences in their communities and of the Anishinaabe stories that informed their lives. There are continuity and shifts in the ongoing dialogue about land happening at the community level. The fundamental aspects of the Anishinaabe worldview, manner of teaching, and philosophy accentuate a fluid and dynamic society. An Anishinaabe society in a process of excessive social change, but still maintaining core Anishinaabe knowledge(s). In this worldview, we have agency: Anishinaabekwe are not muted.

Anishinaabekwe are invigorating processes for life for Indigenous societies. Settler knowledges theorize about feminist futures; Anishinaabe societies practise this women-balanced world. Imagine a future time when Indigenous societies exist, Indigenous societies based on Anishinaabe lands and waters secured with the help of our allies. The strength of this vision can help us with the challenges resulting from ongoing colonialism of our lands and ourselves. Family stories maintained by Anishinaabekwe serve our memories for all of us. Morrisseau's Miskwi onaman stories from his grandparents about land records and rock paintings were the inspiration for the beauty of his work. The Anishinaabe with stories about thunderbirds, renewal and growth, are critical to our understandings of who we are and who we can be in this present life and in our future existence. It is time for Anishinaabe to have acknowledgement of the Indigenous knowledge(s) informing who we are. The social transformations from these knowledge(s) enact our resiliency and celebrate our ancestors' vision. It is a path we must choose for decolonizing and Indigenizing our scholarship. It is a path that requires allies who seek to change the current relationships they have with us and to change their societies in the process.

DISCUSSION QUESTIONS

1. What ideas contained in this chapter about Anishinaabekwe, women, are new information for you?

2. What parts of this article make sense to your understanding about Indigenous histories and why?

3. How can students contribute to gendered understandings of Indigenous histories?

GLOSSARY

Anemki Wajiw: Refers to where Thunder Beings live. Fort William First Nation is the caretakers of the Sacred mountain close to Thunder Bay.
Animipeegoong, Animbiigoo: The body of water now called Lake Nipigon.
gii Aanikoobijigan: Refers to your past, present and future ancestors.
Misakamigokwe: Translated as Great Earth Woman.
nii daajiibaa: Refers to the land where you are from.
nii dodem: Refers to your clan within Anishinaabe.
nii intawem: Means you have a relation with.
patriarchy: A social system developed and maintained which privileges men.

FURTHER READINGS/WEBSITES

Cote-Meek, S. (2014). *Colonized classrooms: Racism, trauma and resistance in post-secondary education.* Winnipeg, MB: Fernwood Publishing.

Eddo-Lodge, R. (2017). *Why I'm no longer talking to white people about race.* London, UK: Bloomsbury Circus.

Manuel, A., & Derrickson, R. (2017). *The reconciliation manifesto: Recovering the land, rebuilding the economy*. Toronto, ON: James Lorimer & Company.

McFarlane, P., & Schabus, N. (2017). *Whose land is it anyway? A manual for decolonization*. Vancouver, BC: Federation of Post-secondary Educators of B.C.

Vowel, C. (2016). *Indigenous writes: A guide to First Nations, Metis & Inuit issues in Canada*. Winnipeg, MB: HighWater Press.

REFERENCES

Childs, B. J. (2012). *Holding our world together—Ojibwe women and the survival of community*. New York, NY: Penguin Books.

Conway, T. (1993). *Painted dreams—Native American rock art*. Wisconsin: North Word Press Inc.

Erdrich, L. (2003). *Books and islands in Ojibwe country*. Washington, DC: National Geographic Society.

Geniusz, W. M. (2009). *Our knowledge is not primitive: Decolonizing botanical Anishinaabe teachings*. St. Paul: University of Minnesota Press.

Indian Act, 1876. R.S.C. 1985. Retrieved December 29, 2018, from http://laws.justice .gc.ca/eng/acts/I-5/FullText.html

Morton, R., & Gawboy, C. (2000). *Talking rocks—Geology and 10,000 years of Native American tradition in the Lake Superior region*. St. Paul: University of Minnesota Press.

Rajnovich, G. (1994). *Reading rock art: Interpreting the Indian rock paintings of the Canadian shield*. Hamilton, ON: Dundurn Press.

Sinclair, L., & Pollock, J. (1979). *The art of Norval Morrisseau*. New York, NY: Methuen.

University of Minnesota, Department of American Indian Studies and American Libraries. (n.d.). *Ojibwe People's dictionary*. Retrieved from http://ojibwe.lib.umn .edu/

CHAPTER 3

Reconciliation through Métissage

Bryanna Rae Scott

INTRODUCTION AND SITUATING SELF

I am deeply rooted in the cultural experiences of my childhood where I grew up in a small northwestern Ontario community. I am a half-breed, a **Métis** woman, a citizen of the **Métis Nation of Ontario**, born and raised within the historic Treaty 3 area—the only numbered Canadian treaty where the Métis people are recognized as signatories through an adhesion. I have parents with both European and Aboriginal ancestry. I am also a mother to a daughter who is a First Nations registered member with family from the Lake Helen reserve located within the Robinson-Superior treaty of 1850. I do not represent the typical, dominant culture of European or mainstream students within doctoral studies, or maybe even those of contract lecturers in Indigenous learning degree programs, both of which I am. I am a Métis student and a first-generation learner; I do not have educated parents. I am positioning myself within this context because it will represent the way in which I have taken in information and the way in which I choose to share information: as a representative of a "**Métissage**" or blended context. "Métissage has been used to denote cultural mixing or the hybridization of identities as a result of colonialism and transcultural influences" (Donald, 2009, p. 7). My contribution as an emerging academic moving forward will use the hybridization of my identity to explore education through a Métissage approach, or that of a mixed worldview, so that others like me will have the opportunity to experience an education that is reflective and responsive to who they are as a Métis person.

My passion lies with the concept of reconciling education through a "Métissage" approach and what this means for myself as an emerging Métis academic. **Reconciliation** in education allows the opportunity to challenge past discourse and allows for Métis content to enter the curriculum. "To help with rereading, reframing, and reimagining the relationships connecting Aboriginal peoples and Canadians, and thus facilitate the decolonization process in educational contexts" (Donald, 2009, p. 5): Donald calls this "Indigenous Métissage."

As referenced by Alfred (2015), "there is a whole school of Indigenous scholarship emerging around the theme of Indigenous resurgence, where a critical view of the decolonization process as it has been manifested in Canadian society is a main thrust. The other thrust is the question of what you do about it" (p. 6). I see myself placed here as one of these emerging scholars asking questions and looking for answers to better address Indigenous knowledge content in regards to curriculum gaps, so the next generation of learners have an accurate historical story of the Métis people in Canada infused within curriculum across all levels of education. I believe that with this "resurgence," opportunities exist for emerging scholars like me to reclaim our identity with the ability to address the effects of colonization on Métis people.

The time has come to reconcile relationships between the Métis and Canadian peoples and to gain a deeper understanding of Indigenous education in Canada. "Reconciliation is about establishing and maintaining a mutually respectful relationship between Aboriginal and non-Aboriginal peoples in this country. For that to happen, there has to be awareness of the past, acknowledgement of the harm that has been inflicted, atonement for the causes, and action to change the behaviour" (Truth and Reconciliation Commission of Canada, 2015b, p. 113). It is critical and timely that through education, the absence of Métis perspectives can be reconciled, paving a new path of learning for future generations of students. Reconciliation does not heal the wounds or accept the behaviour of the past, but it does allow for change. In particular, it allows change in one important system: the education system, where all come together to learn.

WHO ARE THE MÉTIS?

There are many current "claims" used to describe who the Métis are in Canada. Métis identity is often thought of in various ways: the political, the legal, and the social. To understand who the Métis are, it is best to consider each of the ways in which they may be referenced. This is important because the average Canadian is unaware of these competing definitions, which creates further confusion about who the Métis people are and pan-Indigenizes the Métis and does respect their distinct culture as a people.

The Political Métis

While the first major Métis communities were established around the Red River in Manitoba, others were later established in Saskatchewan, Alberta, around the Mackenzie River in British Columbia, around the Great Lakes in Ontario, parts of Quebec, and up to the Northwest Territories (Canada's First People, n.d.). Geography is geography; people of mixed blood are known throughout the world, but in Canada, they are known as the Métis people. "Written with a small 'm,' métis is a racial term for anyone of mixed Indian and European ancestry. Written with a capital 'M,' Métis is a socio-cultural or political term for those originally of mixed ancestry who evolved into a distinct Indigenous people during a certain historical period in a certain region in Canada" (Métis National Council, Opening Statement to the United Nations Working Group of Indigenous Populations, cited in Peterson & Brown, 1985, p. 6). The term *Métis* was used to describe those of mixed Indian and European ancestry, especially those with mixed French and Indian blood, while the term *half-breed* was used to describe those of mixed British and Indian blood (Davies, 1980, p. 4). There has been a lack of awareness and understanding of what is known about the Métis people, but what is most imperative is that the Métis are a people with a distinct history, culture, language, and way of life within Canada.

Anderson (2014) explores Métis identity as "a form of difference that powerfully shapes indigeneity in Canada. Many continue to hold up Métis hybridity as evidence of our not-quite-Aboriginal-ness" (p. 28). He further claims that "Métis are classified as a hybrid—with all the denigrating connotations of the term—in ways that deny that which we seek most, an acknowledgement of our political legitimacy and authenticity as an Indigenous people" (p. 38). I take pride in my hybridity, which allows me to claim both my Indigenous and non-Indigenous heritage. For those well versed in the history of First Nations people in Canada, it is well known that the Indian title is negotiated through treaties and the oppression faced by First Nations people enforced through legislation like the Indian Act (p. 40). Most Canadians are unaware of the scrip system, established by the federal government as a way "to extinguish the Métis' Aboriginal title to the land before a settlement could occur on the Prairies" (Dorion & Prefontaine, n.d., p. 2). In this system, each Métis person filled out an application for their entitlement and was awarded a certificate redeemable for money or land, which ultimately led to grievances over land and political representation, causing the Métis people in Manitoba to form a provisional government, which became incentive for the federal government to enter into negotiations with the Métis people (Augustus, 2008). This history is important to understand the Métis people in Canada, as they have a unique story and relationship with both the land and the federal government. This political history, however, is just one part of the story.

The Legal Métis

There is much dispute within the Métis nation about who is Métis and who is not. A more contemporary definition of Métis references both the French word *Métis*, which is derived from the Latin word *mixtus*, meaning "mixed," and the English expression "half-breed," meaning mixed blood of European and Indian people (Canada's First People, n.d.). The Métis Nation of Ontario (MNO), in its Statement of Prime Purpose (2015), offers one interpretation of who "counts" as Métis:

> We are a Nation, born of independence, and self-sufficiency whose teachings are founded on the value of honesty and truth. We are proud of our rich heritage. We are inspired by the values and traditions of our ancestors. The strength of our society is based on democracy, freedom, fairness, equality, generosity, justice and the customary and written law of our people. Above all, we cherish harmony and peace.

The Métis Nation of Ontario—along with various other provincial Métis Nation organizations across Canada—claims that "the Métis Nation is a distinct nation among the Aboriginal peoples in Canada and as such our Aboriginal and treaty rights are recognized and affirmed under Section 35 of the Constitution Act, 1982" (Métis Nation of Ontario, 2015). Gaudry and Leroux (2017) describe the Métis people in the following way:

> The Métis people have been marginalized for some time within Canada's colonial management regime. Until recently, the Métis were confined to provincial jurisdiction and were often lumped in with other unrecognized Indigenous people—non-status Indians—in Canada's legal framework. As a result, the Métis were typically regarded as mixed-descent people, not as a self-governing Indigenous nation that predates the formation of Canada.

These colonial strategies, as well as the common belief that the Métis are already at least partly European, have made Métis identity more open than that of other Indigenous peoples to settler appropriation and more easily re-conceptualized as an outcome of the white settler project. (p. 118)

The Cultural Métis

As Métis people with "a unique culture, traditions, language (Michif), way of life, collective consciousness and nationhood" (Métis National Council, n.d.), we are brought together and are distinguished from our European and First Nations relatives. Culture is often associated with belonging to a specific group. I have personally been accepted by my Métis community and belong to the MNO as a citizen. I am a mixed-blooded, half-breed woman from Treaty 3 lands. I am a direct descendant of both a Cree Indian-blooded woman and a European Norwegian man. I am the result of a genesis of a new people called Métis! My family was mobile, living in Métis settlements along the shores of the Hudson Bay, moving south to Fort William and Lac Seul, later settling in Fort Frances. I have strong family connections and a shared collective history. I am a testament to my family's genealogy of Métis culture.

Métis are a mixed hybrid race of people and want to be identified similarly to other Indigenous peoples like the Anishinaabe or Mi'kmaq, in a way that is not merely about their mixedness that defines who they are as a people, but rather their "Métisness," which is about belonging to a larger Métis nation of people (Anderson, 2014; Gaudry & Leroux, 2017). Bringing Métis perspectives forward in post-secondary education is unknown territory; however, with support from our larger community, we can use our voice and share our collective story within the larger Canadian society. With this in mind, I believe that the "average" Canadian is unaware of Métis people, their ongoing contributions to Canadian society, and the uniqueness of their culture, language, and way of life. The question to ask, then, is how could the history of the Métis people ever be integrated within higher education?

Davies (1980) reminds us that after the Battle of Batoche in 1885, where the Métis were defeated by fighting with the Canadian government and army for land title, three-quarters of a century passed before the Métis were to be heard from again. For this reason, the Métis have often been referred to as Canada's "forgotten people." Many of the Métis went to unsettled areas of the continent, usually along waterways and into the United States as refugees, and many changed their names so they would not be found guilty for

36 Decolonizing and Indigenizing Education in Canada

their role in the Northwest Rebellion. With the settlement of immigrants, many Métis lost their land and, although living off the land, there were new laws controlling how much and where they could harvest. The Métis moved around, looking for employment and schooling for their children. Alcohol became a problem for those who faced depression, and stealing became the answer to those who were hungry. Many Métis were forced to adapt to new conditions in Canada and found pride in becoming farmers, ranchers, and fishers. Overall, throughout the twentieth century, the Métis people lived in poverty, humiliation, and time of conflict (Davies, 1980, pp. 78–79).

> Over the centuries [the Métis] developed into a strong, vigorous, hybrid race that spread throughout the West and evolved into a nation. In Western Canada, they made their stand against the advancing Europeans, fought well, and lost. The evolution, the stand, and the loss are fascinating and tragic stories of North America. Their subsequent history, their constant seeking for a place in Canadian society, their desire to enter into it with the dignity of men imbued with a deep sense of history shows how a people, even a defeated and forgotten people, continually search for a future. (Sealey & Lussier, 1981, pp. 9–10)

Today, in a contemporary time of Métis people, we know a great deal more about the population.[1] After a 17-year battle, which ended on April 14, 2016, in *Daniels v. Canada*, the Supreme Court of Canada ruled that the Métis are "Indians" and entitled to rights under Section 91(24) of the Constitution Act, 1867 (Indigenous and Northern Affairs Canada, 2016). Although the details of this case will take time to work out, there is a renewed sense of hope for the Métis people. After much time and ongoing legal and political fights, the political landscape is changing as the Métis continue to move their people forward and claim their constitutional rights.

RECONCILIATION

Thinking about Canadian "willful ignorance" and the "self-serving and erroneous interpretations of key historical events [that] have been used to dispossess Aboriginal peoples for hundreds of years" (Godlewska, Moore, & Bednasek, 2010, p. 420), I became passionate about reconciliation and what this would look like for teacher education programs and the teaching of Métis history. Education has historically not made significant reference to Indigenous perspectives, histories, and cultures within the curriculum. I wanted to focus on defining "reconciliation" to explore how this could provide new ways to rethink policy and practices of education as the repair that acknowledges past errors in education, as well as addresses inconsistencies and gaps in current curriculum and pedagogies. I see "reconciliation" as a way of changing personal and institutional policies and practices to create more equitable educational outcomes and to share in Canada's Indigenous story, which is important for all students. "Reconciliation" through a Métissage approach with teachers, faculty, and students will benefit all because Canada has a Métis history and everyone deserves the opportunity to learn in the context of global citizenship and social justice education. Work needs to be done to further explore teachers' definitions of reconciliation and how they can address Métis content in all levels of education, from kindergarten through to post-secondary studies, which will further support the success of Métis learners. As we are aware, few post-secondary institutions have Indigenous content requirements, and students do not voluntarily take credits in Indigenous histories or perspectives. It is not too late, though, for post-secondary institutions to provide the opportunity for students to learn about Métis perspectives. Teaching Métis perspectives earlier, in kindergarten through to Grade 12, would be beneficial, but the provincial ministries of education do not currently prioritize Métis content. We want to see our Métis people educated and graduating high school and post-secondary studies, reaching their educational goals and employed in the work force.[2]

On one level, reconciliation is a deeply individual process that requires time and space to define what is significant and how we can best educate those students of today with an accurate history and understanding of Canada's colonial past, as well as the impact of that past on Indigenous people and all people in Canada. We do this to ensure both stories, those of settler-Canadians and those of the Indigenous peoples, can be shared and taught to all our students. Reconciliation can address inconsistencies and gaps in the current curriculum and pedagogies that continue to impact or hinder the success of all learners. On another level, reconciliation is also a concept that educators and faculty need to think about and address so we can make a connection with all our students, specifically those who have historically been segregated and oppressed within the education system. The Truth and Reconciliation Commission (2015b) defines reconciliation as an ongoing individual and collective process [that] will require commitment from all those affected including First Nations, Inuit, and Métis former Residential School (IRS) students, their families, communities, religious entities, former school employees, government and the people of Canada. Reconciliation may occur between any of the above groups. (p. 186)

For hundreds of years, Indigenous and non-Indigenous peoples have been divided on every level, enduring much conflict specific to politics on rights, in education, and in health care, and today we have the opportunity to correct misinformation and inaccuracies of the past and move toward a more shared Indigenous-Canadian story, which will only benefit all learners, including those in post-secondary studies. I envision the Métisized-Canadian story shared across the curriculum in all grade levels through to post-secondary institutions.

As a starting point, the **Truth and Reconciliation Commission** of Canada's (TRC) Calls to Action (2015a) speak to reconciliation in education occurring through the development of "age-appropriate curriculum on residential schools, Treaties, and Aboriginal peoples' historical and contemporary contributions to Canada [as] a mandatory education requirement for Kindergarten to Grade Twelve students" (p. 7). We are not telling the Indigenous chapter on the history of Canada, especially through the perspectives of Indigenous peoples. Our teachers and faculty generally know one Western history of people in Canada, and many fail to know the history from an Indigenous perspective, thus perpetuating a sense of ignorance. Ball (2003) comments,

> Culturally conditioned values and practices are caused and reflected in post-secondary studies by those who create and deliver curriculum, and it would appear as though this is especially clear in the social sciences, teacher training and other human service programs. Lack of representation of values, content and other methods at all levels of education outside of North America has educators around the globe expressing concern. (p. 86)

We need to get the Canadian history of Aboriginal peoples right, so everyone understands the relevance of the content. Osborne (2003) brings forward a strong argument that, by the end of the 1990s, the teaching of Canadian history was under debate: "Its starting point was the asserting that

Canadians did not know their history, that as a result of the quality of citizenship and the future of Canada were endangered, and that this sorry state of affairs was due in large part to the schools' failure to teach Canadian history, or to teach enough of it, or to teach the right sort of history, or to teach it effectively" (p. 589). With the TRC as a guide, we can move forward in our country to address reconciliation in education that demonstrates appropriate and acknowledging content reflective of Indigenous perspectives. Naturally, our teacher education programs need to equip upcoming teachers with Indigenous perspectives, and ideally, we would have more Indigenous faculty within post-secondary institutions to teach Indigenous content, which would include learning opportunities specific to Métis people, culture, and history.

Todd (2016) reminds us "in this time of reconciliation, not to lose sight of the importance of thinking, carefully and deliberately, about the impacts of our words, stories and philosophies as scholars upon the very communities we are part of and which are affected by how we articulate ideas about Métis peoplehood, governance, politics and existence" (p. 47). Todd reminds us of the TRC's Calls to Action (2015a), focusing on section 45, which emphasizes the need to reconcile Aboriginal and Crown constitutional and legal orders (p. 5):

> Our duty is not only to rebuild thriving, dynamic legal orders for today, but to envision futures for ourselves to carry Métis people forward into another 154 years and beyond. Contending with the Canadian courts to demand jurisdictional clarity, as is the case with the Daniels decision, is of course a part of the struggle to assert a better future for Métis people and communities. However, we cannot wait for the courts alone to revive and rebuild the stories, laws and governance practices that Métis carried with them. (Todd, 2016, p. 55)

Métis people have been held hostage by the federal government through the rebellions, the formation of the Manitoba Act, the residential school and the Sixties Scoop experiences, land scrip fraud, creation and recreation of political organizations, the wrongful execution of Louis Riel, and the time when the Métis were considered "Canada's forgotten people"; it is time to move forward in the spirit of reconciliation while sharing the Métis story within post-secondary studies, so Métis students and all students can learn, be empowered, and be proud of this historical legacy in Canada.

RECONCILING EDUCATION THROUGH MÉTISSAGE

Donald (2004) explains Métissage as an approach to research that is "a metaphor for both the fluid and discordant mixture of race, language, culture, and gender that constitutes as postcolonial experience and identity" (p. 24). Marshall, Marshall, and Barlett (2015) insist that "First Nations peoples all have to be able to walk in two worlds: that of their Native community and that of the newcomers of the white people, whose ways are the ways of mainstream society" (p. 17). As a person of mixed ancestry, I have to walk between both worlds, carving out my path to best represent my worldview and values appropriately in education and my mixed culture. Furthermore, Métissage involves "the ethical desire [that] is to reread and reframe historical understanding in ways that cause readers to question their own assumptions and prejudices as limited and limiting, and thus foster a renewed openness to the possibility of broader and deeper understandings that can transverse perceived cultural, civilizational, and temporal divides" (Donald, 2009, p. 5). My academic journey has provided several opportunities for me to explore my assumptions and judgments about education, to come to a place of reconciling traditional curriculum and content while gaining a deeper theoretical foundation of education through my cultural background and emerging scholarship. For non-Métis educators, assumptions and judgments may be made in regards to Métis students within their classrooms, and these may include:

1. A belief that there are no Métis students in post-secondary education.
2. A lack of awareness about Métis culture; a belief that the culture is the same as that of First Nations and/or Inuit people and using a "pan-Indigenous" approach to group all these cultures together is acceptable. It is not; they each have their own history as Indigenous peoples of Canada.
3. A belief that there is no one in the community to reach out to and learn about the Métis people. This is a myth as many communities in Ontario now have local Métis councils and citizens of the MNO. Many of these Métis people are professional people, and some are even teachers or educators at local community colleges.
4. There is an understanding that education is free for Métis students, so it does not matter if they pass or fail. This is also not true. There are many one-time education and training programs for Métis people, but education itself is not something supported by the federal

government, and the Métis people currently do not have the same rights as First Nations people do in accessing funds for education.

5. For Métis students that receive funding, there is an assumption that they may not attend, and this is the reason behind the mandatory attendance forms they are required to have completed for their funding. The attendance forms and grades are related to successfully completing their education program, and this is an understanding each Métis student makes as they commit to their education program. Similarly, there is an assumption that Métis students are not high achievers and likely to fail or drop out of post-secondary studies as they are first-generation students without educated parents. The truth is that Métis students are resilient, and they are achieving college diplomas and university degrees.

6. There are assumptions about what students know in relation to their culture. For example, there is the mistaken idea that all Métis students know their history, culture, and traditions well. In fact, many students have been removed from these things and are just learning them now.

Teachers themselves feel out of place based on their lack of self-reflection, knowledge, and awareness of the Métis people, culture, and history. Teacher education programs are not educating teachers about Métis history, perspectives, or content. Overall, classrooms and spaces within academic institutions are not inclusive and diversity is not respected, and therefore "those Métis" students do not have a place and are not welcome. This is fuelled by administrative people not knowing the Métis culture and all support going to First Nations students. Métis students continue to be left out of various initiatives and academic supports, and there are often no Métis people working with academic post-secondary institutions that can be called upon as a resource or to provide culturally relevant support as Métis initiatives emerge. It is very difficult to claim reconciliation in education for Métis students when there is no one inside, no Métis voice within academic institutions to assist.

Like the Métis sash, which is woven of a blend of colourful threads into a beautiful garment, my academic research, life experiences, culture, and academic-doctoral education are coming together string by string. Other educators have the opportunity to learn and reflect upon their assumptions and judgments to be in a better place to best educate their students. "Despite our common colonial reality, theorists have, through the internalization of

42 Decolonizing and Indigenizing Education in Canada

Métis-ness by Canadians, been able to construct a Canadian identity premised on a supposed mixed-ness—Métissage—represented by Louis Riel and the Métis people, and a kind of Métis-ized Canada" (Gaudry, 2013, p. 66), and this vision is what I hold dear to my heart and academic work. As a Métis student, I had to sift through readings, articles, and research that I had to read, review, and apply my cultural standpoint and worldview to critically analyze and make decisions on information reflective of my values. I had to attempt to address how various domains in education were missing, present, or revisited throughout my academic journey, reflected in my coursework experiences and scholarly activities. Before post-secondary studies, I had not considered many of these roles as belonging to my identity, nor did I realize the significance of my journey through reconciliation in academia. It is crucial for other academics to do the same, embracing their Indigenous students and a better understanding of First Nations, Métis, and Inuit histories in Canada, which are all different and deserve ongoing recognition as part of the Indigenous history of Canada.

Ladson-Billings (1995) is noted for supporting "culturally relevant pedagogy which occurs when teachers have really engaged Indigenous students in their learning" (p. 160). Three criteria compose culturally relevant pedagogy: academic success as experienced by students, cultural competence developed and maintained by students, and a critical consciousness developed by students as a way to challenge the status quo (p. 160). This engagement takes place only once faculty have accommodated for the values students bring to learning, their patterns of communication and behaviours; the sources of knowledge they see as a priority; and their histories of living and learning. Once these things have been recognized, then faculty can authentically engage students in their learning. When a student's culture is utilized in the learning process and students can maintain cultural integrity, as well as achievement in school, you know they have been engaged by a culturally relevant teacher (p. 160–161). If faculty continue to ignore the cultural and linguistic backgrounds of students, there is resistance and lack of engagement experienced by the student.

> While many Métis students grew up in the supportive and nurturing atmosphere of Métis communities and lifeways, a disproportionate number of us have not. A critical part of developing Métis pedagogies that are well-rounded and consistent with Métis ways of life is the re-establishment of relationships with the land and with Métis communities. This does not mean simply going hunting and fishing, or gardening, or ranching, but rather an immersion in Métis worldviews that sustain these practices. This

cultural immersion has a pedagogy of its own, a way of relating between knowledge-holder and learner that is based on respect, patience, and responsibility. This land-based Métis pedagogy described above respects the ability and individual attributes of the learner, while the knowledge holder must embody profound patience as the learner struggles. All of this is premised on the idea of responsibility—that learners are capable and responsible individuals who are tasked with contributing a social or material benefit back to the family or community. (Gaudry & Hancock, 2012, p. 20)

Indigenizing teaching curriculum, let alone exploring a Métissage approach, is tough work because Indigenized curriculum has gone unmandated by the government that establishes curriculum standards, learning objectives, and outcomes. We have more recently settled for "token" pieces of Indigenous content randomly placed in certain grades and subject areas. We have never fully committed to incorporating Indigenous ways of knowing and learning or content across all curriculum and grade levels, including post-secondary studies, in our country. Indigenous people have never been a priority in our education system. Métis people have never been a priority. We have always settled for what has been dictated by Western mainstream educators and policy-makers, and, if fortunate, we may have had a teacher that may have tried to do a bit more within the classroom. We live in a country filled with rich diversity and Indigenous people who have always lived here, yet we ignore and deny educational experiences and opportunities that speak to this history. We have allowed colonized practices to dictate the content our children learn in classrooms since the beginning of Canada's formation as a country. In the spirit of reconciliation, we must correct this colonial and historical error. It might be true that while

there is an initial awareness of the need for Aboriginal Education within Ontario Faculties/Schools of Education, this awareness is not necessarily impacting practice. Course directors report that they often do not include Métis content in their courses due to their lack of knowledge and understanding. The most pressing challenge confronting those working in the field is the dominant belief that Métis Education is only relevant to teachers who intend to teach in communities where there is a significant population of Métis people. (Dion, 2012, p. 5)

I know this not to be true, as people in all areas of Canada must learn about the First Nations, Métis, and Inuit history to have a complete Indigenous story of Canada.

CONCLUSION

Maria Campbell, Métis, Canadian, author, and playwright (1978), reminds us that

> history calls [the Métis] a defeated people, but the Métis do not feel defeated, and that is what is important. Today, as in the old days, they play their fiddlers, sing, dance, and tell their children the old stories. They work hard, as they have always done. They do not mind when they are called Métis, half-breeds, mixed bloods, Canadians or bois-brules. They know who they are: "Ka tip aim soot chic"—the people who own themselves. (p. 46)

Although many Métis children were sent to residential school, many remained at home to maintain the family unit. These children were able to engage in a culturally relevant education as they learned songs and dance, history, and the values of their people. As a result, these children were able to be proud of who they were and their culture.

In 2016, the Ontario government published the document "The Journey Together: Ontario's Commitment to Reconciliation with Indigenous Peoples," noting that the government needs to work with Indigenous partners and "is committed to teaching coming generations about our shared history and ensuring that survivors [of residential schools] and communities are the ones sharing these stories. Children [youth and adult learners] in Ontario must be given the opportunity to effect change and work to build a better province. This can only happen if we equip them with the truth of our entire history" (p. 16). This applies not only to children in Ontario, but to all in kindergarten through to Grade 12 and into post-secondary education systems throughout Canada, and includes an appreciation of First Nations, Métis, and Inuit peoples. As noted by Kearns and Anuik (2015), the lack of awareness of Métis history and culture continues in schools and school boards because appropriate resources need to be created that bring forward an understanding of the historical Métis people, specifically in regards to their role in the Federation of Canada and the legacy of Louis Riel (p. 26). "The Journey Together" states that

> education remains a key component of reconciliation. Through the Initial Teacher Education Program, accredited teacher-education programs offered by Ontario's faculties of education are required to provide mandatory

Indigenous content. The Province is also working with Indigenous partners to enhance the Ontario curriculum to support mandatory learning about residential schools, the legacy of colonialism and the rights and responsibilities we all have to each other as treaty people. (p. 19)

The time has come to address the curriculum absence of the Métis people, and the education system must allow for space to learn and share about the historical and contemporary Métis people, while teachers can find a relational position in regards to the Métis culture that will support in celebrating this unique culture of people (Kearns & Anuik, 2015, pp. 26–27).
In addition, "The Journey Together" (2016) says that

> through the Ontario-Métis Nation of Ontario (MNO) Framework Agreement signed in 2008 and renewed in 2014, Ontario and the MNO agreed to advance reconciliation between the Crown and the Métis people through actions including the Métis Voyageur Development Fund, announced with MNO in 2011; the declaration of 2010 as the Year of the Métis by the Ontario Legislature; and the passage of the Métis Nation of Ontario Secretariat Act in the Legislature in December 2015. (p. 43)

Although all these acts are not specific to education, progress is being made toward reconciliation between the government and Métis people. As an upcoming Métis academic, providing further research into the needs of teachers and faculty in regards to embedding a Métissage lens in education from kindergarten through to post-secondary education is a critical piece of work as part of the reconciliation/reconcile-action process in education, along with the sharing of the Métis story in Canada.

NOTES

1. According to Statistics Canada (2017), in 2016, there were 1,673,785 Aboriginal people in Canada, which accounted for 4.9% of the total population. Of this population, 587,545 identified as Métis people, accounting for 1.7% of the total population. The Indigenous population of Canada has grown by 42.5% since 2006, a growth rate four times faster than the rest of the population. Ontario and the Western provinces have the majority of the Métis people living within them (80.3%). Ontario reported the highest Métis population (120,585), one-fifth of the overall Métis population in Canada. Métis people were the most likely to live in a city, and 62.6% of the Métis population reported living in a metropolitan area of at least 30,000 people

in 2016. Winnipeg was the city with the largest reported Métis population, with 52,130 Métis people, a 28.0% increase from 2006.

2. Statistics Canada (2018) reports that in regards to education, one in four Métis people (25.6%) between the ages of 25 and 64 completed a college diploma in 2016, compared to one in five (21.1%) in 2006. An additional 13.2% completed a bachelor's degree or higher in 2016, as compared to 8.9% in 2006. There was a slight rise in high school diploma completion in 2016, with 26.5% Métis people completing high school diplomas as compared to 2006, when there were 24.3%.

DISCUSSION QUESTIONS

1. Who are the Métis? How has the definition changed over time?

2. Do Métis perspectives deserve to be included in post-secondary studies as a course all to themselves? Why or why not?

3. Why are the Métis historically significant?

4. Why do today's textbooks include more material on First Nations people than Métis people?

5. Have our perceptions of the Métis people changed in the last few decades? What were the turning points in Canadian history for the Métis people?

6. What reconciliation efforts have been made in your province to advance education on the Métis story?

7. Where are the historical Métis communities in your province?

8. What percentage of the overall Canadian population is Métis in your province?

GLOSSARY

Daniels v. Canada: A Supreme Court of Canada case that affirms the constitutional rights of Métis people in Canada under Section 35.

Métis: A distinct Indigenous group of people in Canada.

Métis Nation of Ontario (MNO): An Aboriginal government for Métis people living in Ontario.

Métis National Council: A representative body of Métis people living in Canada.

Métissage: A mixed cultural worldview, a blend of First Nations and European ancestry.

reconciliation: Understanding Canada's colonial past through Indigenous perspectives, creating equitable educational outcomes.

Truth and Reconciliation Commission: A component of the Indian Residential School Settlement that has a goal to educate Canadians about residential schools.

FURTHER READINGS/WEBSITES

The Canadian Encyclopedia, "Métis": https://www.thecanadianencyclopedia.ca/en/article/metis

First Peoples of Canada: http://firstpeoplesofcanada.com/fp_metis/fp_metis1.html

Gabriel Dumont Institute: https://gdins.org

Indigenous and Northern Affairs Canada—Métis: https://www.canada.ca/en/crown-indigenous-relations-northern-affairs.html

Indigenous and Northern Affairs Canada—Métis Rights: https://www.aadnc-aandc.gc.ca/eng/1100100014413/1100100014414

Louis Riel Institute: http://louisrielinstitute.com

Métis National Council (http://www.metisnation.ca) provides links to various Métis Nations in Canada.

Our Legacy: http://digital.scaa.sk.ca/ourlegacy/exhibit_metisculture

Statistics Canada, Aboriginal Peoples in Canada: https://www12.statcan.gc.ca/nhs-enm/2011/as-sa/99-011-x/99-011-x2011001-eng.cfm

REFERENCES

Alfred, T. (2015). Cultural strength: Restoring the place of Indigenous knowledge in practice and policy. *Australian Aboriginal Studies*, 3–11.

Anderson, C. (2014). *Métis: Race, recognition, and the struggle for Indigenous peoplehood.* Vancouver, BC: UBC Press.

Augustus, C. (2008). Our legacy: Métis scrip. Retrieved from http://digital.scaa.sk.ca/ourlegacy/exhibit_scrip

48 Decolonizing and Indigenizing Education in Canada

Ball, J. (2003). Incorporating Indigenous knowledge in post-secondary teaching. In M. Cherian & R. Y. Mau (Eds.), *Teaching large classes: Unstable practices from around the world* (pp. 84–101). Singapore: McGraw-Hill Education.

Campbell, M. (1978). *Riel's people: How the Métis lived*. Vancouver, BC: Douglas & McIntyre.

Canada's First People. (n.d.). Métis. Retrieved from http://firstpeoplesofcanada.com/fp_metis/fp_metis1.html

Davies, C. (1980). *We built Canada: Louis Riel and the new nation*. Agincourt, ON: The Book Society of Canada Limited.

Dion, S. (2012). *Our place in the circle: A review of Métis content in Ontario faculties of education*. Toronto, ON: York University.

Donald, D. (2004). Edmonton Pentimento: Re-reading history in the case of the Papaschase Cree. *Journal of the Canadian Association for Curriculum Studies, 2*(1), 21–54.

Donald, D. (2009). Forts, curriculum, and Indigenous Métissage: Imaging decolonization of Aboriginal-Canadian relations in educational contexts. *First Nations Perspectives, 2*(1), 1–24.

Dorion, L., & Prefontaine, D. (n.d.). Métis land rights and self-government: Métis scrip system in Canada. Retrieved from http://www.metismuseum.ca/media/db/00725

Dorion, J., & Yang, R. (2000). Métis post-secondary education: A case study of the Gabriel Dumont Institute. In M. Brant Castellano, L. Davis, & L. Lahache (Eds.), *Aboriginal education: Fulfilling the promise* (pp. 176–189). Vancouver, BC: UBC Press.

Gaudry, A. (2013). The Métis-ization of Canada: The process of claiming Louis Riel, Métissage, and the Métis people as Canada's mythical origin. *Aboriginal Policy Studies, 2*(2), 64–87.

Gaudry, A., & Hancock, R. (2012). Decolonizing Métis pedagogies in post-secondary studies. *Canadian Journal of Native Education, 35*(1), 7–22.

Gaudry, A., & Leroux, D. (2017). White settler revisionism and making Métis everywhere: The evocation of Métissage in Quebec and Nova Scotia. *Critical Ethnic Studies, 3*(1), 116–142.

Godlewska, A., Moore, J., & Bednasek, C. (2010). Cultivating ignorance of Aboriginal realities. *The Canadian Geographer, 54*(4), 417–440.

Government of Ontario. (2016). The journey together: Ontario's commitment to reconciliation with Indigenous peoples. Retrieved from https://www.ontario.ca/page/journey-together-ontarios-commitment-reconciliation-indigenous-peoples

Indigenous and Northern Affairs Canada. (2016). The CAP/Daniels decision frequently asked questions. Retrieved from https://www.aadnc-aandc.gc.ca/eng/1460635873455/146063594694

Kearns, L., & Anuik, J. (2015). Métis curricular challenges and possibilities: A discussion initiated by First Nations, Métis, and Inuit education policy in Ontario. *Journal of the Canadian Association for Curriculum Studies, 12*(2), 6–36.

Ladson-Billings, G. (1995). But that's just good teaching! The case for culturally relevant pedagogy. *Theory into Practice, 34*(3), 159–165.

Marshall, M., Marshall, A., & Bartlett, C. (2015). Two-eyed seeing in medicine. In M. Greenwood, S. de Leeuw, N. Lindsay, & C. Readings (Eds.), *Determinants of Indigenous peoples' health in Canada: Beyond the social* (pp. 16–24). Toronto, ON: Canadian Scholars' Press.

Métis National Council. (n.d). Who are the Métis? Retrieved from http://www.metisnation.ca/index.php/who-are-the-metis

Métis Nation of Ontario (MNO). (2015). Statement of prime purpose. Retrieved from http://www.metisnation.org/media/652666/mno-sopp-2015.pdf

Osborne, K. (2003). Teaching history in schools: A Canadian debate. *Curriculum Studies, 35*(5), 585–626.

Peterson, J., & Brown, J. (Eds.). (1985). *The new peoples: Being and becoming Métis in North America.* Winnipeg: University of Manitoba Press.

Sealey, D., & Lussier, A. (1981). *The Métis: Canada's forgotten people.* Winnipeg, MB: Pemmican Publications.

Statistics Canada. (2017). Aboriginal peoples in Canada: Key results from the 2016 Census.

Statistics Canada. (2018). First Nations People, Métis and Inuit in Canada: Diverse and growing populations.

Truth and Reconciliation Commission of Canada. (2015a). *Truth and Reconciliation Commission of Canada: Calls to Action.* Retrieved from http://trc.ca/assets/pdf/Calls_to_Action_English2.pdf

Truth and Reconciliation Commission of Canada. (2015b). *What we have learned: Principles of truth and reconciliation.*

Todd, Z. (2016). From a fishy place: Examining Canadian state law applied in the Daniels decision from the perspective of Métis legal orders. *TOPIA, 25*, 43–57.

CHAPTER 4

Indigenous Thinkers: Decolonizing and Transforming the Academy through Indigenous Relationality

Candace Kaleimamoowahinekapu Galla (Kanaka Hawai'i) and Amanda Holmes (Kanien'keha:ka)

SITUATING OURSELVES

Candace Kaleimamoowahinekapu Galla (Kanaka Hawai'i) is Associate Professor in the Department of Language & Literacy Education and the Institute for Critical Indigenous Studies at the University of British Columbia. She taught in Ka Haka 'Ula O Ke'elikōlani College of Hawaiian Language at the University of Hawai'i in Hilo, and was the Program Coordinator of the American Indian Language Development Institute at the University of Arizona. Her research emphasizes (1) Hawaiian language and Indigenous languages at the intersection of education, revitalization, digital technology, well-being, traditional and cultural practices, and/or policy and planning, and (2) decolonizing and Indigenizing the academy to create pathways for Indigenous scholars and scholarship.

Amanda Holmes is Kanien'keha:ka (Mohawk) on her mother's side, Highland Scottish on her father's side. She grew up in the Hudson River Valley of New York. She has had her Clan returned to her. She is Turtle Clan. She recently graduated with her doctorate in Language, Reading and Culture from the University of Arizona's College of Education. Her dissertation, *Geographies of Home, Memory, and Heart: Mohawk Elder Praxis, Land, Language, and Knowledge Woven in Place*, won the Frederick Erickson

ENCOUNTERING THE ACADEMY: CONTEXTS OF RESISTANCE

Outstanding Dissertation Award from the Council on Anthropology and Education in 2018.

The Western academy has constructed itself—on top of Indigenous lands, knowledge systems, memories, and ancestors—as the "privileged center of meaning-making in this hemisphere dominated by imperial nation-states" (Justice, 2004, p. 101). As academia continues to entrench and expand the colonialist project, other knowledge systems are excluded, marginalized, invisibilized, and de-legitimated as inferior (Battiste, 2000; Henderson, 2000; L. T. Smith, 2012). Western research and knowledge production "assumes its own superiority, [and] functions to silence, erase, appropriate, dominate, own, and oppress that which it encounters in the world—be it people, knowledge systems, or alternate visions of how the world could be" (Brayboy et al., 2012, p. 433). And yet Indigenous scholars remind dominant society and the academy that "this is Indian Country" (Justice, 2004, p. 102). It should go without saying, though it still needs to be stated explicitly, that Indigenous Peoples, knowledges, and ways of knowing *belong here* on Turtle Island—and in the academy.

The educational journey is challenging for Indigenous students who enter a Western academy that still refuses to recognize the impact of colonialism and the self-determination and sovereignty of First Peoples, their relationships with traditional lands, and Indigenous ways of knowing-being. Finding little space for Indigenous epistemologies and practice, Indigenous Thinkers (IT)[1] was created in 2004 by a handful of Indigenous doctoral students at the University of Arizona (UA) in response to the dearth of Indigenous scholarship, research, curricula, pedagogies, methodologies, and representation in Indigenous education they found in the College of Education. Members of IT enacted an Indigenous decolonizing methodology that attempted to "make the academy both responsive and responsible to First Nations goals of self-determination and well-being" (Justice, as cited in Mihesuah & Wilson, 2004, p. 5), and to "[establish] a continuous, visible, and active presence" (Mihesuah & Wilson, 2004, p. 5) in the academy. IT formed a grassroots response of Indigenous graduate students in education to survive the academy by Indigenizing it.

IT was, in fact, an Indigenous "resistance initiative" (G. H. Smith, 2000, p. 211)—an act of "survivance" (Vizenor, 1999), a practice of survival and resistance, and a sustaining relational network in the foreign territory of Western academia. In the academy, "knowledge production has historically been embedded within a framework driven by colonialist and imperialist interests" (Brayboy et al., 2012, p. 428), yet many Indigenous scholars assert that "the academy is worth Indigenizing" (Mihesuah & Wilson, 2004, p. 5) as a space of critical engagement and transformative resistance (hooks, 1990; G. H. Smith, 2000; Yosso, 2005).

This chapter reflects the experiences of Indigenous graduate student members of IT, who created a space for Indigeneity within the academy while navigating this unfamiliar terrain. IT began as a way to promote scholarship around Indigenous education and knowledges; to engage Indigenous knowledges and languages; to offer mutual support; and to provide resources for participating in academic practices. IT confronted a hegemonic and homogenizing academic space that neither included nor fully understood the importance and relevance of Indigenous knowledge systems and practices.

We are Kanaka Hawai'i (Galla) and Kanien'keha:ka (Holmes), scholars from Hawai'i and New York, respectively, who received our doctoral degrees with a focus on Indigenous language revitalization and education from Language, Reading and Culture in the College of Education at UA. As Indigenous scholars who resided away from our traditional homelands during our graduate studies, we acknowledge the personal and professional experiences gained while living on the traditional lands of the Tohono O'odham. Currently, Galla is Associate Professor in the Department of Language and Literacy Education and in the Institute for Critical Indigenous Studies at the University of British Columbia. As a recent graduate, Holmes's research theorizes Indigenous "Elder Praxis," the transformative capacity of intergenerational relationships, mediated by Elders, for the restoration, renewal, and resurgence of Indigenous languages, knowledges, and practice.

The experiences we gained through IT provided us with long-lasting relationships that have been critical to our success in academia and to decolonizing our graduate education. We claimed space within the academy, asserted our own self-determining aspirations and ways of knowing, resisted dominant practices of the Western institution, and created opportunities to thrive as Indigenous graduate students.

Through IT, we (re)defined the meaning of "success" for ourselves and each other, holding on to the aspiration of a doctoral degree that would be useful and relevant to our communities, as well as privileging Indigenous knowledge systems in the academy. Centring the perspectives and voices of past IT members, we discuss practices of exclusion experienced by Indigenous students within the academy, followed by how IT members actively resisted this exclusion, taking on roles of responsibility for each other's well-being and embodying an Indigenous ethic of sharing, relationality, and collectivity through Indigenous decolonizing methodologies. This was our own way of Indigenizing the academy and our graduate program.

EXCLUSIONARY PRACTICES

Western knowledge production—its processes, structures, methodologies, and ideologies—arouses a host of exclusionary practices and violences of the subtle, implicit, and unstated (and oftentimes unconscious) in its exercise of authority and dominion over the knowledge-making world. The hegemonic function of academic knowledge production makes individualism, competition, commodification, and ownership (and its practices of exclusion in the academic everyday) *normal*, reifying the colonialist project by forcing the ongoing marginalization of Indigenous knowledges, ways of knowing, and scholarship to the peripheries of what is considered valid. "The academy has much invested in maintaining control over who defines knowledge, who has access to knowledge, and who produces knowledge" (Mihesuah & Wilson, 2004, p. 5), a reminder of just what is at stake and why those stakes, and the constant (re)entrenchment of Western knowledge production, are so high.

We are reminded of the need "to write back to the academy, especially to our colleagues who in many ways have maintained an iron grip on the gates of power and authority" (Mihesuah & Wilson, 2004, p. 2). From the perspectives and positionalities of the graduate student members of Indigenous Thinkers, some of the practices we experienced that maintained inaccessibility within the academy were: little access to teaching; little access to authoring/co-authoring (or to information about how this process happened); little access to doing research with professors; little access to physical space where we could work within our department (e.g., no office, no desk, no room); little access to graduate academic positions (e.g., Teaching Assistantships, Graduate Assistantships, Research Assistantships). While our non-Indigenous graduate student colleagues *expected* to hold positions that supported them through the duration of their academic programs, none of the Indigenous students had a similar expectation.

Western academic knowledge production asserts the power to define and control, excluding other knowledge systems, framing them as illegitimate, and thus silencing other ways of knowing-being. Education in the context of **settler-colonialism** carries a long legacy of violence (physical, emotional, spiritual, cognitive/intellectual) for Indigenous Peoples, with residential/ boarding schools experienced as part of the genocidal practices of the US and Canada at the centre of **intergenerational trauma**. When cognitive, intellectual violences and macro/microaggressions (Solorzano, Ceja, & Yosso, 2000) are encountered again in new contexts of education, the impact is compounded, as layers of colonizing sediment are freshly deposited on thick layers of traumatic experiences and histories of schooling. Mihesuah (2004) asserts that higher education, though lacking the physical oppression of residential school, too often continues the ideological oppression of that experience, as students are "forced to conform to differing worldviews, values, and social skills" (p. 192). "The painful denial of self necessary for many to be successful in white academic institutions has been referred to by some scholars as 'forced racial suicide'" (Wilson, 2004, p. 80). Practices of academic exclusion created a deep sense of isolation and marginalization, a sense of feeling inferior, for many IT members.

SOCIOCULTURAL CONTEXT OF INDIGENOUS THINKERS

The state of Arizona is home to 22 Indigenous Nations and 19 Indigenous languages (Arizona Department of Education Research & Evaluation Division, 2017; Governor's Office on Tribal Relations, n.d.). Over 25 percent of the total area of the state is tribal reservation land, with two of the largest reservations in the country, that of the Diné and Tohono O'odham (Arizona Department of Education Research & Evaluation Division, 2017; Governor's Office on Tribal Relations, n.d.). American Indians and Alaska Natives make up 4.6 percent of the population of the state (US Census Bureau, 2010). The University of Arizona in Tucson, established as a land-grant university and the territory's first university in 1885, is located on the traditional homelands of the Tohono O'odham Nation. Even today, there is very little recognition in UA discourse that the university is located on O'odham homelands and what this means. Unrecognized in dominant discourse about land-grant

56 Decolonizing and Indigenizing Education in Canada

institutions is the fact that, since its inception, the US has been in the business of dispossessing Indigenous Peoples from their homelands, confiscating and stealing Indigenous land that would then become federal land. As Mihesuah and Wilson (2004) assert, "Since every academic institution sits on Indigenous land, that oppression was first corporeal; ultimately, the institutions exist because Indigenous peoples were first dispossessed" (p. 5). "The peculiarity of settler colonialism is that the goal is elimination of Indigenous populations in order to make land available to settlers" (Wolfe, as cited in Dunbar-Ortiz, 2014, p. 10).

Arizona's Racist and Racialized Policies and Practices

"Arizona's coercive—and byzantine—language and education policies" (Combs & Nicholas, 2012, p. 102) are reflective of Arizona's perception of threat from brown people within its borders and brown people pushing from outside its borders. Indigenous Thinkers was active in the context of these racist laws, policies, and practices in Arizona. The repressive policies that have unfolded in Arizona reveal dominant White supremacist attitudes toward the languages, cultures, curricula, and literatures—even the very existence—of communities of colour in the state. While Arizona has a long history of repression against people of colour, the state has become increasingly emboldened to carry out racist and reactionary policies against marginalized communities of colour.

Targeting students and communities of colour, Proposition 203 effectively eliminated bilingual education in 2000, replacing it with a new, untested "Sheltered English Immersion" program that forced English-language learners to become academically proficient in English in one year (Combs et al., 2005; Combs & Nicholas, 2012; Iddings, Combs, & Moll, 2012). In 2006, Arizona voters passed Proposition 103, making English the "official state language" by a large majority of the vote. Since then, Arizona has continued to experiment with and enact virulent anti-immigrant laws and policies targeting people of colour for heightened surveillance and policing in virtually every aspect of life. In April 2010, Arizona Senate Bill 1070 (Support Our Law Enforcement and Safe Neighborhoods Act) was signed into law, giving police the mandate to "check the immigration status of any person they reasonably suspect of being in the country illegally as part of every lawful stop, detention, or arrest" (Santos, Menjívar, & Godfrey, 2013, p. 81). Less than one month later, Arizona House Bill 2281 banned Ethnic Studies (Mexican American, Native American, Asian American, and

Women's Studies) courses in Tucson public schools in grades K–12 (Otero & Cammarota, 2011). In January 2012, Tucson Unified School District's ban of Ethnic Studies went into effect, targeting Mexican American Studies. These measures can be understood as part of Arizona's Whitestream (Denis, 1997) assertion of dominance and its assumed right to control, oppress, define, and delegitimize "transgressive knowledges" (hooks, 1994). Collective histories, knowledges, and languages are silenced with the passage of exclusionary English-only language legislation, which erases a diversity of voices and experiences with the banning of identities, literatures, curricula. This context of oppression and marginalization provides some texture for understanding the political climate and discourses of dominance in Arizona, which formed a significant part of the backdrop of IT and our graduate school experiences.

UNIVERSITY OF ARIZONA COLLEGE OF EDUCATION

At the same time that these changes were imploding in Arizona, on the University of Arizona campus, there was talk of collapsing the multicultural centres representing the diversity of cultures at the university (Native American Student Association, African American Student Affairs, Asian Pacific American Student Affairs, Chicano/Hispanic Student Affairs, LGBTQ Affairs, Women's Resource Center) into a single centre. In 2009, the College of Education's Department of Language, Reading and Culture (LRC), recognized internationally as maintaining a strong commitment to diversity and social justice in education, was merged with Teaching and Teacher Education to become a new department of Teaching, Learning and Sociocultural Studies.

A RELATIONAL NETWORK

Indigenous Thinkers was founded by Indigenous LRC doctoral students in 2004 (and invited non-Indigenous allies to participate), in a department with a history and academic genealogy of working for social justice with and in marginalized communities. In writing this chapter, we have had to confront tensions that call for nuance and care: On the one hand, the graduate students who made up IT hold great respect for LRC, respect that is based on strong and enduring relationships each of us developed with faculty, staff, and our fellow graduate students; and yet the experience imposed by the Western academy as a totality was bigger than LRC, often drowning out our local experiences and casting a shadow over the things many of us appreciated most about our department, both individually and collectively.

While the Indigenous graduate students who founded IT struggled initially to find ways to locate agency in the academy, they were given messages that, for example, they shouldn't worry because "academic socialization just happens," as one professor told a group of IT members. Yet academic socialization did not "just happen"; in fact, the *lack* of academic socialization was one of the reasons IT was formed, as a response to a lack of presence, an experience of invisibility and marginality. Although the professor's thoughts were not *intended* to exclude, to wound, to further separate, the *impact* of their ignorance of privilege served to further marginalize and diminish students' experience, because academic socialization did not happen for many of us. Indigenous realities and struggles were erased in this easy assertion of entitlement, the assumption of being brought into the academic clubhouse simply because of acceptance into a graduate program and existence in the department.

The graduate students who formed Indigenous Thinkers entered academia with the goal of earning a doctoral degree, carrying the needs of their communities close at heart and attempting to undo some of the damage of colonialism, which for many of us meant focusing on the revitalization of our languages, cultural practices, and knowledge systems. Once in academia, however, we found ourselves having to make space for Indigenous epistemologies, fighting for "the right to an intellectual life" (Parker, as cited in Brayboy et al., 2012, p. 425) for ourselves and our communities. It is our hope that our engagement in academia as Indigenous thinkers and scholars might create a different outcome for our Peoples: "Perhaps our activism and persistence within the academy might also redefine the institution from an agent of colonialism to a center of decolonization" (Mihesuah & Wilson, 2004, p. 5).

Indigenous Thinkers responded to the exclusionary practices we experienced in ways that restored health and well-being, by connecting with and supporting each other. IT embodied an emancipatory project that responded to Western "**cognitive imperialism**" (Battiste, 2000, p. 198); the Western academy enacted a certain exclusivity via academic gatekeeping, hegemony, and silencing, practices that IT members found suffocating. We worked diligently to overcome colonialism in ourselves, within our discipline, and for our respective communities by truth-telling to "[create] the crucial connections that generate the sense of community—love—that is needed to overcome the disconnection and division and mutual hatreds that reinforce colonialism" (Alfred, 2004, p. 91). IT was more than a "speaking back" or "writing back" to the academy (C. Smith, as cited in L. T. Smith, 2012, p. 38); it emerged as a local "resistance initiative" (G. H. Smith, 2000) of self-determination, enacting the six Rs of Indigenous decolonizing methodologies: **relationality**, respect, responsibility, relevance, reciprocity, and resiliency (Galla, Kawaiʻeʻa, & Nicholas, 2014; Kirkness & Barnhardt, 1991; Pidgeon, 2016). In its very assertion of Indigenous presence and legitimacy, Indigenous Thinkers embodied collective self-determination.

Within this Decolonial Space (Holmes, 2018), it was safe to be real, to be honest and open, to be vulnerable, to be flawed, to *not* know or understand—all characteristics that are perceived as weaknesses in the academy. This "living network" of critical caring, support, nurturance, and sustenance embodied by IT grew out of the practices of traditional Indigenous relationality, forming an implicit collective practice from within the worldviews and knowledge systems of its members. While the academy promoted exclusivity and heightened forms of individualism, IT created a very different paradigm, one rooted in collective, community-centred Indigenous ethics, epistemologies, and pedagogies.

As members of IT, we developed a critical consciousness (Freire, 1972) of "how we might meaningfully challenge ... oppression" (Wilson, 2004, p. 72). We reminded and supported each other to make academia relevant and useful for our respective communities by continuing to engage our traditional knowledge systems, languages, and cultural practices. At the same time, IT raised consciousness within the department, the college, and beyond, extending outward into the university, about the necessity and legitimacy of Indigenous education, scholarship, and epistemologies, "[compelling] institutional responsiveness to Indigenous issues, concerns, communities" (Mihesuah & Wilson, 2004, p. 2). With the fluctuation of incoming graduate students, students graduating, and students returning home to continue research and work in their communities, Indigenous Thinkers, as a grassroots resistance initiative, remained active at the University of Arizona through 2012.

ENACTING RELEVANCE

Well-Being, Safe Space, and Community

Participation in Indigenous Thinkers emerged out of the need for cultural coherence, for shared understandings of collective histories, and for survivance in the Western academy. As one founding member of IT reflects,

"We got there [to grad school] and we realized that we only had ourselves ... we didn't know what we were doing. We were 'the blind leading the blind.' We were alone. There was no support system. But we had each other, so we decided to get together and meet." Another founding member recalls encountering roadblocks when navigating the foreign academic terrain and having difficulty finding Indigenous role models at UA in the field of education who were familiar with the "struggles of being connected to our heritage and fighting the annihilation of our languages that had survived reservations or occupation of our homelands." Indigenous Thinkers provided critically needed collectivity, support, and relationship; one member says it offered "a place for us to cry, laugh, and cheer each other on." Another member reflects how the community that became IT created a sense of belonging and wholeness: "It gave us a home, a safe haven, a touchstone, a place to *be*, and to be *ourselves*." Group members talk about the way that, because of Indigenous Thinkers, it became possible to remain (and remain engaged) in academia: "My support came from the Indigenous Thinkers.... Without their encouragement and support, I would have *never* graduated" and "In a nutshell, it saved my sanity."

Indigenous Thinkers created Indigenous community (Cajete, 2015) and allowed for the cultivation of Indigenous presence, the nurturing of well-being, and the articulation of voice within an experience of marginality and the homogenization of Western academia. "Indigenous Thinkers was very significant because it provided me a safe harbour [where] you did not have to spend all your time explaining yourself to people," about assimilation, racism, culture and language loss, which were common lived experiences of IT members. Having to justify "my way of thinking required an inordinate amount of explanation when I shared it ... Indigenous Thinkers allowed me to shift the uncertainty from 'my problem' to critiques of the Western academic space."

Collectivity, relationality, and generosity formed the core ethic of Indigenous Thinkers, cultivating well-being within this community. Group members formed a *relational* response to the absence of Indigenous knowledges, discourses, and engagement in the academy, a *healing* response to the disconnection, competition, and individualism of academia, a *collective, cooperative* response to Western hierarchies and control: "IT made me feel like I *am* part of the university, I *am* gonna make a difference—for ourselves and for the department that we are coming out of." Indigenous Thinkers created a space where we nurtured and sustained our own "critical mass" of Indigenous scholars and non-Indigenous allies, becoming our own little pulsing nucleus of presence, resistance, and survivance: "As Indigenous graduate students, we took control of our education at a time when the institution wasn't meeting our needs, bringing the visibility of Indigeneity to academia in a profound way." We created our own pathways for our own definitions of success.

Knowledge, Epistemology, and Relationships

While Indigenous Thinkers spent much energy developing skills needed for survival and persistence (Nicholas, 2014) in the academy, the group simultaneously asserted the relevance of Indigenous knowledge systems and epistemologies in academia. Indigenous Thinkers "just by its presence and existence called for an awareness of, and an end to, the marginalization and de-legitimization of Indigenous knowledges, epistemologies, etc." As another member shares, "We should be allowed to write about what we want to write about and what we care about. We are *going* to write what we are *going* to write. We have a voice. They shouldn't hinder our voice because we have voices to be heard from our point of view. And *no one* has heard our point of view." This struggle around silencing and invisibility required IT members to work hard to prove that Indigenous knowledges were not only valid but relevant in academia, at times having to educate our colleagues, professors, department, college, and university.

The strength and special quality of Indigenous Thinkers were found in its rootedness in each other. One member shares, "IT created the space for real, enduring relationships, which meant the difference between dropping out and finishing [the doctoral program].... Perhaps this is due to the fact that out of places of great struggle, the most lasting bonds are made. It is a statement about Western academia as a site of profound struggle for Indigenous people ... that it brought us together in such deeply meaningful ways." Through its assertion of presence, its assertion of the legitimacy and relevance of Indigenous knowledges, Indigenous Thinkers members found ways to feel healthy—connected, whole, fed, and sustained: "IT was significant in a Western academic space of higher education because it gave credence to our voices ... and it provided a space to ... learn to cultivate a different, and much-needed, perspective on what it means to be educated." Education for IT members was not just about attaining the degree, but served multiple purposes that included legitimizing and asserting the relevance of Indigenous knowledges *and* that we were going to be drawing from these knowledges in our academic work, giving voice to Indigenous ways of knowing, creating a path for future Indigenous thinkers and scholars, and, most fundamentally, giving back to our communities.

PRACTICES

Writing on Indigenous methodologies, Sandy Grande (2008) maintains, "Indigenous scholars have no choice but to negotiate the forces of colonialism, to learn, understand, and converse in the grammar of empire as well as develop the skills to contest it" (p. 234). While Indigenous Thinkers developed the skills to negotiate and contest "the grammar of empire," the group was more than this; Indigenous Thinkers was about *forming relationships* as the centring orientation of knowledge production, about nurturing and sustaining Indigenous ways of knowing-being. These practices centred around sharing knowledge and resources, fundraising, academic capacity-building, and mentorship. Unlike the individualism and commodification that adhere to Western knowledge production, Indigenous Thinkers enacted generosity and sharing around knowledge and resources, reflecting an Indigenous understanding that "knowledge is relational" (Brayboy et al., 2012, p. 433). Indigenizing our experiences of the academy, "we shared literature we found, including copies of books and articles, literally passing them around. We were sharing resources ... if we found a resource, we shared it with everyone."

Fundraising was another practice fundamental to IT, primarily through frequent fry bread sales on campus, at powwows, and at fairs. Monies raised through sales gave the group opportunities we had not found through "normal" channels to attend and present at academic conferences like the Stabilizing Indigenous Languages Symposium, American Anthropological Association, and American Educational Research Association. "I was going to [the] National Indian Education Association conference ... so the [group] gave me some money to eat up there ... We had that fundraising ... to support each other through the sales of fry bread." Fundraising gave IT members a greater chance to participate and engage in academic practices that were not otherwise readily accessible to us. Additionally, the sale of fry bread meant that the group could invite Indigenous scholars in the field of Indigenous education to fill the void of there being no Indigenous faculty at that time in the College of Education: "We began to bring in Indigenous guest speakers from other universities ... because our department lacked Native faculty ... who could serve as mentors, advocates, and academic role models."

Funds also meant the ability to hold social gatherings where we would get feedback on our papers and presentations, celebrate passing our various exams, sponsor Indigenous events and gatherings, and so forth: "We needed money for guest speakers, books, conferences, and various other support. We wanted work-study jobs, but they were not easy to find." Fundraising in our own way provided an opportunity for us to access resources otherwise unavailable.

Indigenous Thinkers offered the opportunity to give each other crucial feedback on class and academic presentations, academic program requirements, and papers. Presentations were often practised in front of our peers, "to share with each other what we were working on. We did mock presentations complete with possible Q & A in preparation for qualifying exams, comps, and dissertation defences. We did demonstration lessons of things we hoped to present if we got a chance to teach." Additionally, some members of IT offered workshops on "technology to increase our skills in presentation, language preservation, and research." The group modelled an Indigenous pedagogy of mentorship, where those who had experience and expertise guided less experienced learners: "The people who are already there can show them the way and the policies and procedures of what to do and how to do it … 'Do it this way?' 'I don't know.' 'Do it this way?' 'I don't know … Just do it anyway! If it's wrong, it's wrong, if it's right, it's right, and then we'll be on the right pathway!' We developed [IT] so we could support incoming people to show them the way. Because we know the way now!" We created a sustained and sustaining network and pedagogy (Paris & Alim, 2017) of Indigenous Thinkers that mentored and supported each other through our academic program: "Without Indigenous Thinkers, I would have walked away from the struggle to be heard."

CREATING A PATH FORWARD FOR RESISTANCE, RESILIENCE, SURVIVANCE, AND TRANSFORMATION

Recognizing that resistance initiatives emerge from local particularities of context (G. H. Smith, 2000; L. T. Smith, 2000), it should be acknowledged that IT was no different. IT developed strategies for decolonization that were unique to us and to our experiences at UA. The community that Indigenous Thinkers became might be useful as a model of engagement in academia, as a self-determining resistance initiative that "[refines] or [adapts] analytical frameworks and models that have been developed for specific communities"

(Brayboy et al., 2012, p. 424). IT and the experiences we gained within IT are not a blueprint for what will work in other institutions—but it is our hope that sharing what we experienced in the academy, and the collective response that became IT, might serve as the seed of an idea, one that might be useful and relevant to other Indigenous students struggling in similar ways in the Western academy. IT, as a relational decolonizing methodology and pedagogy, became an Indigenous community of resistance, resilience, and survivance, "[engaging] in the transformation of scholarly inquiry" (Brayboy et al., 2012, p. 430), its processes, approaches, and structures, and illuminating the deep significance of relational practices that surround knowledge production for Indigenous Peoples.

We extend the theorizing of Critical Indigenous Research Methodologies (Brayboy et al., 2012) beyond research, by developing it as a relevant framework for thinking about Indigenous Decolonial Spaces (Holmes, 2018) of collectivity and community that might support and sustain Indigenous students' abilities to persist within the Western academy and, ultimately, Indigenize and transform this space. Shifting "inward, outward, and throughout the spaces-in-between" (Grande, 2008, p. 233), these methodologies hold the potential to enact collectivities of relational practice within a framework of social justice, decolonization, and self-determination for Indigenous graduate students negotiating the everyday of the Western academy.

Indigenous Thinkers became an Indigenous community of resistance and resilience, a means of survivance within the Western academy, ignited out of necessity. Western knowledge production and "research grounded in these methods [have] functionally served to vivisect the world, cutting across interconnections, lives, cultural knowledge, and bodies" (Brayboy et al., 2012, pp. 428–429), and have been used to effectively discredit and eradicate Indigenous knowledge systems. Indigenous Thinkers was a critical Indigenous decolonizing methodology in the practice of everyday resistance through connection, enacted through a supportive, nurturing, and sustaining Indigenous relationality that operated *within its own self-determining space and consciousness*. Perhaps the unifying orientation of Indigenous Thinkers was "a conscious desire we have as Indigenous people to transform the world around us because we are dissatisfied with the status quo, because we are tired of the tremendous injustices occurring around us, and because we are hungry for a change that will bring respect to our rights as Indigenous peoples" (Mihesuah & Wilson, 2004, p. 5).

We hope that the remarkable story of Indigenous Thinkers might serve as a model for the academy to consider in supporting and sustaining Indigenous graduate students throughout their program, as well as in taking transformative action that engages and privileges decolonizing methodologies and pedagogies. Most of all, it is our collective hope to support and encourage other Indigenous graduate students, in whatever institutions they find themselves, to form their own "ITs," their own local "resistance initiatives" (G. H. Smith, 2000), in whatever ways make sense for them, *regardless of institutional support*. We believe that a critical part of the beauty and power of IT has been in its very *lack* of institutionality, its grassroots nature, its inability to be contained, defined, or controlled by hierarchies of power within the academy. This occupation of liminal space was a critical element as to why IT worked so well, existing outside of academia while simultaneously situated within an academic context. We pushed against—and transgressed—boundaries and borders so as to widen the academic spaces for Indigenous scholarship, education, knowledge systems, ways of knowing, and languages. And, in the process, we became whole, together.

NOTE

1. Indigenous Thinkers was formed in 2004 and remained active (as the group that we were part of and that is the subject of this chapter) until 2012. It should be noted that in 2018, after a period of dormancy, IT was revived at the University of Arizona, though in a very different, more institutionalized framework than the IT whose incarnation we discuss here.

ACKNOWLEDGEMENTS

We would like to thank our fellow Indigenous Thinkers who have contributed to this chapter: Indigenous scholars Dr. Maxine Baptiste, Jodi Burshia, Dr. Angie Hoffman, Dr. Depree Shadowwalker, Dr. Philip Stevens, Carmen Tirado-Paredes, and ally Dr. Duffy Galda. We would also like to acknowledge the network of Indigenous Thinkers from 2004 to 2012 who contributed to decolonizing our collective experience of the academy.

DISCUSSION QUESTIONS

1. How is your department, program, college, and/or university supporting the success of Indigenous graduate students? How is it deepening and engaging wider meanings of "success" for Indigenous students and communities?

2. How is the Western academy acknowledging Indigenous "funds of knowledge" (González, Moll, & Amanti, 2005) and Indigenous ways of knowing-being?

3. What are the resources that are currently available to support the success (physical, mental, emotional, spiritual) of Indigenous graduate students? How do these resources differ from their counterparts?

4. What are some of the ways to foster this kind of a support network within academia, especially in institutions that do not have an already-established relationship with traditional landholders?

5. How can community-centred Indigenous graduate students make Western academia relevant and useful for their respective communities?

6. How can community-centred Indigenous graduate students engage their traditional knowledge systems, languages, and cultural practices within Western academia? How can Western academia support this?

7. How can Indigenous epistemologies and knowledges be engaged critically, as legitimate, relevant, and valid, within the context of cognitive imperialism (Battiste, 2000) that defines Western academic knowledge production?

8. What strategies for decolonization and Indigenization are relevant to your experiences at your particular institution?

9. How might IT be useful as a model of engagement in academia? What might an "IT model" look like in your local context?

10. How might your local context develop self-determining resistance initiatives, "[refining] or [adapting] analytical frameworks and models that have been developed for specific communities" (Brayboy et al., 2012, p. 424)?

GLOSSARY

cognitive imperialism: The hegemonic function of Western knowledge production has operated through "cognitive imperialism" (Battiste, 1986) to silence, oppress, and dominate other ways of knowing and knowledge systems, including those of Indigenous Peoples. In its relentless assertion of Western knowledge production as the only valid form of knowledge, the one and only Truth, cognitive imperialism has attempted to erase and eviscerate the richness and depth of Indigenous community knowledge systems.

intergenerational trauma: Also known as historical unresolved grief, historical trauma (Brave Heart, 1998; Brave Heart & DeBruyn, 1998). Settler-colonialism has been an everyday experience of genocide for Indigenous Peoples since contact with Europeans. This ongoing experience of massive, pervasive violence has left "a legacy of chronic trauma and unresolved grief across generations" (Brave Heart & DeBruyn, 1998, p. 60), stemming from the theft and destruction of lands, the removal from homelands, the attack on languages, the targeting of cultural and spiritual/religious practices, the desecration of sacred sites and species, and the cleaving apart of families and communities through the educational system.

relationality: "The ways in which relationships are enacted and connected" (Brayboy et al., 2012, p. 433).

settler-colonialism: "The governing settler-colonial imperative being the acquisition and retention of territory, its transfer from Native ownership requires the mobilisation of technologies of violence together with the social relations that underpin their deployment" (Wolfe, 2016, p. 15); the ultimate purpose of the settler-colonialist project is the taking of Indigenous lands through the removal and extinction of Indigenous Peoples (Dunbar-Ortiz, 2014, p. 10).

FURTHER READINGS/WEBSITES

Brayboy, B. M. J., Fann, A. J., Castagno, A. E., & Solyom, J. A. (2012). Postsecondary education for American Indian and Alaska Natives: Higher education for nation building and self-determination. *ASHE Higher Education Report, 37*(5).

Cajete, G. (2015). *Indigenous community: Rekindling the teachings of the seventh fire.* St. Paul, MN: Living Justice Press.

Coulthard, G. S. (2014). *Red skin, white masks: Rejecting the colonial politics of recognition.* Minneapolis: University of Minnesota Press.

Greenwood, M., de Leeuw, D., Lindsay, N. M., & Reading, C. (2015). *Determinants of Indigenous peoples' health in Canada: Beyond the social.* Toronto: Canadian Scholars' Press.

Simpson, L. B. (2017). *As we have always done: Indigenous freedom through radical resistance.* Minneapolis: University of Minnesota Press.

Smith, L. T., Tuck, E., & Yang, K. W. (Eds.). (2019). *Indigenous and decolonizing studies in education: Mapping the long view.* New York, NY: Routledge.

United Nations. (2008). *United Nations Declaration on the Rights of Indigenous Peoples.* https://www.un.org/development/desa/indigenouspeoples/declaration-on-the-rights-of-indigenous-peoples.html

Wolfe, P. (2016). *Traces of history: Elementary structures of race.* New York, NY: Verso.

REFERENCES

Alfred, T. (2004). Warrior scholarship: Seeing the university as a ground of contention. In D. A. Mihesuah & A. C. Wilson (Eds.), *Indigenizing the academy: Transforming scholarship and empowering communities* (pp. 88–99). Lincoln: University of Nebraska Press.

Arizona Department of Education Research & Evaluation Division in collaboration with the Office of Indian Education. (2017, March). *Arizona 2016 Indian education annual report.* Retrieved from http://www.azed.gov/oie/files/2017/03/arizona_2016_indian_education_annual_report_final_3-23-17.pdf

Battiste, M. (1986). Micmac literacy and cognitive assimilation. In J. Barman, Y. Hebert, & D. McCaskill (Eds.), *Indian education in Canada: The Legacy* (pp. 23–44). Vancouver, BC: UBC Press.

Battiste, M. (2000). *Reclaiming Indigenous voice and vision.* Vancouver, BC: UBC Press.

Brave Heart, M. Y. H. (1998). The return to the sacred path: Healing the historical trauma and historical unresolved grief response among the Lakota through a psychoeducational group intervention. *Smith College Studies in Social Work, 68*(3), 287–305.

Brave Heart, M. Y. H. & DeBruyn, L. M. (1998). The American Indian holocaust: Healing historical unresolved grief. *American Indian and Alaska Native Mental Health Research, 8*(2), 56–58.

Brayboy, B. M. J., Gough, H. R., Leonard, B., Roehl, R. F., & Solyom, J. A. (2012). Reclaiming scholarship: Critical indigenous research methodologies. In S. D. Lapan, M. T. Quartaroli, & F. J. Riemer (Eds.), *Qualitative research: An introduction to methods and designs* (pp. 423–450). San Francisco, CA: Jossey-Bass.

Cajete, G. (2015). *Indigenous community: Rekindling the teachings of the seventh fire.* St. Paul, MN: Living Justice Press.

Combs, M., Evans, C., Fletcher, T., Parra, E., & Jiménez, A. (2005). Bilingualism for the children: Implementing a dual-language program in an English-only state. *Educational Policy, 19*(5), 701–728.

Combs, M., & Nicholas, S. (2012). The effect of Arizona language policies on Arizona Indigenous students. *Language Policy, 11*(1), 101–118.

Denis, C. (1997). *We are not you: First Nations and Canadian modernity.* Peterborough, ON: Broadview Press.

Dunbar-Ortiz, R. (2014). *An Indigenous peoples' history of the United States.* Boston, MA: Beacon Press.

Freire, P. (1972). *Pedagogy of the oppressed* (M. Bergman Ramos, Trans.). New York, NY: Continuum.

Galla, C. K., Kawaiʻaeʻa, K., & Nicholas, S. E. (2014). Carrying the torch forward: Indigenous academics building capacity through an international collaborative model. *Canadian Journal of Native Education, 37*(1), 193–217.

González, N., Moll, L., & Amanti, C. (Eds.). (2005). Funds of knowledge: Theorizing practice in households, communities, and classrooms. Mahwah, NJ: Lawrence Erlbaum.

Governor's Office on Tribal Relations. (n.d.). *Tribes of Arizona.* Retrieved from https:// gotr.azgovernor.gov/gotr/tribes-arizona

Grande, S. (2008). Red pedagogy: The un-methodology. In N. Denzin, Y. Lincoln, & L. T. Smith (Eds.), *Handbook of critical and Indigenous methodologies* (pp. 233–254). Los Angeles, CA: Sage Publications.

Henderson, J. (2000). Postcolonial ghost dancing: Diagnosing European colonialism. In M. Battiste (Ed.), *Reclaiming Indigenous voice and vision* (pp. 57–76). Vancouver, BC: UBC Press.

Holmes, A. (2018). *Geographies of home, memory, and heart: Mohawk elder praxis, land, language, and knowledge woven in place.* Unpublished doctoral dissertation, University of Arizona, Tucson, Arizona.

hooks, b. (1990). *Yearning: Race, gender and cultural politics.* Cambridge, MA: South End Press.

hooks, b. (1994). *Teaching to transgress: Education as the practice of freedom.* New York, NY: Routledge.

Iddings, A., Combs, M., & Moll, L. (2012). In the arid zone: Drying out educational resources for English language learners through policy and practice. *Urban Education, 47*(2), 495–514.

Justice, D. H. (2004). Seeing (and reading) red: Indian outlaws in the ivory tower. In D. A. Mihesuah & A. C. Wilson (Eds.), *Indigenizing the academy: Transforming scholarship and empowering communities* (pp. 100–123). Lincoln: University of Nebraska Press.

Kirkness, V. J., & Barnhardt, R. (1991). First Nations and higher education: The Four Rs—respect, relevance, reciprocity, responsibility. *Journal of American Indian Education, 30*(3), 1–15.

Mihesuah, D. A., & Wilson, A. C. (2004). Introduction. In D. A. Mihesuah & A. C. Wilson (Eds.), *Indigenizing the academy: Transforming scholarship and empowering communities* (pp. 1–15). Lincoln: University of Nebraska Press.

Mihesuah, J. (2004). Graduating Indigenous students by confronting the academic environment. In D. A. Mihesuah & A. C. Wilson (Eds.), *Indigenizing the academy: Transforming scholarship and empowering communities* (pp. 190–199). Lincoln: University of Nebraska Press.

Nicholas, S. (2014). "Being" Hopi by "living" Hopi, redefining and reasserting cultural and linguistic identity: Emergent Hopi youth ideologies. In L. Wyman, T. McCarty, & S. Nicholas (Eds.), *Indigenous youth and multilingualism: Language identity, ideology, and practice in dynamic cultural worlds* (pp. 70–89). New York, NY: Routledge.

Otero, L. R., & Cammarota, J. (2011). Notes from the ethnic studies home front: Student protests, texting, and subtexts of oppression. *International Journal of Qualitative Studies in Education, 24*(5), 639–648.

Paris, D., & Alim, H. S. (Eds.). (2017). *Culturally sustaining pedagogies: Teaching and learning for justice in a changing world*. New York, NY: Teachers College Press.

Pidgeon, M. (2016). More than a checklist: Meaningful Indigenous inclusion in higher education. *Social Inclusion, 4*(1), 77–91.

Santos, C., Menjívar, C., & Godfrey, E. (2013). Effects of SB 1070 on children. In L. Magaña & E. Lee (Eds.), *Latino politics and Arizona's immigration law SB 1070, immigrants and minorities, politics and policy* (pp. 79–92). New York, NY: Springer.

Smith, G. H. (2000). Protecting and respecting Indigenous knowledge. In M. Battiste (Ed.), *Reclaiming Indigenous voice and vision* (pp. 209–224). Vancouver, BC: UBC Press.

Smith, L. T. (2000). Kaupapa Maori Research. In M. Battiste (Ed.), *Reclaiming Indigenous voice and vision* (pp. 225–247). Vancouver, BC: UBC Press.

Smith, L. T. (2012). *Decolonizing methodologies: Research and Indigenous Peoples* (2nd ed.). London, UK: Zed Books.

Solorzano, D., Ceja, M., & Yosso, T. (2000). Critical race theory, racial microaggressions, and campus racial climate: The experiences of African American college students. *The Journal of Negro Education*, [Special issue] *69*(1/2), 60–73.

US Census Bureau. 2010. Arizona: Race and Hispanic or Latino origin. Retrieved from https://factfinder.census.gov/faces/nav/jsf/pages/index.xhtml

Vizenor, G. R. (1999). *Manifest manners: Narratives on postindian survivance*. Lincoln: University of Nebraska Press.

Wilson, A. C. (2004). Reclaiming our humanity: Decolonization and the recovery of Indigenous knowledge. In D. A. Mihesuah & A. C. Wilson (Eds.), *Indigenizing the academy: Transforming scholarship and empowering communities* (pp. 69–87). Lincoln: University of Nebraska Press.

Wolfe, P. (2016). *Traces of history: Elementary structures of race.* New York, NY: Verso.

Yosso, T. J. (2005). Whose culture has capital? A critical race theory discussion of community cultural wealth. *Race Ethnicity and Education, 8*(1), 69–91.

CHAPTER 5

Thinking with Kihkipiw: Exploring an Indigenous Theory of Assessment and Evaluation for Teacher Education

Dr. Evelyn Steinhauer, Dr. Trudy Cardinal, Dr. Marc Higgins, Dr. Brooke Madden, Dr. Noella Steinhauer, Dr. Patricia Steinhauer, Misty Underwood, and Angela Wolfe, with Elder Bob Cardinal

INTRODUCTION AND SITUATING OURSELVES

As a collective of Indigenous and ally scholars who lead and teach within the Aboriginal Teacher Education Program (ATEP) at the University of Alberta, we came together over a seven-month period to explore the intentions: How do the norms of knowledge and measurement that circulate in our faculty of education act as a barrier to decolonizing, Indigenizing, and reconciliation efforts?;[1] and how are Indigenous theories of education informing how we conceptualize evaluation and design assessments for Indigenous education coursework? Our process centred a series of four listening circles and was guided by ceremony and the wisdom of Elder Bob Cardinal. We invite readers to engage this chapter in the spirit of circlework that permeated our inquiry. Circlework is distinct from focus groups in the traditional and sacred meaning it holds in many Indigenous societies and in the transformational potential for individual participants, as well as the human collective in relation (Lavallee, 2009; Nabigon et al., 1999). With cautious adaptation for research use, Indigenous theories of holism, balance, and interconnectedness directed inquiry and formulation of the intentions presented above. With guidance from Elder Bob Cardinal, we attempted to honour the tradition of circlework through engaging long-standing local protocols: particular opening and closing practices; use of sacred objects, medicines, prayer, and ceremony; a specific number and direction of circle rounds; and the participants' physical location in circle. A series of four listening circles was audio-recorded, transcribed, and relationally coded. Of the last process, each co-author spent time with the words of the person who sat to the left of them in circles; witnessed their most salient contributions given our collective intentions; and offered input regarding which of the gifts they shared might appear, and in what order, in our collaboratively written chapter. As such, the body of our chapter offers glances at what co-authors shared in circle through a format that reflects the original medium, though, in many cases, circle excerpts[2] have been reorganized and edited for clarity and flow. Not every co-author contributes to each round, nor are rounds a complete record of inquiry. Rather, we have chosen to focus on issues that educational researchers and practitioners might find resonant or relevant as they explore their own construction and enactment of evaluation and assessment when designing Indigenous education coursework. We hold that this approach works toward creating an "ethical space of engagement" (Ermine, 2007), wherein readers are supported to generate multiple meanings from their own unique positionality and relations of power; honour the diverse and embodied ways of knowing and being they bring to the text; and translate and adapt findings when considering their own educational context, roles, and responsibilities.

THEORETICAL FRAMEWORK: TRADITIONAL TEACHINGS AS PHILOSOPHICAL UNDERSTANDINGS FOR INDIGENOUS ASSESSMENT AND EVALUATION

Patsy Steinhauer: To begin I would like to share a quote from the late Lakota Elder/Scholar/Uncle Lionel Kinunwa, who stated, "We have to stop minimizing our Indigenous languages" (personal communication, 1998). He reminded us that there is precise knowledge and multidimensional intelligences that cannot be articulated in the unidimensional nature of English. I want to talk about an important nehiyaw context that operates within the processes articulated in the word kihkipiw and how I've come to understand kihkipiw, in this case, as a philosophical understanding for Indigenous assessment and evaluation. The word kihkipiw in nehiyawewin could be related to the beginning translation processes of sitting with something sacred, sitting with sacred knowledge, sitting in a sacred circle. I like to think of kihkipiw as a learning context or an Indigenous learning community, one that has physical and spiritual contexts and—if we can consider that even a little bit further—a ceremonial context of learning guided by Natural Laws. So, in this understanding, kihkipiw comes with a very ancient and rigorous system. Another understanding that is so important in this relational reality is an interconnected understanding of our kinship to all things. Our language systems perpetuate this kinship consciousness of all entities being related and interdependent in a spiritually governed reality. So, past, present, and future are interconnected in time and space in a living interconnected relationship with all our human, earthly, and cosmic relationships, which connect to all ancestral and spiritual relations. Through this teaching, we arrive at a deep understanding of the responsibility of learning.

When I was a teacher in my home community of Onihcikiskowapowin, Saddle Lake Cree Nation, our schools engaged in a community consultation that honoured ceremonial protocols to articulate the meaning and vision of education for our community.[3] The consultation unfolded the process realities of teaching and learning and informed fuller understandings of teacher, learner, curriculum, pedagogy, outcomes, and assessment as they are embodied and operate in nehiyaw pedagogical constructs of kiskinohamâkosowin—which is about teaching through a Cree understanding or in a Cree context; kiskinohamâsowin—which is the responsibility of engaging in the learning process; and kiskinwahamâtowin—teaching and learning together whereby everyone can make a valuable contribution to the collective learning. The words related to teaching in our systems inform us succinctly about what teaching and learning mean; underneath these words are spiritual contexts inherent and instinctive by our Cree mind.

In 2002, Anishinaabe Elder Jim Dumont gathered a beginning list of Indigenous intelligences that are cultivated through our systems and can be considered as we think about schooling and assessment. Briefly, our Indigenous intelligences operate through the following ways: (a) a centredness; (b) a consciousness; (c) a capacity for total responsive connectedness to the whole collective; (d) a connectedness to the total environment; and (e) Indigenous value-based seeing, relating, knowing, and doing.

In one of my first graduate school courses I had the privilege of being taught by Lakota Elder/Scholar and Uncle Dr. Lionel Kinunwa. Although

I was fluent in the language, I learned the complexity of how language IS our knowledge system. The significance of context and relationality was crystalized. I have come to learn its intricacies are fundamental to the contextual knowing and thought processes of nehiyawewin. Our language is not merely a functional tool for communication that can be relegated to linguistic classification. As a nehiyaw scholar our Elders have always reminded me of the responsibility we have in honouring the spiritual life and multidimensionality of nehiyawewin left to us by our ancestors. It is at this juncture that we make critical choices as educators to honour the gifts inside our ancient language systems and that we must take great care in upholding the spiritual essence of our Indigenous languages.

As I think about assessment and evaluation, they must be thought of through Indigenous philosophy and knowing, as well as within a context of wholeness. We might ask ourselves: Who is/are teacher(s) and what is teaching and learning? What does *being responsible* to one's peoples, ancestors, culture, language, self, and relationships as a teacher look like? What does *being responsible* look like as a learner? How important is it for us as Indigenous educators of Indigenous students to have opportunities to learn from each other, from our ancestral knowledge, and in our languages? As we consider these questions, we must ask, What is the context (kihkipiw) in which we're designing assessment?

METHODOLOGICAL FRAMEWORK: DESIGNING INDIGENOUS ASSESSMENT AND EVALUATION RESEARCH WITH TRADITIONAL TEACHINGS

Marc Higgins: At the undergraduate level, there is often flexibility in what and how you teach. Yet assessment pieces often have to be the same across course sections. The implicit message is that you can only teach so far from these norms: Assessments become challenging choke points to negotiate and navigate. So what does it mean to divert this singularizing pathway and honour the diverse ways in which people become teachers and teacher educators? To me, this isn't only a conversation about assessment but also about methodology and the ways in which the two come together and pull apart. How might we also design, carry out, analyze, and represent research in ways that align with our theoretical framework and educational commitments?

As I understand it, there are many spaces of congruency between assessment and methodology. Conventionally, methodology is understood as the methods through which knowledge is generated as well as validated through concepts such as objectivity, reliability, rigour, and reproducibility. This resembles questions of assessment: How do we know what students know and how do we measure that? Considering the overlap is critically significant: Linda Tuhiwai Smith and colleagues (2016) state methodology continues to be an important site for the work of decolonizing because "conventional" knowledge claims are often constructed and validated against the motif of an Indigenous Other. If Western knowledge and how we "measure" knowledge is defined in opposition to Indigenous ways-of-knowing-in-being, there are similar consequences for assessment as well. The work of decolonizing assessment is, however, not only a move that displaces colonial logics beyond simple reversal but also an invitation to think with Indigenous practices, peoples, places; to pull them through how we think about methodology and assessment. It is as an ethical call, to which we are accountable in terms of the ways in which we respond.

Methodology is to research as assessment is to pedagogy and curriculum. Methodology is never just a method: it's always an entangled relationship in which theory, practice, ethics, ways-of-knowing-in-being coalesce. It's the same for assessment. We can see assessment as method/ology: a test, an exam, or a writing project, for example. However, entangled within the assessment method, there's already multiple assumptions, beliefs, and practices about whose knowledge counts, what counts as knowledge, how knowledge counts, and how knowledge has to be represented in order to count.

EMERGING UNDERSTANDINGS

Round One: The Weight of Evaluation and Assessment

Evelyn Steinhauer: We are judged from the day we are born. When my first daughter was born, family members were quick to mention the colour of her skin. Why did that matter so much to them, and why did I interpret these comments as judgments? Were they telling me that "whiter was better"? There is an energy associated with that judgment that's internalized, even though it might be difficult to name or understand.

78 Decolonizing and Indigenizing Education in Canada

Imagine other children with similar experiences who are constantly being judged, both generally and through assessment in K–12 and post-secondary systems. They're going to react in ways that are linked to that negative energy. It is often assumed they are not as cognitively capable, when that is often so far from the truth. They just have a different way of being. Think of kihkipiw and Indigenous intelligences, thought processes, and types of analysis that are cultivated in this scared context and rarely acknowledged, let alone valued, in mainstream education. We are slotted into a box that sets us up for failure.

The only way that I survived as a student was through memorization. I remember my dad being called in for a parent–teacher interview and told, "Evelyn doesn't participate." When he shared this, I didn't know what participate meant, and I don't think he fully did either. For me, it was more than a lack of participation on their terms; it was an attempt to become invisible. At a very young age, I had already learned to be ashamed of who I was. I was already very familiar with judgment, maybe even comfortable with knowing that I was always going to be judged.

I've thought about my experience of a master's course for a long time. I was the only Indigenous graduate student. The professor would ask a question to start discussion and then everybody would jump in. I never had the opportunity to jump in because that's not my way, my spirit wouldn't allow it. We have been socialized to wait, to be invited, to really think through what we need to say rather than just throw out a quick response. That was a really difficult class for me until I had the opportunity to do a presentation that created space for my gifts; the professor and students noticed and started to deliberately call on me to contribute. As Patsy shared, as educators we need to design assessment that nurtures and assigns value to a broad range of intelligences and processes of analysis, like comparing and translating saturated knowledge and our peoples' knowledge.

Noella Steinhauer: Assessment is one of those things that we had to start figuring out the day we started our formal schooling. As Evelyn said, in many ways assessment is a judgment of your ability to perform at a given interval. As the oldest in the family, you have to figure out what assessment is for your siblings, that's your responsibility. So when I went to school, I had to understand what testing was about. I figured out quickly that testing did not consider my prior cultural knowledge; it was irrelevant. Testing measured how good I was at recall; I was no longer responsible for honouring the social and cultural norms of conversation and behaviour.

When I went home my grandmother would say to me, "acimow," which means, tell me the story. I knew that she meant I had to recall my entire day and I couldn't get away with saying "nothing" because I had a responsibility to provide a full review of all aspects. This review included what subjects were covered in school and who I interacted with. As I recalled the day, she might tell me how I was related to people I had interacted with and if I had interacted properly with people, all the important things for a Grade 1 child to know. These skills were different than the rote responses I was expected to perform at school. Over time I lost the ability to provide the fulsome responses to my grandmother because that was not was expected at school; all I needed to know was a bunch of information and people would think that I was smart.

When I was in Grade 6, the student with the highest mark on a particular standardized test got their test back first. I was always a reader and realized that people would think you were smart if you could regurgitate the information. I got mine back first and the teacher immediately said, "Who did you copy from?" The person who got the next-highest mark sat at the front of the class. I knew then exactly where I stood in terms of assessment. As a Cree kid, I wasn't supposed to do that well. I went through school and university with that view of myself, that I didn't deserve to do as well as others. As a student I doubted myself. Even in university, I used to think, "When are they going to catch up with me? That mark I got, maybe that wasn't my real mark."

I think of how assessment does injustice because it becomes so deeply embedded in how we think about ourselves as learners in a system so fixated on numbers to demonstrate how "smart" someone is.

Round Two: The Limitations of Normative Notions and Enactments of Evaluation and Assessment

Trudy Cardinal: Throughout the whole education system we over-privilege readers and writers and we panic if we have a child for whom this narrow version of literacy is not their gift, or if the gift does not arrive in the predetermined time. We look at the child—so full of other strengths, gifts, and promise—and say, "Your life is going to be a struggle because you are not yet reading at grade level." When we pay attention to the increasing number of

80 Decolonizing and Indigenizing Education in Canada

children who hate school and all the children who aren't surviving this life,[4] never mind surviving schooling experiences, and we choose to narrow our focus and only zoom in on "the goal of reading," especially in Indigenous communities, I know we are absolutely missing something.

As Indigenous educators we have an opportunity, a responsibility, to do something brilliant and push back against this single story of schooling success, of life-success, as only achievable via reading skills. I am not dishonouring reading. We, as Indigenous Peoples, covet these skills—reading and writing English—and see their value. However, much harm is done in this narrowly focused quest and much lost when we don't notice how much more complex lives are. I think about Elder Bob's teachings. He held up two books—one a Cree Language dictionary and the other a Western curriculum textbook—and spoke about how we can master both. As Indigenous Peoples we can master the Western curriculum but we need to also need to honour our Indigenous languages, knowledges, and wisdoms. They bring life back into what we are doing through schooling.

As we come together to think collectively about how we're assessing in ATEP over two years,[5] we have to consider that maybe we too are missing something. Have we narrowed our focus too much as well? Maybe in the first year the goal is not regurgitation of textbook Western knowledge. Maybe it is asking students, "How are you learning to balance your life? Who will help support when crisis happens?" Maybe it is making explicit how we all chose to be in this Western institution, and we must learn to navigate the institutional processes and policies and admit that they do not always align with Indigenous ways of being, knowing, and honouring of relationships. As a program, one of the goals at the very heart of all we do is our responsibility, our desire, to guide all pre-service teachers to know that as Indigenous Peoples our children are not to be harmed by schooling practices anymore. Our children are to survive and even thrive.

Noella Steinhauer: In class discussions on assessment my graduate students often struggle with the question, "What are we really teaching kids?" Mainly because standardized test scores are directly linked to a school's performance and ability to meet learner outcomes. Schools are forced to meet the targets; therefore, they must find creative ways to meet the targets because they are directly tied to funding.

So when we speak of standardized testing, it does not really exist because of this pressure to perform. Still, what is expected is authentic assessment;

therefore, I think ATEP has an important role to play in changing how assessment takes place. For example, so many of our students are so fixed on marks and have lost sight of their responsibility as learners. We need students who are engaged in deep learning. Deep learning moves beyond measuring students who are good at test taking to those who can apply knowledge in the real world (Fullan, Quinn, & McEachen 2017). It further begs the questions: What are we really teaching?; How are we really teaching?; and Are we doing a good job of doing it?

Round Three: Reconceptualization of Evaluation and Assessment

Misty Underwood: My relationship to assessment has come full circle since teaching the classroom assessment course. I'm realizing the tremendous gaps, the inherent biases, and the systemic racism that exists within standardized examinations. Through circles, I encouraged my students to spend the semester thinking about assessment differently.

The way that we assess now is primarily mental. Occasionally you may have an emotional aspect, occasionally you may have something creative, or where they're maybe doing something more physical. Hardly ever do we even know how to bring in that spiritual element, especially within an institution that lacks spirit. So I guess, as instructors we have to go back to the first question we are taught to ask: "What is it that we're assessing?"

In academia, what we're assessing is knowledge, basically, memory and the ability to retain information. Occasionally it goes beyond that, but it's all about what the person knows now, it's not how they live. And for teachers, it should be more. A teacher should go through the kind of intensity that our old medicine people went through because it's important.

In the courses I teach, my students have the opportunity to present their learning in a format or medium of their choosing. Many of our students choose to present their learning orally. I think that is where we're headed. If we are going to truly be here and our knowledge system valued, and our languages valued, then the next step is to figure out how to do oral assessments in our own way. We have to do whatever we can in our own way, when we have the power to do it.

Trudy Cardinal: As I think about my own pedagogy and practice, I notice how teacher education courses are about the healing work that I have heard Elder Bob talk about. It is about trust. I'm asking pre-service teachers to trust me, to feel safe. I acknowledge that I am restricted to an abstract B+ average (an unwritten but practised policy) and to what the institution deems is an A+. I try to be more transparent in how I am making sense of this story of grades and how we are going to get there.... In the process of being transparent, in my assessment practices, I am asking them to trust me, to just try, to just start.

This focus stems from a realization of how much fear resides in our educational system at all levels. Fear is not just in the students. It also lives in some of us as teacher educators and creeps all the way up to the top, reaching those we are accountable to in institutional hierarchies. We are held accountable to ethics that often feel dehumanizing and not relational. I think about how worried I get if my students thrive and succeed in my courses because, in my five years as professor, if too many undergraduate students achieve a grade of A or A+ in my course, this phenomenon has been viewed with unease. This unwritten but enforced policy is a foreign concept to me because for over 13 years as an elementary classroom teacher I created assessments and experiences designed to get children to succeed, to aim for the A+.

These differences are especially clear when I invite Indigenous knowledge holders and Elders into my courses as a way for pre-service teachers to build relationships with Indigenous Peoples and deepen understanding of Indigenous ways of being and knowing. In these moments, the ethic and sensibility I am hoping for them to achieve is *not* average. I am looking at whether they show up with their whole being. Learning course "content" is important but we are learning from the wisdom that the knowledge holders have over the written text. What matters now is also how well they treat all the humans that I bring in. Because they are going to teach people that I love—the next generations of Indigenous and non-Indigenous youth—this matters. Sometimes, as students begin to heal and to trust and to thrive in my courses, grades are too high. I submit them anyway and I see what happens. Sometimes I am called to account for this "unusual" trend. When I am questioned, I respond by asking, "What are you scared of? What is your worry? Who is it that we have to stand up against? I'll stand up with you. What do we need to do?" Sometimes I am trusted to have professionalism, rigour, and to be doing my due diligence when it comes to assessment and am not questioned. Either way the whole process continues to be very tension-filled for me. But I too am healing from the harm assessment can do to both assessor and assessee alike.

Round Four: Examples of Assessments That Mobilize Evolving Understandings

Marc Higgins: Just as with this circle methodology, in which we're trying to honour Indigenous oral traditions and giftedness beyond written text, I attempted to do something similar with assessment through doing an oral midterm. Part of it was to honour the oral tradition, like we're doing here, but also to recognize that different learners had different gifts. It seems so simple, yet difficult to put into practice in higher education. Towards this end, I offered big open-ended questions that recognized students had a whole background of schooling and pre-existing relations to educational assessment.

Preparing students for an oral midterm entailed offering them road signs rather than a road map: I offered questions in advance to allow for the space and time to be in relation. I suggested particular texts that they might want to reread. Further, and in the spirit of kihkipiw, questions were framed to foster kiskinohamâsiwin and kiskinwahamâtowin. Specifically, significant lived experiences in relationship to midterm questions and insights from fellow classmates were granted the same status as academic literature as it is important to demonstrate learning from one's self and from others. Instead of a written take-home exam, a 30-minute conversation was held. To begin and set the tone, I'd make a pot of tea, pour two cups, and ask how they prepared for our conversation. My favourite answer? "I've been ready for this all along. I've been to every class, I've done all the readings, I'm there, I'm present, and I'm engaged. I'm ready for this."

Through the exam, students told all sorts of stories; I wanted to know more. It wasn't a question of them attempting to anticipate my desires as assessor—we were there together, having a conversation, then another, using a descriptive rubric. I'd offer students different models: "You can grade it, I can grade it and then you speak up if you don't agree, or I can just do it." While there's no escaping the many power relationships at play, there's value in co-constructing assessment with learners and attempting to honour the diverse gifts they bring.

Angela Wolfe: Survival as a student is so common. As an Indigenous person I have had to survive more in my life as a student than in any other situation. This was especially true for me as an undergraduate student. When I think back to my undergraduate years and what I learned from the many

84   Decolonizing and Indigenizing Education in Canada

courses I took—I cannot recall much. However, what I remember vividly are the professors that were human and who treated me as such. Professors who could see the whole picture of me: beyond the student ID number, beyond the course syllabus and assignments, and beyond the cookie-cutter institutional expectations and experiences. I remember because I was asked, What do you know?; How do you feel?; and Who are you? What are your intentions with this knowledge? These are experiences I want our ATEP students to have.

To embrace our students as whole beings, we have to be able to give them space to express all aspects of themselves. As an instructor for a previous cohort I greeted each student as they came in the classroom. I saw them as whole beings. To have the students work together and be a cohort, I had to work with the complexities of who they were as a small community cohort. I realized that's how they learned how to work through their dynamics. Being from a particularly small Aboriginal community, they had all the different levels of relationship. Many of them grew up together, some were relatives, some had long histories from grade school on, while others had troubled or jilted relationships. The only way I could get to a common learning ground was if they bridged new relationship, and we did that through circle.

I literally had to put aside the course outline and how we do things as an institution, and I said, "Okay. Put the books down. Bring your chair, let's sit in circle." I pulled out a grandfather rock and shared how the *grandfather rock* was going to support us in our circle. I told them they also have to take care of him and that each of them will take turns taking mosom home when we were not in class. Then I explained to them how I understand the circle; how each person comes into a space with all they are at the moment and that in circle we are equal to share and hear each other. I said, "look in the middle of our circle, I want you to put what you're bringing that's heavy for you, put it in the middle. Then we can make a little room in our whole person to make new relationship and a space to learn." The circle became an essential pedagogical foundation for our cohort of students to be themselves. And it didn't take long, I'd say two weeks, you could feel the change when they came in the room. They were, as a cohort, different. They sat differently with each other, they talked a little differently with each other, they bonded as a cohort. As we advanced in the program we continued with each course starting in circle—professors committed to have part of their class start with circle.

We were able to use the circle not only to check in with what was challenging them but also as a place of self and group assessment. We were able to have the circle be the place we could call them out on their lack of meeting their responsibilities. For example, as instructors we were challenged with the students being on time, completing the required readings, and showing up to the class with their whole selves. I started to ask a purposeful question after the first round of checking in. I asked them: What does it mean to be late and not prepared? What does that mean to you? What's the personal consequence as well as the impact on others around you? They self-assessed in gentle, yet more firm ways than I could have as their instructor. They checked themselves and shared how if each of them did not show up committed to the class, it was hard to be a cohort learning alongside each other. Being able to do this in circle was safe and productive. No one left the circles alienated or negative. Often students ended circles with hugs and laughter. Students shared how they really depended on the circle in each class. The circle helped each student navigate their complex lives not only as students, but also as community members. Some of the students started their own classes during practicums in circle and shared how amazing it was to see Grade 1 students embracing the experience. The circle is not mine personally—it is an essential pedagogical foundation and teaching of our Aboriginal ways of being. I have always loved and trusted the process of circle and I also know how important the circle is to a classroom.

Evelyn Steinhauer: I really have come to recognize the importance of circle. Not only as a self-assessment approach that Angela raises but also as tool for creating space for participants to think about their future classrooms and selves as teachers. Transitioning from student to teacher can be really hard, so offering pre-service teachers opportunities to think about, design, and practice assessment individually and collectively gives them a head start. They get to listen to and learn from the collective and end up with multiple plural, diverse, relational images of teacher and pathways for teaching that Marc mentioned.

Brooke Madden: In attempting to blur the line between teacher and student and the hierarchical relationship therein, I involved students in designing the assessment for the required course in Indigenous education I facilitated. The teaching that we are all responsible for nurturing, investigating, and assessing our individual and collective engagement cultivated student agency.

I asked students if they wanted to consider an option other than multiple choice exams and was surprised when only about half did. I responded that since there weren't enough students who desired change, we would not revise the course assessment. One student asked, "What if we could all write the exam that best represented our learning?" We ran with this idea! With support from Technologies in Education, we co-developed midterm and final "Choose Your Own Adventure" exams. They directed students to select the components they wanted to complete for a total of 20 possible points (e.g., multiple choice for 10 or 20 points, fill in the blank for 5 points, short answer for 5 points/question up to 15 points, and essay for 10 points/question up to 20 points). There was a 10 percent increase in the class average compared to the previous year and, perhaps more importantly, I perceived a shift in responsibility for student learning. Instead of commenting that "the exam was hard," students shared things like, "I made the wrong choice. Next time I am going to trust myself and what I know and choose an essay question!"

We also co-developed a "take-away" exam. The students generated significant areas of growth and skill development (e.g., positionality in relation to Canada's colonial history and Indigenous Peoples, anticipated contributions to Indigenous education). I then generated a prompt for each area/skill to support them in detailing their engagement and a fun rubric. Level one was "I'm not moving a muscle!" and level five, "I can barely recognize the person I was when I began this course." We went back and forth—the students offering feedback to inform my revisions—and then they completed and assessed the assignment. I kept reiterating, "Who is better positioned to evaluate your process and progress than you?" and communicated that I would honour the grades they gave themselves. This approach gave way to meaningful conversation about knowledge, learning, and assessment. I stressed that while they were gifting me with their learnings and I was recording a grade, this assignment was an opportunity for them to mark what they were taking away. The class average was right around 78–80 percent. There were a few instances where I disagreed. If I thought a grade should be higher, I let students know but, for the most part, they were in alignment with what I would have given.

CONCLUSION

In this chapter, we represent what we have come to know about how conventional approaches to evaluation hinder our decolonizing, Indigenizing, and reconciliation efforts. We demonstrate how Indigenous theories of kihkipiw, teacher/teaching, intelligences, and analysis have inspired us to reconfigure research methodology, challenge knowledge and measurement norms that circulate in our faculty of education, and design creative assessment for Indigenous education coursework. We provide glances at our engagement in related circlework in four rounds: (a) the weight of evaluation and assessment, (b) the limitations of normative notions and enactments of evaluation and assessment, (c) reconceptualization of evaluation and assessment, and (d) examples of assessments that mobilize evolving understandings. Teacher educators are encouraged to bear witness to our relational theory through carrying these stories forward in their respective coursework. Our goal is for this chapter to serve as an invitation into our circle. We wonder what it might look like if teacher educators were to participate in circle rounds themselves and support pre-service teachers and teachers in doing the same, differently.[6] What ideas and experiences resonate, provoke, and/or challenge? Why? How do contributions from differently positioned, placed, gifted, and committed readers/practitioners inflect and enhance the theory developed herein? What additional rounds might be included? We suggest focus on assessment creates space to challenge under-examined colonial relations of power that generate inequity and entrench deeply learned divides in Indigenous–Canadian relations. An Indigenous theory of evaluation and assessment must be deeply rooted in and advance educational change that serves local Indigenous epistemologies, ontologies, and community priorities.

NOTES

1. We do not intend to suggest that these three terms can and/or should be used interchangeably. We understand that the assumptions, discursive practices, key scholars, purposes, and approaches are distinct across these related fields and work is required when they are put in conversation. Instead our usage signals the diversity of our collective, who, to varying degrees, engage and contribute (combinations of) Indigenous, decolonizing, and reconciliation scholarship.

2. We use "excerpt" because the contributions do not, and cannot, offer the full research context or comprehensive description of the data and associated positional, theoretical, methodological, and ethical contexts.

3. The Kihew Asiniy Education Center, our junior and senior high school, opened in 1993. The following is the initial version of the school philosophy: "We the people of Saddle Lake First Nation have a firm belief in the Natural Law (Kindness, Honesty, Sharing and Determination) which guides and maintains our distinct way of life. We are committed to kiskinohamâkosowin, ekwa kiskinohamâsowin, ekwa

mina kiskinohamâtowin as a lifelong learning process that involves the cooperation of Elders, Parents, Children, Teachers and Chief and Council of the Saddle Lake First Nation. We believe that kiskinohamâkosowin, ekwa kiskinohamâsowin, ekwa mina kiskinohamâtowin guided by Natural Law will ensure esohkahk nehiyaw mâmitoneyihcikan."

4. Nationally, "suicide rates are five to seven times higher for First Nations youth than for non-Aboriginal youth" (Government of Canada, 2018, para. 4).

5. With the exception of our urban cohorts, students must take their first 60 credits (two years) through a partner college before enrolling in ATEP for the final two years of their degree. Thus, as a team, we work closely to align education coursework over a two-year period.

6. Significant differences that might be explored include, but are not limited to, educational context (e.g., higher education vs. school-based education), educational constraints (e.g., university assessment and grading policy vs. standardized testing), and educational experiences of assessment (e.g., dissertation defence vs. application to undergraduate program).

DISCUSSION QUESTIONS

1. How do you story your relationship to assessment and evaluation?

2. What are the touchstones that inform how you engage assessment and evaluation? (How) are they shaped by colonial systems, logics, and practices?

3. Through invitation into our circle, what ideas and experiences resonate, provoke, and/or challenge? What and how will you carry forward what you have witnessed?

4. What are Indigenous teachings/theories of education that are informing how you are reconceptualizing evaluation and assessment? What are examples of assessments that animate your attempts to mobilize evolving understandings in your particular educational context?

GLOSSARY

Indigenous education coursework: That which comprises initial teacher qualification programs designed specifically for Indigenous students and contexts (e.g., ATEP), as well as coursework designed for all students that centres Indigenous perspectives, histories, knowledges, and pedagogies.

listening circles: Following our Chickasaw Elder and colleague Dr. Eber Hampton, we use the term listening circle (as opposed to talking or sharing circle) to reflect our commitment to relational and respectful listening as the central purpose and process of engaging circlework.

FURTHER READINGS/WEBSITES

Dumont, J. (2002). Indigenous intelligence: Have we lost our Indigenous mind? *Native Americas, 19*(3&4), 14–16.

Goulet, L. M., & Goulet, K. N. (2014). Ininee mamitoneneetumowin, Indigenous thinking: Emerging theory of Indigenous education. In *Teaching each other: Nehinuw concepts and Indigenous pedagogies* (pp. 170–217). Vancouver, BC: UBC Press.

Graveline, F. J. (1998). *Circle works: Transforming Eurocentric consciousness.* Halifax, NS: Fernwood Publishing.

Steinhauer, E. (2002). Thoughts on an Indigenous research methodology. *Canadian Journal of Native Education, 26*(2), 69–81.

REFERENCES

Dumont, J. (2002). Indigenous intelligences: Have we lost our Indigenous mind? *Native Americas, 19*(3&4), 1–15.

Ermine, W. (2007). The ethical space of engagement. *Indigenous Law Journal, 6*(1), 193–203.

Fullan, M., Quinn, J., & McEachen, J. (2017). *Deep learning: Engage the world change the world.* Thousand Oaks, CA: Corwin Press.

Government of Canada. (2018). Suicide prevention. Retrieved from https://www .canada.ca/en/indigenous-services-canada/services/first-nations-inuit-health/ health-promotion/suicide-prevention.html

Lavallee, L. F. (2009). Practical application of an Indigenous research framework and two qualitative Indigenous research methods: Talking circles and Anishnaabe symbol-based reflection. *International Journal of Qualitative Methods, 8*(1), 21–40.

Nabigon, H., Hagey, R., Webster, S., & MacKay, R. (1999). The learning circle as a research method: The trickster and windigo in research. *Native Social Work Journal, 2*(1), 113–137.

Smith, L. T., Maxwell, T. K., Puke, H., & Temara, P. (2016). Indigenous knowledge, methodology and mayhem: What is the role of methodology in producing Indigenous insights? A discussion from mātauranga Māori. *Knowledge Cultures, 4*(3), 131–156.

Wilson, S. (2001). What is an Indigenous research methodology? *Canadian Journal of Native Education, 25*, 175–179.

Wilson, S. (2008). *Research is ceremony: Indigenous research methods*. Halifax, NS: Fernwood Publishing.

CHAPTER 6

Centring the Lived Struggle of Indigenous Women in the Academy: A Performance Autoethnography

Celeste Pedri–Spade

What truths would be written if academics weren't afraid of losing their jobs? What truths would be written if you followed through, in practice, the type of sovereignty and decolonization you theorize in journals?
—*Lee, 2016*

Kwe kwe Celeste

Just over a year ago you gave an inspiring panel presentation about "Centering the Lived Struggle of Indigenous Women in the Academy: Identifying and Addressing Violence Towards Safer and Equitable Learning Environments" at the Maamwizing Indigeneity Conference held at Laurentian University.

At this time Taima and I are preparing an edited book on *Decolonizing and Indigenizing Education in Canada* and are inviting some of the keynotes and presenters at that conference to consider submitting an abstract for chapter proposal. I have attached the call for your reference.

We would be honoured if you would consider this invitation.

Miigwech & best wishes,
Sheila

Celeste (thinking): What have I gotten myself into?
Celeste (thinking even harder): Shit.

~

A lot of good teachings start from that little voice inside your head that goes "shit." I have learned over the years that this common reaction can tell us a lot about ourselves. Sometimes it can tell us about things that we are afraid of outside ourselves, and other times, when we dig a bit further, it can help reveal our own self-doubt and insecurity. I've had some time to reflect on what my initial reaction to the invitation to write this chapter meant ... what it still means. Why it is difficult for me to write all of this down?

This invitation takes me back to a talk I gave two years ago. It takes me back a time when I was less experienced in the realities of academic life. It takes me back to a specific time when I was trying to find my way and encountering various challenges that were helping to show me what it really meant to be an Indigenous woman, a proud and strong Anishinabekwe from Lac des Mille Lacs First Nation, in the academy. I recall thinking, *What does it mean to centre the lived struggles of Indigenous women in the academy? Why does it matter? Why do I think this is important to talk about? What does it mean for/to me, as an Anishinabekwe in the academy, to write about this? How do I write about this in a way that keeps me accountable to myself, my family, my community and nation? Will I write something that matters to others? Will I contribute something meaningful? Will this writing hurt or help me/others?*

I'm still thinking all these things. I mean, I am new to all this! I only have five years of experience as Assistant Professor navigating the often tumultuous and confusing staircases and hallways of the academy. But even though it has been a short time, I have had many stumbles along the way. I love my job. I love learning, sharing, and creating knowledge. I love being able to work with my own family members and other **Anishinabe** community members, facilitating opportunities for our people to come together and do the important work of sharing our stories and other kinds of cultural and historical marks that are important for future generations. I love my job because I know that what I am doing is grounded in a love for nin goosuk (my sons) and a commitment to making sure they grow up to be intelligent, healthy, safe, and kind **Anishinabeiniiwug** (native men). While I do love my job, what I don't love about my time in the academy, besides the obvious piles of marking that accumulate by late November, is ...

Feeling unsafe.

In my career as an Anishinabekwe academic, I have felt unsafe. I have felt physically and emotionally unsafe as an Anishinabekwe academic. Despite our academic freedoms, I have felt "unsafe professionally" as an Anishinabekwe academic. I have felt unsafe through an intentional act committed anonymously, an act that may not have inflicted physical harm but literally made me look over my shoulder continuously for some time. I have felt unsafe through an intentional act committed in the open, an act that targeted me directly as an Anishinabe woman. I have felt unsafe through the times that I've witnessed other **Anishinabekwewag** (native women) in the academy harmed.

This stuff is personal.
Deeply personal.

I know that there are many brilliant academics and/or activists and/or politicians who continuously remind us through their hashtags and op-eds that "unsafe" has and continues to be a reality for Indigenous women in **settler** colonial states like Canada. *We know* that violence against the land and water begets violence against Indigenous women (Laboucan-Massimo, 2018). *We know* that given our roles, responsibilities within our communities as caretakers/stewards of life, we are the targets of so many colonial strategies aimed at destroying life—land, water, kinship systems. *We know* that there is no such thing as "cultural safety" for Indigenous Peoples within any institution entrenched in colonial histories or "comfortable" in present-day structures and policies that work against core Indigenous values and beliefs.

In my short time in the academy, I have continued to both experience and witness colonial violence, and what I have found is that Indigenous women continue to bear the brunt of this violence; thus, when I was presented with an opportunity two years ago to propose a topic of importance related to institutional efforts to "indigenize" or implement Truth and Reconciliation, I felt compelled to do something that drew attention to the lived struggles of Indigenous women in the academy.

It is one thing to speak about this topic in a familiar environment surrounded by your peers at a conference, and it is an entirely another thing to write about it in a book that will go out into the world and be experienced by people with whom you have no relationship. I have thought about this over and over again … how to address this subject through writing in a way that keeps me accountable to my own experiences and the experiences of others. After much thought, I come back to a few things. Writing effectively and responsibly means ...

To write from the heart.
To share my own stories.
To contribute my own truth.
To honour my own voice.

To centre the lived struggles of Indigenous women in the academy is to create spaces where an Indigenous woman can come and say, "I have struggled here, I have witnessed or learned of the experiences of many other Indigenous women who have struggled here. I believe them, and I believe that they are important enough to do something about it." It is about centring my own struggles and connecting these struggles to the broader cultural, historical, and social realities affecting the struggles of other Indigenous sisters, aunties, and grandmothers. For me, it is about writing in a way that seeks to reach not only the minds of those who take in my words, but their hearts as well. And so what follows is not a third-person, detached analysis.

It is part performative testimony.
It is part manifesto.
It is part fear.
It is part hope.

It is a struggle.

It is what some may term an Indigenous (performance) autoethnography (Madison, 2011). As such, I acknowledge, draw from, and contribute to an emerging body of qualitative research that explores Indigenous autoethnography as a distinct, legitimate, and respectful means of collecting and producing knowledge that combines the tradition of storytelling with the practice of academic research (McIvor, 2010; Whitinui, 2010).

As an Anishinabekwe, I embrace performance autoethnography as personal poetic narrative: stories about authors who view themselves as the phenomenon and write evocative narratives specifically focused on their academic, research, and personal lives (Pedri-Spade, 2015, 2016; Goodall, 2006; Tillman, 2009). Personal narratives seek to "understand a self or some aspect of a life as it intersects with a cultural context, connect to other participants as co-researchers, and invite readers to enter the author's world and to use what they learn there to reflect on, understand, and cope with their own lives" (Ellis, 2004, p. 46). Moreover, as Anishinabekwe, I accept performance autoethnography into my Anishinabe knowledge system for its congruence with Anishinabe philosophies. Specifically the concept of "W'kikaendaun" or knowing/sharing as it is experienced by the speaker of the lived knowledge (Sinclair, 2013). Telling stories is a practice in many Indigenous cultures, which has sustained communities and validates the experiences of Indigenous Peoples and epistemologies (Iseke, 2003).

The following pages enact performative autoethnography as a meaningful way to centre the lived struggle of Indigenous women in the academy. I organize my contribution and present it as a **layered text** that co-mingles poetic inscriptions based on personal memories, which are interspersed with social science writing and separated with divider lines (Denzin & Lincoln, 2002; Rambo, 2005). This genre/style of writing is intentional on my part as it seeks to make visible the very challenging and messy business of negotiating what it means to "research" my "inner" story as it relates to the "outer" social and cultural realities I continue to navigate. In presenting this **performance autoethnography**, I participate in, and contribute to, the important work of making visible/knowable the overt and insidious ways that colonial violence takes place against Indigenous women in the academy. By sharing my voice, I actively participate in anti-colonial resistance and the maintenance of my own intellectual, emotional, spiritual health (Iseke, 2003).

Okay, here we go.

~

THE TRICK OF TRC

TRC
          Committees
TRC
          Advisory Groups
TRC
          Working Groups
TRC
          Courses

TRC
            Workshops

We want to Indigenize!
We want to decolonize!

We've got the Indian now!

            And she has a PhD
Check the box ...
Truth

            Check
                        Reconciliation
                                    Check
The

Truth
            Of   Reconciliation

We've got an indian!
We've got an indian!
We've got an indian!
We've got an indian too!

Indian
On
Our
Team

                        Check!
Praise us

We've got this TRC down
We've done our job

She is here
We've made a space

We will feed her

                Her Rations

We will give her

                Her Rights

Token

ism

She is our prize
Our entry
way

to reconciliation

after all
you can't have reconciliation without the indian

                right?
Tell us what to do
Use your voice

                We will listen

Good on us!!

She's our gal

                This will be good for her

Great experience

We know
We know
We know

She will learn a lot   *What's going on?*
She is lucky   *How did I end up here again!?*

| She won't get tired | *I'm so exhausted* |
| She is amazing | *I feel helpless* |

Don't worry, she is one of "the good ones"

This ain't our first rodeo, folks

This ain't our first parade

~

When I originally gave my talk back in 2016, a member of our senior administration was in attendance. After the talk, this individual approached me in what I felt to be an honest and "good way" and stated that he was committed to working toward making the workplace a safer and more equitable place for Indigenous women. This exchange instigated a number of questions for me: *Who is responsible for making the necessary changes to put a stop to the kinds of overt and covert ways that Indigenous women are made unsafe in the academy? What are some effective strategies that can be implemented to really make a difference? Should we even try to change a system that continuously shows us that its existence is dependent on our erasure?*

I've had a few years to think about these kinds of questions. I've been in many meetings where people genuinely want me to propose changes that could be implemented ... through strategic planning, through advisory committees, through ad hoc groups. I've been part of many engaging and hopeful discussions on how we can work toward centring and addressing the challenges and needs of Indigenous students, faculty, staff, and community members. I have been fortunate to be part of many groups that have been able to organize smaller projects and initiatives that created supportive and safe spaces for community to come together to do great work, spaces that privileged the voices and experiences of Indigenous women, including their stories of struggle, resistance, and survival. You would be surprised (or maybe you wouldn't be surprised) at how often I have heard people respond with "I had no idea!" or "I didn't know!" This brings me to my first point.

If we are to effectively address colonial violence, we must commit to the ongoing work of revelation, of acknowledging it is a persistent issue everywhere, and yes, it affects our Indigenous women in specific, intense ways. I say this because when these issues arise in discussions with my non-Indigenous peers in the institution, they are often followed by comments of surprise, then followed with ways in which people struggle to acknowledge that what has happened is not, actually, gendered colonial violence. There is this rush toward denial, an urge to argue that gendered colonial violence is something that happens "out there" and certainly not within the sophisticated and civilized university community.

Let's be clear it happens *everywhere*.

~

OFFICE DOOR GRAFFITI

Teacher
Mentor
Researcher

Speak back
Re write
Re right

His

               Stories

His

               Theories

You owe this to your ancestors
You owe this to your children

Honour them!

Be strong
Work hard
Show them new pathways
That
Respect

all life

Fight Back
Against Colonialism

Envision
Decolonial
Futures

Present
Represent

Alternative
Realities

I will
I will
I will

STOP!

Who are you to do this?

Isn't it time YOUR PEOPLE got over this?

I am going to RE WRITE YOU!

WRITE
          Over you
Invade
Your Space

Weaponizing Words

Covertly
Overtly

Terrorize your thoughts
Wage war on your mind

You won't know me
But you will fear me

Constantly looking
Behind/Forward
Wondering where I exist
Who I am
When I will come back
If I am watching

With/On my Mark
You will forget your ancestors

Constant fear
Constant panic

Will

Erase

Them

~

Within academic institutions, colonial violence often goes unaddressed because it is legitimized through various existing systems developed to uphold unequal social relations. In other words, in institutions like the academy, colonial violence is often hidden because it is enacted through **structural violence** (Kennedy, 2010). In the academy, structural colonial violence is enacted through various strategies and policies that continue to uphold the interests and power of privileged groups because their continued comfort and success depend on ignoring and denying the rights and interests of Indigenous Peoples on their own lands.

These kinds of colonial violence are often legitimized through settler colonial logic that takes many shapes and forms. It is when attempts to make change like allowing Indigenous Peoples to smudge on campus are continuously undermined through the rationale that if this were to happen, it could potentially harm those who don't participate in the cultural practice. This logic, of course, fails to acknowledge the harm that Indigenous Peoples may experience when their cultural practices are prevented while the apparent safety and comfort of settler peoples are upheld. It is when the physical environments where Indigenous faculty and staff work are repeatedly vandalized with racist content, and subsequent requests to install equipment that will help restore their sense of safety and well-being are denied based on the logic that it will violate the privacy of the public and create an undesirable environment.

When we centre the lived struggles of women, we also need to work on *decentring* everything that is working against us—all of the ineffective policies that do not contribute to or restore our sense of safety or well-being.

~

VERDICT

Verdict in

NOT GUILTY

I knew this was coming
There was no surprise

So why am I

Hit
Hurt
Harmed

Through/with/by

~~Justice systems~~   violent racism

I sit
I cry
I think

What do I tell my children?
How do I explain this?
How do I love them enough …
        in a society

that tells them
their lives

don't matter?

This scares the shit out of me

I know this is nothing new
Why does the world around me feel

Altered ...

I think
I cry
I stand

I go through the motions

Another work day

I am tired
I am angry

So angry

Raw
Real
Raging

I am mad at every mind that hasn't thought about her today

I am mad at every heart that doesn't ache for her family

I am mad at every body that moves confidently and freely

I am mad at every spirit that isn't carrying grief

Today

I refuse to accept your ignorance
I refuse to accept your privilege

Today

There will be no business without tears
There will be no agenda without prayer

You will never know how this feels

But you will learn her name
You will speak it out loud

She was/is loved

Her life mattered

~

Sarah Hunt (2013) reminds us that colonialism relies on the widespread dehumanization of all Indigenous people, yet this dehumanization is felt most acutely in the bodies of Indigenous girls, women, and two-spirit and transgender people, as violence against us continues to be normalized within our communities.

For Indigenous women surviving in colonial institutions like universities, this dehumanization is often expressed as a form of decontextualization. Anishinaabekwe scholar Sheila Cote-Meek (2014) addresses how Indigenous Peoples in the academy are decontextualized by their non-Indigenous peers and superiors. As an Anisihinabekwe often working in environments comprised primarily of non-Indigenous white men, I have experienced this stripping of context and displacement/dislocation from any personal or cultural context that points to my identity and experiences as an Anishinabekwe. I have been in meetings where I have voiced my thoughts and opinions as an Indigenous woman only to be responded to in a way that suggests that my non-Indigenous male "peers" do not view me as Anishinabekwe. I've come to realize how they need to erase my Indigeneity in order to "deal with me" in various situations, permitted by the duty to collegial university governance. I have also come to realize that this frequent phenomenon has nothing to do

Chapter 6 | Centring the Lived Struggle of Indigenous Women in the Academy **105**

with me at all and everything to do with what Tuck and Yang (2012) have termed "settler moves to innocence." **Settler moves to innocence** are strategies settlers use to relieve themselves of feelings of guilt or responsibility without giving up land or power or privilege, or "without having to change much at all" (p. 10). In this case, the strategy drawn upon is what Tuck and Yang (2012) refer to as the **a(s)t(e)risk(ing) of Indigenous peoples**: a process whereby the settler can imagine an Indigenous person only as culturally and socially bereft (on the brink of extinction) or actually extinct in order to relieve them from having to take my suggestions seriously and commit to changes that would, indeed, compromise the system and processes that uphold their power and privilege.

~

PROGRAMS

It is not okay

That every voice here

Speaks against

Programs
     Schools

Designed
     To
         Develop
Irresponsible
Blind
Unaccountable

"~~Do-gooders~~"   Colonial Agents

Lacking critical thought
Responsibility
Reflexivity

But I'm not the only one opposed to this

There are many around the table

                        Except one

And that one

Finds me
Isolates
                                    me
My voice
My face
My body

And STRIKES

He won't stop addressing
                        only me
He won't turn to look at another
His gaze is locked
His voice rises
As if no one else exists in the room

I shift in my seat
Should I get up?
My heart races
I don't know where to look
Why isn't anyone else saying anything?

To him
I embody
All that he seeks to help

Civilize
            Change
                        Empower

I frustrate him

I should not be here
I should not have a voice here

In his mind

I don't exist here

I only exist

out there

Displacement

Through
Colonial Imagination
Colonial Disbelief

It is not okay
That his peers speak against this too
But to him
I am the sole cause

Of why things aren't going his way

~

To centre the lived struggles of Indigenous women in the academy is to understand how many of the policies and strategies to help or protect people in university environments or to promote/respect democratic and collegial processes are so entrenched in Eurocentric worldviews and corresponding beliefs and values that they actually strengthen broad systems of colonial power, which are in and of themselves violent. That many of the mainstream systems and policies meant to help "all of us" do very little other than ensure the privileges of those who designed them are upheld.

Tuck and Yang (2012) address how directly and indirectly benefiting from the erasure and assimilation of Indigenous Peoples is a difficult reality for settlers to accept because it makes them uncomfortable and impels them hastily toward reprieve. I have been in meetings where people want to know the answers to reconciliation, want suggestions, want a plan they can implement. I've been in meetings where people pat each other on that back for developing such amazing ideas, but are entirely unprepared to accept or commit to the fact that bringing the ideas to fruition will inevitably require them to give something up in return. In this era of truth and reconciliation and the move to increase Indigenous presence across university campuses, Indigenous faculty and students are always asked *what they want* without the accompanying important question of what others who are part of the university community are *willing to give back.*

~

I want to say miigwetch (thank you) to my peers for providing me the opportunity to share my voice. This invitation has encouraged me to share my own experiences, in my own way, as an Anishinabekwe who continues to navigate the challenges of *being Anishinabekwe* in the academy. I am reminded of the teaching of the late Alex Skead, a respected Elder in my home territory, who spoke about the importance of sharing *what you know* and the importance of not trying to talk about something *you don't know* that much about. I think when you can find that balance, that is wisdom. That's what I am working toward.

I opened this chapter with a quote from Erica Violet Lee, a phrase taken from a brilliant piece she wrote to acknowledge the importance and role of her "academic aunties" in helping keep her safe as a **Nehiyaw** graduate student in the academy. I am fortunate to have several academic aunties, and I have learned that my relationship with them has been integral to my well-being as an Anishinabekwe scholar. I have learned that the most powerful strategy or weapon against any activity that threatens our safety and well-being as Indigenous women is the collective efforts of powerful grandmothers, mothers, sisters, daughters, and aunties.

Academic aunties (Lee, 2016) are instrumental in providing safe and supportive learning and working environments for every Indigenous person who sets foot on a university campus. They have walked the path. They have hit the roadblocks and have the bruises/scars to prove it. They have built bridges. Found alternative routes. Learned how to carry on with the blisters. And have done so with integrity, grace, and strength. While academic aunties are our superheroes, what I am noticing is how tired our aunties are getting. This raises the question of,

Who is looking after them?

Chapter 6 | Centring the Lived Struggle of Indigenous Women in the Academy 109

or perhaps the question should be,

What are we, as Indigenous women, doing to look after each other?

Yes, a lot can be learned from that little voice that goes "shit" in your head. I suppose in the end, it was an important reminder for me, as Anishinabekwe, to never forget the importance of our kinship systems, of our sisterhood as Indigenous women. Indeed, there is nothing more important to our collective well-being than the love and respect we have for each other.

Meeya.
Miigwetch.

DISCUSSION QUESTIONS

Questions Before Reading the Chapter

1. What kinds of things, including lived experiences, do you think Indigenous women are discouraged from talking about in the academy? Why?

2. Indigenous women had distinct roles and responsibilities related to education prior to the establishment of settler colonial post-secondary education institutions. What were some of these?

3. What are some of the specific ways that colonialism has harmed people who identify as Indigenous women?

4. When you hear "gendered colonial violence," what comes to mind?

5. What kinds of questions would you ask Indigenous women working in the academy?

Questions After Reading the Chapter

1. How did the author's poems make you feel? What did they make you think?

2. Did one or two of the poems in the chapter especially catch your attention? Why?

3. What do you think your own relationship and responsibility are to gendered colonial violence in the academy?

4. What are some of the strategies and tools that engender safe spaces for Indigenous women in the place/territory you work and/or live in?

5. What further questions do you have after reading this chapter?

GLOSSARY

Anishinabe: Ojibwe.

Anishinabeininii(wug): Ojibwe man (men).

Anishinabekwe(wag): Ojibwe woman (women).

a(s)t(e)risk(ing) of Indigenous peoples: A term developed by scholars Eve Tuck and Wayne Yang to describe a process whereby the settler can imagine an Indigenous person only as culturally and socially bereft (on the brink of extinction) or actually extinct in order to relieve them from having to take suggestions seriously and commit to changes that would, indeed, compromise the system and processes that uphold their power and privilege.

layered text: A reflexive academic writing style developed by sociologist Carol Rambo that blends conventional social science writing with intimate, narrative, and often poetic first-person texts, using asterisks or other typographic signal symbols to switch back and forth. This experiential method allows the author to open up and critique some social or cultural process they are part of, which is often silenced.

Meeya: That's enough or that's all (signifying one is finished speaking/sharing).

Miigwetch: Thank you.

Nehiyaw: Cree person.

performance autoethnography: A form of methodological inquiry committed to evoking embodied and lived experience in academic texts, drawing upon performative and reflexive writing to decolonize academic knowledge production.

settler: A person whose relationship to a specific place is linked to either their own or an ancestral migration to that place in order to establish a permanent residence there, often to colonize the area.

settler moves to innocence: A term developed by scholars Eve Tuck and Wayne Yang used to identify strategies settlers use to relieve themselves of feelings of guilt or responsibility without giving up land or power or privilege, or "without having to change much at all."

structural violence: A term used to articulate the hidden violence built into the structure of societal organizations and that is difficult to pinpoint and eradicate. The systems, policies, and procedures within these organizations are grounded in unjust social structures that reinforce inequalities, benefiting only the privileged group that created them.

FURTHER READINGS/WEBSITES

Archuleta, E. (2006). "I give you back": Indigenous women writing to survive. *Studies in American Indian literatures, 18*(4), 88–114.

Flower, R. (2015). Refusal to forgive: Indigenous women's love and rage. *Decolonization, Indigeneity, Education and Society, 4*(2), 32–49.

Holmes, C., Hunt, S., & Piedalue, A. (2014). Violence, colonialism, and space: Towards a decolonizing dialogue. *ACME: An International E-Journal for Critical Geographies, 14*(2), 539–570.

Lee, E. V. (2016, February 15). I'm concerned for your academic career if you talk about this publicly. Retrieved from https://moontimewarrior.com/2016/02/05/im-concerned-about-your-academic-career-if-you-talk-about-this-publicly/

Rodriguez, D. (2012). Racial/colonial genocide and the "neoliberal academy": In excess of a problematic. *American Quarterly, 64*(4), 809–813.

Simpson, L. (2014, March 18). #ItEndsHere: Rebelling against colonial gender violence. *Rabble.ca.* Retrieved from http://rabble.ca/news/2014/03/itendshere-rebelling-against-colonial-gender-violence

Simpson, L., Nanibush, W., & Williams, C. (2012). The resurgence of Indigenous women's knowledge and resistance in relation to land and territoriality: Transnational and interdisciplinary perspectives. *InTensions, 6*, 1–7.

Suzack, C., Huhndorf, S. M., Perreault, J., & Barman, J. (2011). *Indigenous women and feminism: Politics, activism, culture.* Vancouver, BC: UBC Press.

REFERENCES

Cote-Meek, S. (2014). *Colonized classrooms: Racism, trauma and resistance in post-secondary education.* Halifax, NS: Fernwood Publishing.

Denzin, N., & Lincoln, Y. (Eds.). (2002). *A qualitative inquiry reader.* Thousand Oaks, CA: Sage.

Ellis, C. (2004). *The ethnographic I: A methodological novel about autoethnography.* Walnut Creek, CA: AltaMira Press.

Hunt, S. (2013, February 14). More than a poster campaign: Redefining colonial violence. *Decolonization, Indigeneity, Education and Society.* Retrieved from https://decolonization.wordpress.com/2013/02/14/more-than-a-poster-campaign-redefining-colonial-violence/

Iseke, J. (2003). Living and writing indigenous spiritual resistance. *Journal of Intercultural Studies, 24*(3), 211–238.

Kennedy, C. M. (2010). Imperialism, colonialism and structural violence: An example of the resistance of Piapot and Big Bear to reserve settlement. Retrieved from University of Manitoba MSpace FGS—Electronic Theses & Dissertations (Public).

Laboucan-Massimo. (2018, March 18). Violence against the land begets violence against women. *The Narwhal.* Retrieved from https://thenarwhal.ca/violence-against-land-begets-violence-against-women/

Lee, E. V. (2016, February 15). I'm concerned for your academic career if you talk about this publicly. Retrieved from https://moontimewarrior.com/2016/02/05/im-concerned-about-your-academic-career-if-you-talk-about-this-publicly/

Goodall, B. H. L. (2006). *A need to know: The clandestine history of a CIA family.* Walnut Creek, CA: Left Coast Press.

Madison, D. S. (2011). *Critical ethnography: Method, ethics, and performance.* San Francisco, CA: Sage.

McIvor, O. (2010). I am my subject: Blending Indigenous research methodology and autoethnography through integrity-based, spirit-based research. *Canadian Journal of Native Education, 33*(1), 137–155.

Pedri-Spade, C. (2015). The drum is my document: Decolonizing research through Anishinabe song and drum. *International Review of Qualitative Research, 9*(4), 385–406.

Pedri-Spade, C. (2016). Four stories of an overtaxed indian. *Indigenous Social Work Journal, 10*, 85–100.

Rambo, C. (2005). Impressions of grandmother: An autoethnographic portrait. *Journal of Contemporary Ethnography, 34*(5), 560–585.

Sinclair, N. J. (2013). K'Zaugin: Storying ourselves into life. In J. Doerfler, N. J. Sinclair, & H. K. Stark (Eds.), *Centring Anishinaabeg studies: Understanding the world through stories* (pp. 81–102). East Lansing: Michigan University Press.

Tillmann, L. M. (2009). Body and bulimia revisited: Reflections on "A Secret Life." *Journal of Applied Communication Research, 37*(1), 98–112.

Tuck, E., & Yang, W. (2012). Decolonization is not a metaphor. *Decolonization, Indigeneity, Education and Society, 1*(1), 1–40.

Whitinui, P. (2010, June). *Indigenous autoethnography: Exploring, engaging and experiencing the self* [PowerPoint slides]. Paper presented at the 4th annual traditional international Indigenous conference, New Zealand. Retrieved from http://canterbury-nz.academia.edu/PaulWhitinui/Talks/64858/ Indigenous_Auto-ethnography_Exploring_Engaging_and_Experiencing_Self

THEME 2
DECOLONIZING POST-SECONDARY INSTITUTIONS

Building Space in the Academy for Indigenous Peoples, Resistance, and Reconciliation

CHAPTER 7

Is Decolonization Possible in the Academy?

Lynn Lavallee

In Canada, there has been a surge of discussion around reconciling, decolonizing, and Indigenizing the academy, particularly in the wake of the release of the Truth and Reconciliation Commission (TRC) final report (Truth and Reconciliation Commission of Canada, 2015). The TRC gathered statements from residential school survivors attesting to their experiences while in residential school. However, for Indigenous academics who have been addressing Indigenous matters in their research, attempting to advance Indigenous epistemology and ethical ways of conducting research with Indigenous communities, and battling the chilly climate for Indigenous people in the academy, this surge is more like a resurgence. As Urban Elder Vern Harper stated, "We were never idle!" and the same holds true for senior Indigenous academics who have been tirelessly working on advancing Indigenous knowledge in the academy while facing anti-Indigenous racism, microaggressions, and deeply embedded systemic racism in the academy. Many recall the 1996 Royal Commission on Aboriginal Peoples and the little, if any, movement that came from its recommendations, so it stands to reason that many Indigenous peoples, and this includes Indigenous knowledge keepers/ Elders and scholars fighting the fight for decades, are a bit skeptical about the current reconciliation, decolonizing, and Indigenizing exercise. However, the current interest in decolonizing, reconciling, and Indigenizing the academy is a wave we can ride while many institutions consider Indigenous achievement a priority. Nonetheless, Indigenous peoples in the academy will continue to make space for their bodies, knowledge, and ways of knowing, being, and doing. This chapter will focus on some of the challenges to consider in the quest to reconcile the academy and offer recommendations that could lead to systemic change.

Using the terminology reconciling, decolonizing, or Indigenizing the academy may indicate a strong commitment to advancing Indigenous knowledge in the academy and an attempt to be inclusive of Indigenous peoples and initiatives; however, institutions need to define what they mean by reconciling, decolonizing, or Indigenizing. Reconciliation, decolonization, and Indigenization provide a well-ordered platform that runs the risk of being interpreted as a box that can be checked off once accomplished, although those advocating for reconciliation continually emphasize this is a life-long process. Further, specific measurables that remain sustainable must be articulated and achieved in order to *check the reconciliation box*. In addition, funding commitments and funds spent must reflect stated priorities with respect to Indigenizing the academy; alternatively stated, it's not just giving lip-service to reconciliation but putting money behind insurgence, resurgence, and transformative change. The terminology is important to define in order to be accountable; however, recognizing the inherent issues with these neatly packaged terms needs further discussion.

Reconciliation at the level of the institution is terminology that has gained momentum. It has become an attractive sound bite that is rarely, if ever, defined by individuals and the institution. What would a reconciled institution look like? Reconciliation is defined as a "restoring of friendly relations" and "the action of making one view or belief compatible with another" (reconciliation, n.d.a). Both of these definitions are problematic. The former implies Canada was founded on friendly relations with Indigenous peoples and that restoration is the goal. Transformational change must be the end goal, not a restoration. We cannot return to friendly relations that never existed in the past. The latter definition is even more problematic in that it affirms colonization and is reflective of the residential school movement goal of assimilating Indigenous peoples and the aim to "kill the Indian in the child" (TRC, 2015, p. 130).

The term—reconciliation—also has significant religious meaning that cannot be ignored, particularly when referring to working with a community of people that were colonized through religion. Reconciliation is a Roman Catholic sacrament of penance (reconciliation, n.d.b). The term *reconciliation* never sat well with me, and when I heard Tracey Lindberg (2017) refer to reconciliation as a religious term, I more fully understood my issue with the terminology. I was raised Catholic and, in particular, my maternal grandmother enforced a shameful, punitive, religious upbringing mixed with what I learned were mutated practices from Indigenous ceremony. It was an odd mix but one that still resonates with me today. I knew little about my grandmother's history and, for that matter, little about all my grandparents' and parents' upbringing; however, I knew my grandmother *went away to school* as a young child. She had siblings but never spoke about them. She came back from school with a "bowl" haircut. They called the school a convent where nuns taught the children. All my grandparents had passed away by the very early 1980s, so the term residential school was never used, but I remember there was always a threat to be taken away by a *white van* or child welfare. I'm not sure how the white van plays in but it was a specific threat by my grandmother: "The white van is going to come and take you away!" I experienced the sacraments of baptism, confession, and confirmation—I am intentionally not capitalizing these terms as a form of resistance. The sacrament of penance, also referred to as the act of contrition, where your sins are reconciled, was one of many experiences that led me to be critical of the church. My last confession was in Grade 7 or 8 with a new priest in a church I attended while at St. Paul's School in Toronto, and he alluded to a sexual act. I ran out of the church without doing my penance (prayers assigned by the priest so your sins can be reconciled with and through christ) so as to not have the priest see me and never set foot in the confessional booth ever again. This is the experience from which I speak when I refer to reconciliation, as it sparks a personal history but also blood memory of my ancestors (parents, grandparents, etc.) being colonized through religion. How can this history be reconciled? No amount of hail marys or our fathers, no number of acts of contrition prayers can undo this colonial history.

The term *reconciliation* is a neocolonial term meant to free non-Indigenous peoples from their sins against Indigenous peoples, but the harms are still happening. The act of contrition states:

> O my god, I am heartly sorry for having offended thee, and I detest all my sins because of thy just punishments, but also because they offended thee, my god, who art all-good and deserving of all my love. I firmly resolve, with the help of thy grace, to sin no more and to avoid the near occasions of sin. (found in my grandmother's catechism)

Contrition is meant to lead to reconciliation through christ, but as stated in the act of contrition, there is an expectation to *sin no more*. Harms, injustices, systemic racism, microaggressions, and outright, blatant anti-Indigenous racism are still happening within and outside of the academy, so how can we begin to use the term reconciliation? The entire concept of reconciliation in the academy can be paralleled with the persuasive techniques of a batterer in an abusive relationship, whereby an abusive person apologizes for harming their partner and in due time the abusive and apologetic behaviour continues in an cyclical fashion (Schutte, Malouff, & Doyle, 2010). From an institutional perspective, reconciliation can relate to the institution and individuals committing to bettering conditions for Indigenous peoples in the academy; yet others, often people with significant power in the institution, perpetuate anti-Indigenous racism, whether intentional or unconscious. Healing, let alone reconciliation, cannot occur in this environment. As such, the academy remains a violent colonial institution for Indigenous bodies.

Decolonization is an overly ambitious term when referring to institutional response to advancing Indigenous achievement in the academy. The process of ongoing colonization requires scrutiny in order to speculate about decolonization. Five stages or steps of colonization have been defined as: (1) denial and withdrawal; (2) destruction and eradication; (3) denigration, belittlement, and insult; (4) surface accommodation and tokenism; and (5) transformation and exploration (Laenui, 2000). The process of decolonization follows as: (1) rediscovery and recovery, (2) mourning, (3) dreaming, (4) commitment, and (5) action. Given the above definition of colonization and decolonization, the academy, while wishing to decolonize the institution, is still operating firmly within the phases of colonization. One need not look further than the experiences of anti-Indigenous racism that permeate the experience of Indigenous academics, staff, and students. While an institution may voice the commitment to decolonize, on a micro level, individuals, often times with significant power, belittle, denigrate, and insult Indigenous peoples and their ways of knowing, being, and doing. Worse yet, in the quest to decolonize the institution, there is a reliance on the Indigenous people within these institutions to do this work—assisting non-Indigenous people in learning, developing curriculum, and assisting in the securing of funding earmarked for Indigenous growth while padding the curriculum vitae of non-Indigenous scholars. The feelings of surface accommodation and the experience of tokenism are all too familiar to Indigenous peoples. Non-Indigenous scholars doing Indigenous work need Indigenous scholars and peoples' involvement more than Indigenous scholars need them. With funding agencies and research ethics now requiring Indigenous participation, junior and even more senior Indigenous scholars, under the guise of *good intentions*, realize they are being tokenized once funds are secured and there is little, if any, further communication by nominated principal applicants. Dr. Barry Lavallee eloquently and directly critiques this notion, stating that Indigenous peoples are not the Sherpas to carry the settler body to the pinnacle of whiteness (Lavallee, 2018).

The process of colonization is well entrenched in the academy, and we need to speak this truth before we can propose to decolonize the institution. The term neocolonial is much more accurate, and a neocolonial state acknowledges that we are still functioning within systems that privilege whiteness and Eurocentric knowledge but might offer hope that Indigenous peoples and knowledges are equally valued. While I feel the ivory tower is a bit more inclusive of other ways of knowing than it was when I first began my academic journey almost 30 years ago and perhaps when I started my tenure as Assistant Professor, it takes one experience to realize that with two steps forward, we can take four steps back. When students stop coming to me expressing acts of violence through microaggression and anti-Indigenous racism, when a visibly Indigenous man who presents as a warrior can come into the academy and not have security called on him, when two-spirit and Indigenous trans academics can be in front of the classroom and not face violent coordination to annihilate their career, only then can I entertain the discussion on decolonizing the academy.

After a presentation where I discussed the university's approach to decolonizing the academy, a well-respected Elder came to me and whispered, "My girl, it can't be done," as she affectionately rubbed my cheek. I already felt that way about the *decolonizing exercise* being undertaken in the academy. While I do not want to damper people's enthusiasm about various initiatives that are undoubtedly advancing Indigenous knowledges in the academy and making spaces more welcoming for Indigenous students, staff, and faculty, I also want to ensure that I am not a pawn in this decolonizing exercise. I realize Indigenous people can be tokens made to speak to the amazing work of the institution and help check off the reconciliation box while hiding issues that may cast a more negative light or the institution not having the budget line up with stated goals about reconciliation. However, taking this opportunity to ride the reconciliation wave to make a little more change in the academy is where I see potential, at least for the time being. *Full stop* on the use of decolonizing the academy!

Indigenization is the least offensive of the three terms but also fraught with tension. Drs. Maria Campbell and Brenda MacDougall (2018) noted that Indigenizing is often interpreted as Indigenizing spaces by adding a few feathers here and there, hanging artwork and paintings, and even hiring more Indigenous peoples, but this does not lead to Indigenizing the institution. What resonated with me most from Drs. Campbell and MacDougall's presentation is that Indigenizing the academy falls on the shoulders of Indigenous people. However, this is no different than the actions of Indigenous academics who have been in the academy for decades attempting to advance Indigenous knowledge. Observations of the curriculum vitae of most Indigenous scholars will demonstrate extensive service to the university. Today, there are a few more Indigenous scholars to take on the work of *being the Indian* on committees and being asked to help advance non-Indigenous scholars' work on Indigenous topics. Having said that, the surge of attempting to Indigenize the academy is exponentially falling on the shoulders of Indigenous academic and non-academic staff, as well as Indigenous students. This also includes **Elders** or **Traditional Knowledge Holders** hired to help Indigenous students advance in a good way through their academic journey now being asked to assist departments and faculties, often in a tokenistic way, by conducting openings of events, sitting on committees, or guest lecturing in classes.

While on the topic of Elders and Traditional Knowledge Holders in academia, let me digress. Many Canadian post-secondary institutions now have positions such as Elder-in-Residence, hired primarily to assist Indigenous students through their journey. How one becomes an Elder comes from community. However, we are seeing people being hired within academia and given the title Elder when the community has not acknowledged this person as an Elder. At one point, I risked being lumped into the category of academic institutions hiring and anointing Indigenous Elders or Traditional Knowledge Holders. The department was given $10,000 of end of fiscal year money from the Aboriginal Education Council to hire an Elder to work with our students. I formed a hiring committee of all Indigenous people: myself, part-time sessional instructors, and students. We interviewed five people, all of whom did not identify as Elders but carried knowledge that I felt could help our students. Some would be helpful to go to classes to speak about Indigenous peoples' history and culture, while others would be instrumental to work directly with some of the Indigenous students. We interviewed five people on a Friday, and by Friday evening, my phone was ringing.

People from the community were challenging the knowledge and character of all five individuals. A colleague and I met with three recognized Elders in Toronto: Vern Harper, Jacquie Lavalley, and Pauline Shirt. The outcome of their guidance was to hold an Acknowledgement Ceremony, whereby the individuals we were considering would bring people to speak to the work they have done and are doing in community, thereby not having the university validate someone's experience but involving community in this validation process. It was a phenomenal ceremony with the three Elders present, as well as Dr. Akua Benjamin, a person considered an Elder in the Black community in Toronto. We hired all five people, with each working in various ways based on their skill set. No one was given the title of Elder.

In summary, the use of these three terms—reconciliation, decolonization, and Indigenizing—is potentially dangerous for Indigenous people as it presents an unrealistic and impossible condition. The terminology offers the institution a superficial checkbox that, given the current, beyond-inclement and chilly climate (see work by Christina Sharpe [2016] on climate in academia), leaves many Indigenous peoples discouraged about the future of next generations.

So where does it leave us if this terminology is problematic? It leaves us exactly where Indigenous scholars have been for decades, advancing Indigenous knowledges and peoples in academia. The wave of reconciliation has taken us a bit further along with a stronger understanding within the academia of the harmful impacts of colonization, that we are functioning with a colonial environment in the academy, and has provided non-Indigenous people with more education about how to contribute to change by supporting Indigenous people beyond performative allyship.

The arguments above present the academy as a colonial or neocolonial institution, and this position may be challenged by some, therefore warranting further elaboration. After all, in 2008, Prime Minister Stephen Harper publicly apologized for Canada's residential schools past (Indigenous and Northern Affairs Canada, 2010) and, at the 2009 G20 Summit, he stated that Canada has "no history of colonialism" (Dearing, 2009). To explore the notion of academia as a colonial institution, I look to the work of Dr. Sheila Cote-Meek (2014), who cites Memmi (1965), noting privilege is at the heart of the colonial relationship. The hierarchy and privileging of knowledges implicate the academy as a colonial institution. That a hierarchy of knowledge exists in the academy is not an assumption. That discussion in and of itself is another chapter or book, but many Indigenous and racialized scholars can attest to their knowledges—even when brought forward with *academic rigour* and defining epistemology, ontology, and axiology—still being discredited without valid argument. Further, Cote-Meek (2014) considers **colonialism** to require a specific set of ideologies (Said, 1993) that involves inferiority, subordination, authority, and dependency, all of which are part of the experiences of Indigenous scholars in the academy. Cote-Meek (2014) furthers this, stating that in the "racialized hierarchy Indigenous people are at the bottom ... as is our knowledge" (p. 20). I wholeheartedly agree with this statement and reflect on something a reputable Black scholar said in a public forum: that until we see the advancement of Indigenous peoples in the academy and society, we cannot progress as racialized people. Of course, I'm paraphrasing but that is what I took away from her words.

To further complicate the colonialism of academic institutions, Cote-Meek (2014) talks about the scars of academic colonialism. When I began considering university as a possibility in my life as a mature student, my father was still alive and although he never attended post-secondary—he did not even complete Grade 1—his words still echo in the hollows of my mind: "Lynnie, make sure it [university] doesn't make you go crazy." I thought to myself, "What can he possibly know about university. He didn't even finish Grade 1!" I came to quickly understand what he meant, and reflect on his words when I feel I'm being swallowed up by the colonial violence that is ever-present in the academy.

Identity politics for Indigenous peoples in the academy is a topic that is becoming part of the discussion related to decolonizing, reconciling, and Indigenizing the academy. One of the most prevaricated acts of viciousness that contributes to colonial scarring in the academy is lateral violence often intersected with the notion of identity—who is Indian enough and who is a pretendian (an informal term for a person who falsely claims to have Indigenous ancestry; pretendian, n.d.)? While we don't often call people out publicly on their misrepresented identities, it is often those that are not secure in their identity as Indigenous people or people who are not completely transparent about their stated Indigenous identity that cause the most lateral violence and disruption that then perpetuates a stereotype that we can't all get along and thrive in the academy—in essence, that we don't belong.

While on the topic of identity, the notion of the *palatable Indian* is a consideration when discussing the topic of Indigenizing the academy. Many Indigenous scholars identify with being called an apple or sell-out from their community once gaining further knowledge in the colonial academy.

Equal pressure on the other end of the continuum is the notion of being palatable to senior administration and academic colleagues. That is, individuals in the academy are often open to having Indigenous people in the institution, as long as their own power and privilege are not challenged and we do not attempt to disrupt the status quo, ivory tower, or the supremacy of whiteness in the academy. The *palatable Indian* is therefore in a position to **not** disrupt the supremacy of whiteness but be the Indigenous person who counts in the diversity statistics, the public-relations poster child, and most detrimental, used by administration and others as the Indigenous voice countering other Indigenous people who are labelled as provocative, agitators, or the *angry Indian*.

One might ask, if I am so critical in stating that the academy is a colonial institution and the terminology of reconciliation, decolonizing, or Indigenizing is problematic, why am I an active participant in these structures? Commissioner and Justice Murray Sinclair is often quoted as saying education is the key to reconciliation and healing. I agree with this statement, that education is important to the health and well-being of Indigenous peoples, but I also believe that our ceremony and culture outside the academy will lead to our healing (Lavallee & Poole, 2010). In addition, education can be harmful if not delivered in a way that values Indigenous knowledges and people and where Indigenous students are not free from anti-Indigenous racism. There is an undeniable correlation between educational attainment and economic status, and I want to see my next generations gain knowledge through the colonial institution and break the cycle of poverty. I want my niece, nephews, and grandnephews to not live in poverty as I did growing up and as their mothers did right up until their passing to the spirit world. What I would like when they enter the academy is that they are free from anti-Indigenous racism, they walk with pride about who they are, and that their knowledges are accepted and valued in the academy. This is why I do what I do and why so many other Indigenous scholars before me have done so. These tangible outcomes are what reconciling, decolonizing, and Indigenizing the academy mean to me.

In my doctoral studies, I became keenly interested in epistemology and the hierarchy of knowledges. Through my undergraduate and graduate studies, I never saw myself reflected appropriately in the literature, even when the topics directly related to my experience and culture. I become *that person* in the class who would question concepts and statements that made other students roll their eyes. During my doctoral studies, I would intentionally sit across from certain people so I could catch their facial exchange with other students when I spoke. I was made to feel like I did not belong because I questioned the dominant knowledge. So, when I was introduced to the study of knowledge and sought out the few readings on Indigenous epistemology, I became intrigued by the hierarchy of knowledge as it related to my experience in the academy. It was a natural progression that, after commencing my tenure as an assistant professor in 2005, each year in my annual report I would emphasize how my research, pedagogy, and service all address an attempt to advance Indigenous knowledge in the academy.

The fundamental raison d'etre of academic institutions is education and research informing education. Linked to education and research, universities and colleges have also long been an environment for social justice. Therefore, inclusion and valuing of Indigenous knowledges are appropriate and vital in education and research. There has been a tremendous amount of work by Indigenous scholars to advance Indigenous knowledges in the academy, and the reconciliation movement would benefit from recognizing these contributions. Again, we were never idle! For instance, many scholars have written about Indigenous knowledges and Indigenous methodologies in research (see, for example, Brant-Castellano [2000]; Cajete, [2000]; Hart [2002]; Kovach [2010]; Lavallee [2009]; Nabigon et al. [1999]; Smith [1999]; and Wilson [2001]). Indigenous scholars in the field of education and Native studies have advanced Indigenous knowledges in the academy for decades. For instance, Dr. Marie Battiste is a prolific writer on the topic of decolonizing education, publishing for over 30 years (Battiste & Barman 1995; Battiste, 2013). Dr. Willie Ermine wrote and presented on the topic of Aboriginal epistemology (Ermine, Battiste, & Barman, 1995). Dr. Laara Fitznor wrote about Aboriginal philosophies 20 years ago (Fitznor, 1998). There is also Dr. Eileen Antone's (2003) scholarship related to Indigenous adult literacy and learning. And Dr. Emma Laroque's book *Defeathering the Indian* was published back in 1975 and, unfortunately, is still relevant today and would be a useful tool in dealing with current microaggressions and anti-Indigenous racism in the classroom. I purposely reflect on these Indigenous scholars to demonstrate, "We were never idle!" and that the current decolonizing exercise needs to build upon the foundational contribution of these scholars. The decolonizing exercise cannot ignore the work of Indigenous scholars that helped pave the path to advancing Indigenous knowledge in the academy over the past three to four decades. Further, we cannot let the focus on decolonizing, reconciling, and Indigenizing distract us from advancing Indigenous knowledges and dealing directly with anti-Indigenous racism on campus.

Ensuring Indigenous knowledges are recognized and valued in the academy and that Indigenous people are free from anti-Indigenous racism in the academy are two objectives that should be the focus of the reconciliation, decolonizing, and Indigenizing exercise. This is a monumental task that requires many approaches, starting with the decision-making bodies of the institution. Fundamental change in the academy is driven by the governance structures of the university, such as the Senate and/or Board of Governors. The most senior decision-making bodies of the institution need to transform beyond a token seat at the table. These positions need to include Indigenous leadership willing to speak to the advancement of Indigenous knowledges in the academy and not be a seat reserved for the palatable Indian. There cannot be only one Indigenous person on these decision-making bodies.

Senior leadership needs to be transformed to include Indigenous people in positions such as president, provost, vice-president, dean, and director. This should also include Indigenous-specific positions, both academic and non-academic, such as vice-presidents focused solely on Indigenous resurgence and senior non-academic positions to ensure we are at the tables where decisions and policies are being made, from how tenure and promotion will be decided to how research funding will be dispersed and how student awards and admissions are conducted. Given the need to have Indigenous leadership at all governance and policy levels of the institution, more than one person is required. It cannot and should not fall on the shoulders of one person. One senior level position cannot effect change and will contribute to unintended tokenism. Making substantial and more lasting change in the academy means making change at the policy level, from the Board of Governors and Senate down to departmental by-laws, and we require Indigenous people at these tables.

Increasing the number of Indigenous academic staff who are taking on the work of advancing Indigenous knowledges in the academy is vital to build a critical mass so we can transform the colonial academy and challenge policies and procedures. Across Canada there is an increased demand for Indigenous scholars. While institutions may boast about the number of new Indigenous hires, for a critical mass to develop, the increase in Indigenous scholars needs to be measured against the ratio of non-Indigenous scholars and account for the attrition and retirement of more senior Indigenous scholars. So, while it may be commendable that there are Indigenous-specific

128 Decolonizing and Indigenizing Education in Canada

hires, we need to look at the overall ratio of Indigenous to non-Indigenous scholars over time.

In the quest to Indigenize the academy, there has been a focus on required or mandatory curriculum. Some disciplines have had mandatory curriculum for decades, primarily due to accreditation standard requirements, such as social work and education in some provinces. There are essentially two models that are discussed with respect to *Indigenizing* curriculum: an infusion model and courses that focus solely on Indigenous content. I am more supportive of courses focusing solely on Indigenous content as it would hopefully require an instructor with the requisite expertise and more likely involve the hiring of Indigenous people to teach these courses. However, I have seen many Indigenous courses being taught by non-Indigenous people, and while these instructors may have the required knowledge and experience, I want to emphasize that we have to build capacity within Indigenous people. Another consideration opposing the infusion model is that instructors with little knowledge, and sometimes little or no interest, are *required* to teach the content. Indigenous topics are complex; it is not simply teaching about Indigenous history or promoting Indigenous culture. Take, for instance, identity. In Canada, one should have a sound knowledge about the Indian Act and changes over time with respect to identity, as well as the legislation and political context of non-status First Nations, Métis identity, and the diverse identities of the Inuit and people of the north. The infusion model encourages instructors who are not experts in the field and has the potential to perpetuate stereotypes, microaggressions, and anti-Indigenous racism in the classroom. The infusion model is probably the most harmful to Indigenous students, who are often called upon to be the expert witness to the delivered content. In essence, the Indigenous students are the Sherpas for the instructor and other students. We need to question the quality of the content delivered in Indigenizing curriculum and the repercussions of infusion and course models. This discussion needs to be explored before we dive into required Indigenous curriculum.

Finally, budgets need to reflect stated commitments to reconciling, decolonizing, and Indigenizing the academy. Rather than boasting about diversity statistics, the statistics that need to be transparent so they can be questioned relate to the money that is being spent to advance stated Indigenous-related goals and strategies. It is not enough to profile a funding envelope for Indigenous achievement; the academy must also report on how much of that envelope has been spent and who benefited from support. As mentioned earlier, we need to move beyond helping non-Indigenous people and instead directly support Indigenous scholars, staff, and students. Metrics attached to reconciliation are needed and the most important metric to report is actuals related to budget.

My conclusions are simply stated but not a simple task. Let not the sound bite—reconciling, decolonizing, or Indigenizing—distract us from ignoring the decades of work by Indigenous scholars on advancing Indigenous knowledge in the academy and dealing with anti-Indigenous racism. We were never idle, and we will continue to advance Indigenous knowledge in the colonial academy for the next generations.

DISCUSSION QUESTIONS

1. Is decolonization achievable within academia? If so, what would decolonized education look like?

2. Is reconciliation possible? If so, what would a reconciled academic institution look like?

3. Should all curriculum in post-secondary education be Indigenized? If so, how can this be accomplished? What would it look like?

4. How can racism toward Indigenous people in the academy be adequately addressed?

GLOSSARY

colonialism: The practice of domination involving political and economic subjugation of one group over another other. In the context of academia, colonialism acknowledges the privileging of Western-dominant knowledge and the minimizing and discrediting of Indigenous knowledge. Colonialism is often used synonymously with imperialism; however, the Latin derivatives indicate colonialism often refers to a transfer of land/territory and a population, while imperialism emphasizes the exertion of power from one group over another. See, for example, the definition in the *Stanford Encyclopedia of Philosophy* (https://plato.stanford.edu/entries/colonialism/).

decolonization: The action or process of a state withdrawing power from a former colony, leaving it independent.

Elders: Within the Indigenous context, individuals who have accumulated a wealth of knowledge and are subsequently recognized by their community as holding such knowledge and given the title of Elder.

Indigenization: A term used to describe incorporating Indigenous worldview, knowledge, and perspectives.

reconciliation: A restoration of friendly relations.

Traditional Knowledge Holders: People who have accumulated a wealth of knowledge from previous Traditional Knowledge Holders or Elders and are recognized by their community as holding this knowledge.

FURTHER READINGS/WEBSITES

Battiste, M., & Bouvier, R. (2013). *Decolonizing education: Nourishing the learning spirit*. Vancouver, BC: Purich Publishing.

Cote-Meek, S. (2017). Supporting the TRC's calls to action. *University Affairs*. https://www.universityaffairs.ca/opinion/from-the-admin-chair/supporting-trcs-calls-action/

Cote-Meek, S. (2018). Making a long-term commitment to Indigenous education. *University Affairs*. https://www.universityaffairs.ca/opinion/from-the-admin-chair/making-a-long-term-commitment-to-indigenous-education/

DiAngelo, R. (2018). *White fragility: Why is it so hard for white people to talk about racism*. Boston, MA: Beacon Press.

Lavallee, L. F. (2019). Recommendations and thoughts regarding Indigenous governance and matters in academia and UofM. *Indigenous Resurgence and Insurgence*. www.lynnflavallee.home.blog

MacDonald, M. (2016, April 6). Indigenizing the academy: What some universities are doing to weave Indigenous peoples, cultures and knowledge into the fabric of their campuses. *University Affairs*. https://www.universityaffairs.ca/features/feature-article/indigenizing-the-academy/

Martin, K., & Mirraboopa, B. (2003). Ways of knowing, being and doing: A theoretical framework and methods for Indigenous and Indigenist research. *Journal of Australian Studies, 27*(76), 203–214. doi:10.1080/14443050309387838

Kanu, Y. (2011). *Integrating Aboriginal perspectives into the school curriculum*. Toronto, ON: University of Toronto Press.

Regan, P. (2011). *Unsettling the settler within*. Vancouver, BC: UBC Press.

Rodriquez, C. O. (2018). *Decolonizing academia: Poverty, oppression and pain*. Halifax, NS: Fernwood Publishing.

Stielgelbauer, S. M. (1996). What is an Elder? What do Elders do? *The Canadian Journal of Native Studies, 16*(1).

Toulouse, P. R. (2018). *Truth and Reconciliation in Canadian schools.* Winnipeg, MB: Portage & Main Press.

REFERENCES

Antone, E. M. (2003). Culturally framing Aboriginal literacy and learning. *Canadian Journal of Native Education, 27*(1), 7–15.

Battiste, M. A., & Barman, J. (1995). *First Nations education in Canada: The circle unfolds.* Vancouver, BC: UBC Press.

Battiste, M. A. (2013). *Decolonizing education: Nourishing the learning spirit.* Vancouver, BC: UBC Press.

Brant-Castellano, M. (2000). Updating Aboriginal traditions of knowledge. In G. Dei, B. Hall, & D. Rosenberg (Eds.), *Indigenous knowledges in global contexts* (pp. 21–36). Toronto, ON: University of Toronto Press.

Cajete, G. (2000). *Native science: Natural laws of interdependence.* Santa Fe, NM: Clear Light.

Campbell, M., & MacDougall, B. (2018). Ceremony, cultural knowledge and the classroom: Indigenizing without further colonizing. Paper presented at the Teaching and Learning Conference, University of Saskatchewan, Saskatoon.

Cote-Meek, S. (2014). *Colonized classrooms: Racism, trauma and resistance in post-secondary education.* Halifax, NS: Fernwood Publishing.

Dearing, S. (2009, October 3). Harper in Pittsburgh: "Canada has no history of colonialism." *Digital Journal.* Retrieved from http://www.digitaljournal.com/article/280003

Ermine, W., Battiste, M. A., & Barman, J. (1995). Aboriginal epistemology. In M. A. Battiste & J. Barman (Eds.), *First Nations education in Canada: The circle unfolds* (pp. 101–111). Vancouver, BC: UBC Press.

Fitznor, L. (1998). The circle of life: Affirming Aboriginal philosophies in everyday living. In D. McCane (Ed.), *Life ethics in world religions* (pp. 21–40). Atlanta, GA: Scholars Press.

Hart, M. (2002). *Seeking Mino-pimatisiwin: An Aboriginal approach to helping.* Halifax, NS: Fernwood Publications.

Indigenous and Northern Affairs Canada. (2010). Statement of apology to former students of Indian Residential Schools. Ottawa, ON: Government of Canada. Retrieved from https://www.aadnc-aandc.gc.ca/eng/1100100015677/1100100015680

Kovach, M. (2010). *Indigenous methodologies: Characteristics, conversation, and contexts*. Toronto, ON: University of Toronto Press.

Larocque, E. (1975). *Defeathering the Indian*. Agincourt, ON: Book Society of Canada.

Lavallee, B. D. A. (2018). "Outing" unconscious bias: Strategies to reconfigure harmful response modes in Indigenous health care. Paper presented at Leaders in Indigenous Medical Education (LIME), Flinders University, South Australia. Retrieved from http://www.limenetwork.net.au/resources-lime-publications/slice-of-lime-seminars/

Lavallee, L. F. (2009). Practical application of an Indigenous research framework and two qualitative Indigenous research methods: Sharing circles and Anishnaabe Symbol-Based Reflection. *International Journal of Qualitative Methods, 8*, 21–40. doi:10.1177/160940690900800103

Lavallee, L. F. & Poole, J. (2010). Beyond recovery: Colonization, health and healing for Indigenous people in Canada. *International Journal of Mental Health and Addiction, 8*(2), 271-281. doi:10.1007/s11469-009-9239-8

Laenui, P. (2000). Process of decolonization. In. M. Battiste (Ed.), *Reclaiming Indigenous voice and vision* (pp. 150–160). Vancouver, BC: UBC Press.

Lindberg, T. (2017). Present and powerful Indigenous women. Paper presentation at the Humanities and Social Sciences Congress, Ryerson University, Toronto, ON.

Memmi, A. (1965). *The colonizer and the colonized*. London, UK: Beacon Press.

Nabigon, H., Hagey, R., Webster, S., & MacKay, R. (1999). The learning circle as a research method: The trickster and windigo in research. *Native Social Work Journal, 2*(1), 113–137.

"pretendian" [Def. 1]. (n.d.). In *Wiktionary.org*. Retrieved from https://en.wiktionary.org/wiki/Pretendian

"reconciliation" [Def. 1 & Def. 2]. (n.d.a). In *English Oxford dictionary online*. Retrieved from https://en.oxforddictionaries.com/definition/reconciliation

"reconciliation" [Def. 2]. (n.d.b). In *Merriam-Webster online*. Retrieved from https://www.merriam-webster.com/dictionary/reconciliation

Royal Commission on Aboriginal Peoples. (1996). *Report of the Royal Commission on Aboriginal Peoples*. Ottawa, ON: Government of Canada. Retrieved from http://www.bac-lac.gc.ca/eng/discover/aboriginal-heritage/royal-commission-aboriginal-peoples/Pages/final-report.aspx

Said, E. (1993). *Culture and imperialism*. New York, NY: Vintage Books.

Schutte, N. S., Malouff, J. M., & Doyle, J. S. (2010). The relationship between characteristics of the victim, persuasive techniques of the batterer, and returning to a battering relationship. *Journal of Social Psychology, 128*(5), 605–610. doi:10.1080/00224545.1988.9922914

Sharpe, C. (2016). *In the wake: On Blackness and being.* Durham, NC: Duke University Press.

Smith, L. T. (1999). *Decolonizing methodologies: Research and indigenous peoples.* Dunedin: University of Otago Press.

Truth and Reconciliation Commission of Canada (TRC). (2015). *Honouring the truth, reconciling for the future: Summary of the final report of the Truth and Reconciliation Commission of Canada.* Ottawa, ON: Author. Retrieved from https://nctr.ca/assets/reports/Final%20Reports/Executive_Summary_English_Web.pdf

Wilson, S. (2001). What is Indigenous research methodology? *Canadian Journal of Native Education, 25*(2), 175–179.

CHAPTER 8

The Dynamics of Decolonization and Indigenization in an Era of Academic "Reconciliation"

Emily Grafton and Jérôme Melançon

INTRODUCTION

This chapter will explore the dynamics of decolonization and Indigenization in the contemporary era of academic **"reconciliation."** We understand decolonization and Indigenization as separate movements with the potential for mutual reinforcement in the liberation of Indigenous peoples from settler colonial **oppression** and the transformation of colonial structures. Decolonization is an emancipatory response to colonial oppression. Indigenization is a process of **resurgence**, a re-centring of **precolonial** and **acolonial** Indigenous ways of knowing and being that never ceased to exist despite colonial structures and processes and their attempts of assimilation and erasure. It is not a response to **colonialism**, but a movement despite colonialism.

Decolonization and Indigenization are not static or universal movements: Their meanings change depending on the Indigenous identity and/or colonial position of those participating in them. For example, settlers cannot Indigenize by themselves, without an application of Indigenous ways of knowing accessed through Indigenous collectivity. They can, however, turn to **anticolonial**, acolonial, or **intercultural** traditions that can facilitate learning from and about Indigenous ways of being. While Euro-Canadian settlers can decolonize settler colonial structures, Indigenous people can only decolonize themselves and Indigenous-centred institutions and not the colonial-centred institutions that uphold the power of the non-Indigenous or **settler** majority. They can, however, create spaces within colonial institutions whence this change can be catalyzed and maintained.

There are also inadvertent or negative outcomes that can arise within each movement in the struggle for liberation and transformation. **Indigenization**, for example, has the potential for cooptation of Indigenous ways of knowing and the legitimization of colonial systems. Decolonization can result in marginalization or the exclusion of Indigenous peoples in colonial institutions. While acknowledging such outcomes, this chapter will argue that the anti-oppressive strategies associated with these two movements will be necessary for reciprocal, respectful relations between Indigenous and non-Indigenous people as articulated by this era of academic "reconciliation."

SITUATING OURSELVES

We are colleagues at the University of Regina, Saskatchewan, which is situated in Treaty 4 with a presence on Treaty 6 lands; these are the territories of the nêhiyawak (Cree), Nakawēk/Anihšināpēk, Dakota, Lakota, and Nakoda, and the homeland of the Métis. This shared territory, and our relationship to it, means different things to each of us. For Jérôme, who grew up in Québec, lived briefly in Ontario on unceded territory, and has lived in Alberta and Saskatchewan in Treaty 6, it means the opportunity to understand and develop different ways of relating to the land, to other persons and other beings, but also to understand and transform what it is to be a settler in Canada. Jérôme's studies in phenomenology and critical political philosophy (with a PhD from Université Paris-Diderot) and his work with Indigenous students, Elders, knowledge holders, and community members are leading him to search for ideas and practices within both families of intellectual traditions that can facilitate truth, justice, and reconciliation.

For Emily, who is a member of the Métis Nation and grew up in Treaty 1, it means the opportunity to strengthen and deepen her understanding of being Métis in settler Canada by building new relationships and experiencing new teachings and ceremonies. With a PhD in Native Studies (University of Manitoba), Emily brings to this chapter expertise on the decolonization, Indigenization, and the truth and reconciliation processes underway in several settler colonial institutions.

This chapter reflects our relationality to this territory, to each other, and to the diversity of theories and practices that form the methodological diversification that is Indigenous Studies (Anderson & O'Brien, 2017, p. 18). Using Sioui's (1992) proposed method for the intercultural communication of intellectual schemas, this chapter is an intercultural exchange between our stated positionalities. Sioui argues that, for change to occur, it is not enough to simply insert Indigenous knowledges into Western theories and practices. It is necessary instead for relations to be created between Indigenous and non-Indigenous collaborators who will come to understand enough about each other's intellectual framework to adapt and translate concepts and ideas for each other and for their own society. Such intercultural exchanges and collaborative cultural transfers can create deep understanding that might then result in transformative change. Further, as Million (2014) argues, theorizing takes many forms, is always related to life, and, therefore, is ever-changing: Theory serves to link different experiences. Million (2014) writes, "The stories, unlike data, contain the affective legacy of our experiences. They are a felt knowledge that accumulates and becomes a force that empowers stories that are otherwise separate to become a focus, a potential for movement" (pp. 31–32). Methodologically, this chapter weaves a literature review of critical colonial theory with creative borrowing from critical political thought and an intercultural exchange to demonstrate the changing theoretical nature of academic Indigenization and decolonization, which are both movements that act as links to experiences, knowledge-building, and transformative change.

Defining Our Terms

We are writing from Treaty 4 lands in a society that we view as inherently shaped by settler colonialism. We understand colonialism as those processes associated with the invasion of a nation that is expected to assimilate to a foreign power's political, legal, economic, social, and cultural ways. The principal motives of imperial colonial projects include **domination** of land and resources to increase profit and benefit for the foreign, colonial power. **Settler colonialism** is similarly based on the premises of invasion, domination, and assimilation; however, as is argued by Wolfe (2006), it is not a historic event, but an ongoing structural process. Veracini (2010, 2015) adds that settler colonialism is distinct, as it requires the economic, cultural, and political marginalization of Indigenous populations; a re-visioning of the history of place; and the physical, cultural, and linguistic displacement or genocide of Indigenous peoples. These characteristics of dispossession frame our understanding of settler colonialism in Canada.

Decolonialism can be thought of as the undoing of such colonial influences. It is typically used to distinguish the period that a colonized nation liberates itself from a colonial power (Ashcroft, Griffiths, & Tiffin, 2000, p. 56). Post-colonialism is a term that evolved in response to the limitations of decolonialism: As colonized nations achieved political independence, the ongoing and insidious nature of colonialism became apparent (Young, 2001), because the languages, political systems, economic practices, legal structures, and cultures of a colonial power often remained in place after such "political liberation" (Ashcroft et al., 2000, pp. 168–169). We use *decolonization* to reference activities that bring decolonialism into practice by restoring diminished rights or equity that is the result of a nation's colonial past or those continuing legacies of colonialism; we are reminded, however, by Tuck and Yang (2012) that "decolonization is not a metaphor" (p. 3): Colonialism takes land, and therefore decolonialism must principally be about returning the land.

Important to Indigenization and decolonialism are precolonial and acolonial practices, which can be used to work outside of colonial constructs or to assist with dismantling colonial structural processes. **Indigenous worldviews** are those knowledge systems that are place-based, oral, and intergenerationally transmitted within Indigenous communities (Frideres, 2011). As Hunt (2014) writes, "Its relational, alive, emergent nature means that as we come to know something, as we attempt to fix its meaning, we are always at risk of just missing something" (p. 31). To truly understand Indigenous worldviews, we encourage participating in languages, ceremonies, and teachings from Indigenous Elders and Knowledge Keepers. These Indigenous-centred knowledge systems often continue to exist alongside or outside of settler colonial knowledge systems (Hubbard, 2008; Simpson, 2004). Thus, traditional Indigenous-centred knowledge systems often remain intact—not assimilated—in settler colonial societies. For example, King (1997) explains that Indigenous peoples' actions or ideologies are not only reactions to colonialism; instead, Indigenous knowledge originates prior to contact and is held intact by many Indigenous peoples through language and traditional teachings. Therefore, Indigenous peoples, knowledge systems, and worldviews are not necessarily destroyed by colonial presence or practice, even though they might need to be pieced back together and transformed in response to the effects of colonialism (Alfred, 2009). It is often these precolonial or acolonial knowledge systems that are used in **decolonial** and Indigenization initiatives.

To understand the political injustice and moral evil associated with set-tler colonialism, many authors have recourse to the concepts of oppression and domination. According to Young (1990), oppression is the impossibility of "developing and exercising one's capacities and expressing one's experi-ence," and domination, the impossibility of "participating in determining one's action and the conditions of one's action" (p. 37). Oppressed people are linked in their lack not of a capacity for self-creation but of what they need to develop and enact it. This oppression can be institutionalized through laws and state practices, and it can also be violent. However, as Harvey (2010) points out, there is a form of "civilized oppression" that "involves very fine-grained actions indeed and they seem utterly trivial to those not repeat-edly at the receiving end" (p. 22). While oppression is a set of constraints on self-development, domination is constraints on self-determination. For Newcomb (2011), domination can be found in the activities described by a series of words whose definition is associated with the term *domination*: invasion, slavery, empire, capture, conquest, colonialism, to vanquish, gov-ernment, subdue, subjugation, reduction, subordination, and lord (p. 580).

The act of overcoming oppression and domination can be expressed by the term "**emancipation**," although with care, as this term lends itself to misunderstandings given its use as a part of the Indian Act, which uses *emancipation* to effectively mean a loss of Indian status. The word thus be-came a euphemism for the termination of rights and assimilation through enfranchisement. The word *emancipation* has a long history and is usually associated with the freeing of slaves. More broadly, it is understood as liber-ation from severe forms of domination. The Canadian government reversed the meaning of the word by using it to refer to the loss of Indian status. Such a use implied that Indigenous persons would be "freed" from their culture. As a result, in the context of colonial relations in Canada, it has come to mean its opposite and to stand for assimilation. Here we use it in its original, rather than falsified, meaning. There is, indeed, another concept of emancipation: For Abensour (2003), emancipation consists in the institution of a free political community. Because domination internally threatens all communities, freedom is never assured and is only ever born out of constant political vigilance. Attention given to emancipation attunes us to the emer-gence of the political question in our situation–that is, the question of the ways of being together that allow each person to remain tied to the others while staying separate from them (Abensour, 2003). We can turn again to Young (1990), who presents emancipatory phenomena as what is liberating and enabling. Emancipatory actions and movements make it possible to fight against oppression and domination. It is through action and participation in movements of struggle and vigilance that emancipation takes place and that freedom and self-determination are experienced and that capacities are developed and deployed.

This understanding of emancipation echoes the phenomenon that has been theorized by Alfred (2009) and Simpson (2011) as resurgence. Alfred (2009) explains that Indigenous peoples can draw on resurgence because it is already present in their communities as they regenerate power, restore social connections, and establish new connections to memory (including Indigenous-centred knowledge systems) and spirit. In other words, resurgence is the re-creation of cultural practices and political identities on the basis of a tradition that needs to be reconstructed and pieced back together, but that cannot exist as it once did. Simpson (2011) takes from Alfred the idea that resurgence is about reclaiming "the *Indigenous* contexts (knowledge, interpretations, values, ethics, processes) for our political cultures" (p. 17), to be able to articulate an anticolonial future. Resurgence consists of living an Indigenous life, creating the conditions to live such a life, and producing more life even as settler colonialism destroys its various forms. It is a practical endeavour that begins with taking on the resurgent practices: a "how" that is at once personal and national change; theory; and a transformation of the mode of production of Indigenous lives (Simpson, 2017). It is a series of processes and outcomes that begin with oneself, at home, in the community, in the nation, in the rest of the social and historical orders. Resurgence is thus at once individualizing and collectivizing—and is the contemporary basis for Indigenization.

The concept of reconciliation fluctuates in its meaning; however, the Truth and Reconciliation Commission of Canada (TRC, 2015b) suggests a definition of reconciliation "as an ongoing process of establishing and maintaining respectful relationships" (p. 11). This process includes apologies, reparations, and concrete actions—but also revitalizing Indigenous legal traditions and notably using them in the process to resolve conflicts, repair harm, and restore relationships (TRC, 2015a). There is no reconciliation without truth, nor without real institutional and political change. We use "reconciliation" cautiously, hence the quotations. In our experience, the concept of truth and "reconciliation" in Canada can raise all sorts of concerns, resistance, or disdain from Indigenous peoples and survivors and intergenerational survivors of the Indian Residential School System (Diabo, 2017; Simpson, 2013).

While attempting to be respectful of these positions, we use "reconciliation" as a framework to discuss academic Indigenization and decolonization because of the increasing prevalence of these three concepts in academia, the overlap in their related initiatives, and the confusion of these movements' distinctions.

Finally, the concept of Indigenization is, similar to decolonization, an attempt to overcome colonial-based oppression; it includes **efforts** to transform colonial-framed spaces, decision-making processes, and institutions/structures from a perspective of Indigenous ways of knowing in an effort to empower **Indigenous peoples and communities** (Aboriginal Advisory Circle, 2015). Based on the prior discussion of Indigenous knowledge systems, Indigenization can be a precolonial or acolonial act, but can also signal decolonial processes as it transforms colonial space by re-centring those marginalized Indigenous ways of knowing.

MUTUAL REINFORCEMENT OF DECOLONIZATION AND INDIGENIZATION

We argue that decolonization and Indigenization, while separate movements, can be mutually reinforcing in the efforts of transformation or liberation from settler colonial oppression. Both movements can, however, result in a number of challenges and even colonial re-inscription. The mutual reinforcement and obstacles that can arise often do so due to the positionality of those involved. In the shared territory of Treaty 4, we hear various ideas about these terms from nêhiyawak (Cree), Anihšināpēk (Saulteaux), Dakota, Lakota, Nakoda, Métis, neighbouring Indigenous nations, newcomer populations, and settler populations. Decolonization and Indigenization are not static or universal movements: Their meanings change depending on Indigenous or settler identity and the colonial position of those participating in them.

Decolonization is an emancipatory response to colonial oppression and thus demands not only actions and the development of relations toward new, free political communities but also new ways of acting and relating. Yet colonialism hinders the possibility for non-Indigenous people to establish new ways of acting and relating that may be appropriate for them and for Indigenous people. For non-Indigenous people, emancipation involves recognizing that they relate to Indigenous people at once through their ethno-cultural background (for instance, French-speaking Euro-Canadian or Cantonese-speaking Han Chinese) and through their colonial and political position as settlers. Colonialism involves giving privilege to white ethnicities and cultures of European origin but also providing political power and legitimacy to all those who appropriate the land by erasing their status as settlers in order to define them as immigrants. In the process, colonial policies and processes cut off settlers from Indigenous people, from their communities, and from those elements of Indigenous cultures that threaten settlers' claim to power and land. Emancipation from colonialism will then mean that in their relationship to themselves (a relationship that is always mediated by the presence of others), settlers can cease the internalized dehumanization that comes from dehumanizing others and the violence against oneself that accompanies violence against others but also learn to draw from Indigenous cultures and knowledge systems. Settlers can respect and enable the self-determination and capacities of Indigenous people by respecting their demands for the space necessary for autonomy and cooperating to share and develop resources. This understanding of emancipation is at the source of current alliances forming among Black, Indigenous, and people of colour who refuse to enact the colonialism that affects them all, and who are establishing relationships and alliances that undermine or stand outside colonialism.

Indigenization is a process of resurgence, a re-centring of precolonial and acolonial Indigenous ways of knowing and being that never ceased to exist despite colonial structures and processes and their attempts of assimilation and erasure. It is a response that draws upon the traditional or ancestral knowledges of Indigenous peoples that have been passed orally and intergenerationally from ancestors over thousands of years through ceremony and Indigenous-centred teaching methods such as storytelling, being on the land, and language use. In this sense, Indigenization is not decolonial because it does not have a colonial reference point. It can be an act that is emancipatory, liberating, and resurgent in the sense that it seeks to overcome oppression and transform those institutions that enforce colonial oppression. There are circumstances, however, where Indigenization is a response to colonial-imposed inequity. This can be, for example, when Indigenization is used to re-centre Indigenous knowledge that is marginalized through colonial activity or to transform colonial structures.

It ought to go without saying that settlers cannot Indigenize universities by themselves without an application of Indigenous ways of knowing accessed through Indigenous collectivity. The inclusion of Indigenous voices, knowledges, materials, and epistemologies requires the inclusion of those who bear them, use them, and develop them. What is more, without the leadership of Indigenous people, this inclusion cannot take place without the decolonization of the structures and spaces necessary to provide the grounds for epistemic and physical coexistence. This inclusion points to the classic problem of representation of underrepresented groups: Should representation be symbolic (where the fact of being Indigenous would suffice to ensure Indigenization) or substantive (where expertise with Indigenous ways of knowing would suffice, even coming from a non-Indigenous person)? However, both forms of representation fall short of meeting the need for settlers to develop connections with specific Indigenous collectivity—to engage with Indigenous *peoples* as nations rather than *people* as individuals in such a way that respects the relationality at the heart of Indigenous ways of knowing, being, and acting.

Some common examples of the shortfalls of such representation include when too much is asked of individuals who do not have the time and resources to participate in university-led initiatives, as the University of Saskatchewan Indigenous Student Council claimed in withdrawing from all reconciliation and Indigenization efforts (MacPherson, 2018). Additionally, too much can also be asked of individuals who do not have the sufficient expertise to do what they are asked to do. As Marshall explains, while Euro-Canadian faculty, students, or classroom guests are requested to intervene based on expertise, the breadth of work that is needed for Indigenization and decolonization means that Indigenous people may be asked to intervene as Indigenous persons rather than as experts. This may tempt those assumed to be Elders or knowledge holders, especially if payment is involved, to "just make it up" (Marshall, as cited in Bartlett, Marshall, & Marshall, 2012, p. 334) and give answers that fit what is expected of them. Settlers, lacking the expertise and knowledge to evaluate their contribution, are then led to take the information they receive at face value.

These two answers also fail to meet the criteria of self-definition of Indigeneity by Indigenous *peoples*. As a result of colonial policies, there exist today a limited number of persons with the recognized credentials necessary to teach in universities, even as Canadian institutions realize the need to include a higher number of Indigenous faculty who can contribute their perspective to teaching and service and who can mentor Indigenous students. Likewise, a push for recruiting a higher number of Indigenous students has been initiated both by a demographic drop in university-age potential students and by well-intentioned responses to the TRC's Calls to

Action to make higher education more accessible (TRC, 2015a). These two phenomena have led universities to recruit Indigenous faculty and students aggressively.

Without the proper attention to Indigeneity as belonging to Indigenous communities (claiming them and being claimed by them), Indigenization repeats the problem of Indian status: Instead of defining Indigeneity too narrowly, universities may be defining it too broadly and missing the mark, all the while taking up the responsibility of definition. Without a clear understanding and adoption of Indigenous processes of recognition of expertise, Indigenization repeats the problem of the colonial knowledge of, rather than by, Indigenous people. These lacunae in Indigenization practices demonstrate the limits of the logic of representation by individuals and point to the necessity of engaging with local Indigenous collectivities, which can range from nearby communities and bands to tribal councils and provincial organizations—and to the communities to which students and faculty belong.

Euro-Canadians can turn to traditions that can facilitate learning from and about Indigenous ways of being and ensure that initiatives are Indigenous-led and informed authentically. Whereas anticolonialism addresses the systemic, political aspects of relationships between Indigenous and non-Indigenous people, interculturalism promotes mutual understanding and collaboration. While Indigenization is about Indigenous ways of knowing, when applied in colonial institutions, such as a university, it is often undertaken by non-Indigenous peoples. In some ways, it has become a practice for non-Indigenous peoples, which can be quite problematic as it can lead to misrepresentation, **tokenism**, and even **cooptation**.

In summary, Euro-Canadians can decolonize settler colonial structures but cannot Indigenize them without Indigenous collectivity. Similarly, Indigenous people can only decolonize themselves and Indigenous-centred institutions—and not the colonial-centred institutions that uphold the power of the non-Indigenous or settler majority over them. They can, however, create spaces within colonial institutions whence this change can be catalyzed and maintained. These limits to decolonization and Indigenization are due to the power dynamics of colonialism, which, after invasion and domination, seek to enforce marginalization and assimilation of Indigenous peoples. Since Euro-Canadian settlers form a broad majority within universities (Henry et al., 2017) and their ways of knowing are at the centre of universities' structures, at this point in time, only they have the numbers and power necessary to decolonize institutions of (Euro-centric) learning.

In this context, where Euro-Canadians do not have an immediate personal interest in Indigenization and decolonization and may indeed feel threatened by them, those among them who define and present themselves as allies can serve to legitimate these goals and amplify the Indigenous voices that may remain rare. Those in administrative positions can encourage the creation of spaces and initiatives and reward those who undertake them, while those who already create relationships with communities can take up some of the epistemic work needed for long-term changes.

OBSTACLES AND PITFALLS THAT KEEP US APART

Indigenization and decolonization efforts can lead to inadvertent or negative outcomes in the struggle for liberation and transformation. Decolonization, for example, can reinscribe colonialism by marginalizing or excluding Indigenous peoples. If Indigenization is thinking and acting from Indigenous ways of knowing, what happens when it is performed by people who are not Indigenous or when Indigenous knowledge is used to inform initiatives in a colonial structure in ways that are not decolonial? Daza and Tuck (2014) argue mainstreaming the disciples of colonial studies and its various sub-fields of critical scholarship leads to potential homogenization, cooptation, and complicities. We agree that academic decolonization and Indigenization can, when increasingly mainstreamed as they are today, lead to legitimation of colonial systems and that Indigenization has the potential for non-transformative change through a range of negative outcomes, including misrepresentation, tokenism, and cooptation.

Decolonization can result in marginalization or the exclusion of Indigenous peoples, because colonialism mobilizes settlers against Indigenous people and peoples, and Indigenization takes place in a society and in institutions that continue to be colonial even as they are slowly decolonized. The creation of decolonized spaces can create a much-needed distinction between Indigenous-centred brave spaces and common spaces, but at the expense of shared spaces or of a more generalized decolonization of a university's spaces. Shared spaces, for example, can then be assumed to be "common" without presenting any concrete signs of decolonization. The attribution of a centre, house, or building can easily become a motive to resist transformation of common spaces. Furthermore, the creation of Indigenous advisory circles or boards can lead to the concentration of Indigenous perspectives in one committee that needs to speak with one united voice to offer strong advice, rather than a plurality of Indigenous voices being included throughout a university's structure. The need and possibility for settlers to decolonize themselves can also lead to a conflation of critical discourse with authentic engagement with Indigenous communities.

Indigenization similarly has the potential for colonial re-inscription. Post-secondary institutions have a long history of misrepresentation through ahistorical accounts, inaccurate cultural depictions, and dismissive understandings of knowledge systems (Kuokkanen, 2007; Battiste, 2013). Because a key feature of settler colonialism is re-visioning, such misrepresentation is tactical for the maintenance of settler colonial structures and processes. This includes those initiatives of Indigenization that lead to tokenism or inauthentic tactics and "symbolic gestures" (Cooper, Major, & Grafton, 2018, p. 55), such as the use of Indigenous peoples, histories, or cultures to further an image of change when no real agenda or will exists for the hard work that is required for the processes of truth and reconciliation, Indigenization, and decolonization. Cooptation can occur when Indigenous-centred struggles are artificially compartmentalized in ways that separate Indigenous peoples' rights and nationhood from Indigenous-based, traditional connections to land, natural resource issues, and political/legal rights (Corntassel, 2008). Indigenous-centred knowledge is often integrated into academic practices by individuals who lack the practical knowledge of Indigenous ways of knowing, and the result is often misrepresentation, tokenism, and cooptation of Indigenous peoples' histories, political rights struggles, and contemporary experiences.

Episodes of misrepresentation, tokenism, and cooptation beg the question of academic institutions and Indigenization strategies: Can Indigenous ways of knowing and representations exist authentically in Western-oriented post-secondary institutions or will they inevitably become exploited knowledge, subsumed and assimilated by the academy? Such episodes often result in maintaining the status quo instead of instigating the transformative change that Indigenization seeks. One such institutional response is to fold Indigenous cultures into Western education systems. Cote-Meek (2014) explains that educational reforms that only take the shape of culture will leave colonial structures intact. Culture alone cannot address the legacies and continuation of colonialism. St. Denis (2007) similarly argues that when cultural difference becomes the focus instead of the resultant systemic inequalities of colonial-informed structures (political, economic, societal, etc.), these structures remain intact and solution-based responses are framed through cultural difference, which places blame on Indigenous peoples (as those who have lost culture) and not settler society or settler colonial structures and processes. This focus on culture allows the very forces of colonialism that stripped culture to escape analysis and redress while the very colonial-disenfranchised are blamed for their own colonial disempowerment.

Indigenization activities, however, can be appropriately undertaken to avoid adverse outcomes and non-transformative change. To begin, ask "who benefits": This work should be about the empowerment, not disempowerment, of Indigenous peoples and communities, be Indigenous-led, and be co-created with Indigenous communities. It can be helpful for settler scholars to use authentic Indigenous voice (by inviting an Indigenous expert, Elder, or knowledge keeper to speak instead of speaking for Indigenous peoples) and to inform scholarly work with Indigenous-centred scholarship and anticolonial theory to understand the history of colonialism and how it has disempowered Indigenous peoples, especially within the academy.

CONCLUSION

While Indigenization, as a process of resurgence and re-centring, and decolonization, a strategy of emancipation, remain distinct strategies of transformation, there is potential for mutual reinforcement. Importantly, this chapter has argued that the anti-oppressive strategies associated with these two movements will be necessary for reciprocal, respectful relations between Indigenous and non-Indigenous people as articulated by the era of academic "reconciliation." Both decolonization and Indigenization pose problems when they are enacted as ledger-balancing acts rather than as transformative processes in which Indigenous peoples and settlers can relate to one another. The above issues with decolonization and Indigenization often emerge from valuing the quantity of efforts and initiatives over their quality: As long as universities support Indigenization and decolonization initiatives that rely on or default to misrepresentation, tokenism, and cooptation, a colonial-framed status quo will remain. It is necessary to let Indigenous *peoples* define the authentic parameters of engagement for decolonization, Indigenization, and truth and reconciliation. The recognition by a university of the traditional territory it resides within can act as a reminder to engage meaningfully with and listen deeply to the nations and communities of the territory. A radical form of Indigenization might, therefore, involve developing joint processes with Tribal Councils to favour the recruitment of local Indigenous students and faculty and facilitate curriculum-development in ways in keeping with Indigenous ways of knowing. For universities to take part in Indigenization and decolonization in a manner that will allow for resurgence and emancipation, they must favour developing and maintaining relationships of collaboration based on mutual need. And they can begin by recognizing and building on the work and commitment of Indigenous and settler students, staff, and faculty who are devoting much of their time to such relationships.

DISCUSSION QUESTIONS

1. Should decolonization precede Indigenization or vice versa?

2. How can Indigenization initiatives exist without misrepresenting, tokenizing, and coopting Indigenous peoples and knowledge systems?

3. How do a university's Indigenization policies benefit it and its non-Indigenous leadership, faculty, staff, and students? Are these benefits less than those to Indigenous students, staff, and faculty and Indigenous communities?

4. How do we ensure that academic Indigenization and decolonization processes remain relevant to Indigenous communities with whom universities share territory?

5. How are settlers of non-European descent and specifically racialized people affected by and involved in Indigenization and decolonization?

6. What elements in non-Indigenous practices and traditions of thought can be brought alongside Indigenous ways of being, knowing, and acting to anchor and further decolonization?

GLOSSARY

acolonial/precolonial: Structures and practices that are independent from those of colonialism, may have pre-existed them, and exist alongside them, usually in conflict. May be Indigenous or non-Indigenous.

anticolonial: Structures and practices deployed in resistance to those of colonialism. May be Indigenous or non-Indigenous.

Chapter 8 | The Dynamics of Decolonization **149**

colonialism: A system put in place to allow for the seizure of land and the control, marginalization, and/or elimination of its Indigenous population.

cooptation: The use of marginalized and repressed ways of being, knowing, and acting and the people who practise them for the benefit of the system that dominates and oppresses them.

decolonial: Structures and practices deployed in order to replace those of colonialism. May be Indigenous or non-Indigenous.

domination: Structures and practices that limit the development and exercise of one's ethical and political capacities.

efforts: Localized and contextualized acts, practices, and policies, as opposed to a stable, final end result.

emancipation: Liberation from domination and oppression; vigilance as to their return; deployment of free structures and practices that enable personal capacities.

Indigenization: Efforts to transform spaces, processes, and institutions founded in non-Indigenous cultures to include Indigenous ways of knowing, being, and acting and the persons who practise them.

Indigenous peoples and communities: Peoples are collectivities that share many attributes (which may include a language, a territory, a culture, a history, institutions) and have the ability to determine themselves; "First Nation" or "nation" in the European sense may be seen as synonymous. Here we refer to the nêhiyawak, Anihšinápék, Dakota, Lakota, Nakoda, and Métis peoples. Communities are networks of relationships that act as contexts for the lives of individuals who know each other; "First Nations," in its use synonymous to "band," are one form of Indigenous community.

Indigenous worldviews: Ways of knowing and interpreting all facets of existence that are place-based and orally transmitted, tied to languages, ceremonies, and teachings. These ways of knowing are attached to ways of being (relating to oneself, other human beings, other-than-human animals, land, water, sky, and ancestors) and acting (ethics and politics).

intercultural: Concerning the relationships between members of two cultural groups, as opposed to multiculturalism, which concerns the relationship of a state or institution to various cultural groups present within.

oppression: Structures and practices that limit the development and exercise of one's cultural and intellectual capacities.

"reconciliation": Efforts to create mutually respectful relationships between Indigenous and non-Indigenous people, or to benefit in terms of power and status from the appearance of such efforts.

resurgence: Re-creation of traditional structures and practices and the contexts and conditions that can make them possible.

settler: A non-Indigenous person, understood in their relation to colonialism. Euro-Canadian settlers stand apart from settlers of non-European origin who are racialized, whose culture is marginalized, and who as a result both suffer the effects of colonialism and profit from settler colonialism for their place on traditional Indigenous land.

settler colonialism: A form of colonialism that depends on appropriation of land and on mass settlement meant to overtake the Indigenous population, rather than on occupation of the land by a minority with ties to a foreign colonial power (as in imperial colonialism).

tokenism: The use of Indigenous people and knowledge to signal efforts and transformation, without meaningful change to structures and practices.

FURTHER READINGS/WEBSITES

Ahmed, S. (2012). *On being included. Racism and diversity in institutional life*. London, UK: Duke University Press.

Alfred, G. R. (1999). *Peace, power, righteousness: An Indigenous manifesto*. Toronto, ON: Oxford University Press.

Battiste, M., & Henderson, J. Y. (2000). *Protecting Indigenous knowledge and heritage*. Saskatoon, SK: Purich.

Battell Lowman, E., & Barker A. J. (2015). *Settler: Identity and colonialism in 21st century Canada*. Winnipeg, MB: Fernwood Publishing.

Burnette, C. E. (2014). Indigenous women's resilience and resistance to historical oppression: A case example from the United States. *Affilia, 30*(2), 253–258.

Burnette, C., & Hefflinger, T. (2017). Identifying community risk factors for violence against Indigenous women: A framework of historical oppression and resilience. *Journal of Community Psychology, 45*, 587–600.

Diabo, R. (2016, July 22). Federal Justice Minister is selling decades old termination plan as a new "reconciliation" framework for First Nations. *The Volcano*. Retrieved from http://thevolcano.org/2016/07/22/federal-justice-minister-is-selling-decades-old-termination-plan-as-a-new-reconciliation-framework-for-first-nations-by-russ-diablo/

Lindroth, M. (2011). Paradoxes of power: Indigenous peoples in the permanent forum. *Cooperation and Conflict, 46*(4), 543–562.

Niezen, R. (2013). *Truth and indignation: Canada's Truth and Reconciliation Commission on Indian Residential Schools*. Toronto, ON: University of Toronto Press.

Regan, P. (2012). *Unsettling the settler within Indian Residential Schools, truth telling, and reconciliation in Canada*. Vancouver, BC: UBC Press.

Simpson, A. (2014). *The chief's two bodies: Theresa Spence and the gender of settler sovereignty* [Video]. R.A.C.E. Network 2014 Conference, Keynote Address. Retrieved from https://vimeo.com/110948627

Sunga, S. (2017) Dealing with oppression: Indigenous relations with the state in Canada. *Ethics and Social Welfare, 11*(2), 135–148.

Vowel, C. (2016). *Indigenous writes: A guide to First Nations, Metis, & Inuit issues in Canada*. Winnipeg, MB: Highwater Press.

Wilson, C. (Ed). (1999). *Civilization and oppression*. Calgary, AB: University of Calgary Press.

Young, I. M. (2005). Self-determination as non-domination: Ideals applied to Palestine/Israel. *Ethnicities, 5*(2), 139–159.

REFERENCES

Abensour, M. (2003). Philosophie politique critique et émancipation? *Politique et Sociétés, 22*(3), 119–142.

Aboriginal Advisory Circle. (2015). *Strategic plan (2015–2020): Working together, strengthening our relationships*. Retrieved from https://www.uregina.ca/strategic-plan/assets/docs/pdf/aac-strategic-plan-2015.pdf.

Alfred, T. (2009). *Wasáse: Indigenous pathways of action and freedom*. Toronto, ON: University of Toronto Press.

Anderson, C., & O'Brien, J. M. (Eds.). (2017). *Sources and methods in Indigenous Studies*. New York, NY: Routledge.

Ashcroft, B., Griffiths, G., & Tiffin, H. (2000). *Post-colonial studies: The key concepts*. New York, NY: Routledge.

Bartlett, C., Marshall, M., & Marshall, A. (2012). Two-Eyed Seeing and other lessons learned within a co-learning journey of bringing together Indigenous and mainstream knowledges and ways of knowing. *Journal of Environmental Studies and Sciences, 2*, 331–340.

Battiste, M. (2013). *Decolonizing education: Nourishing the learning spirit*. Saskatoon, SK: Purich Publishing.

Cooper, E., Major, R., & Grafton, E. K. (2018). Beyond tokenism: Relational learning and reconciliation within post-secondary classrooms and institutions. *Canadian Journal of Native Education, 40*(1), 54–73.

Corntassel, J. (2008). Towards sustainable self-determination: Rethinking the contemporary Indigenous rights discourse. *Alternatives: Global, Local, Political, 33*, 105–132.

Cote-Meek, S. (2014). *Colonized classrooms: Racism, trauma and resistance in post-secondary education*. Winnipeg, MB: Fernwood Publishing.

Daza, S. L., & Tuck, E. (Eds.). (2014). Decolonial, postcolonial, anticolonial and Indigenous education, studies, and theories [Special issue]. *Educational Studies, 50*(4), 307–312.

Diabo, R. (2017, July 12). Trudeau is putting the "con" in reconciliation. Extinguishment disguised as decolonization. *Ricochet*. Retrieved from https://ricochet.media/en/1894/trudeau-is-putting-the-con-in-reconciliation

Frideres, J. (2011). *First Nations in the twenty-first century*. Don Mills, ON: Oxford University Press.

Harvey, J. (2010). Victims, resistance, and civilized oppression. *Journal of Social Philosophy, 41*(1), 13–27.

Henry, F., Dua, E., James, C. E., Kobayashi, A., Li, P., Ramos, H., & Smith, M. S. (2017). *The equity myth: Racialization and Indigeneity at Canadian universities*. Vancouver, BC: UBC Press.

Hubbard, T. (2008). Voices heard in the silence, history held in the memory: Ways of knowing Jeanette Armstrong's "Threads of Old Memory." In R. Hulan & R. Eigenbrod (Eds.), *Aboriginal oral traditions: Theory, practice, ethics* (pp. 139–153). Halifax, NS: Fernwood Books.

Hunt, S. (2014). Ontologies of Indigeneity: The politics of embodying a concept. *Cultural Geographies, 2*(1), 27–32.

King, T. (1997). Godzilla vs. post-colonial. In A. Heble, D. P. Pennee, & J. R. Struthers (Eds.), *New contexts of Canadian criticism* (pp. 183–190). Peterborough, ON: Broadview Press.

Kuokkanen, R. (2007). *Reshaping the university: Responsibilities, Indigenous epistemes and the logic of the gift*. Vancouver, BC: UBC Press.

MacPherson, A. (2018, March 4). Indigenous Students' Council urges "non-participation" in U of S reconciliation efforts. *Saskatoon StarPhoenix*. Retrieved from https://thestarphoenix.com/news/local-news/indigenous-students-council-urges-non-participation-in-u-of-s-reconciliation-efforts

Million, D. (2014). There is a river in me: Theory from life. In A. Simpson & A. Smith (Eds.), *Theorizing Native Studies* (pp. 31–42). London, UK: Duke University Press.

Newcomb, S. T. (2011). The UN Declaration on the Rights of Indigenous Peoples and the paradigm of domination. *Griffith Law Review, 20*(3), 578–607.

Simpson, L. B. (2004). Anticolonial strategies for the recovery and maintenance of Indigenous knowledge. *The American Indian Quarterly, 28*, 373–384.

Simpson, L. B. (2011). *Dancing on our turtle's back: Stories of Nishnaabeg re-creation, resurgence and a new emergence.* Winnipeg, MB: Arbeiter Ring.

Simpson, L. B. (2013). Restoring nationhood: Addressing land dispossession in the Canadian reconciliation discourse. *Leannesimpson.ca.* Retrieved from http://www.sfu.ca/tlcvan/clients/sfu_woodwards/2013-11-13_Woodwards_VOCE_Restoring_Nationhood_12308/

Simpson, L. B. (2017). *As we have always done: Indigenous freedom through radical resistance.* Minneapolis: University of Minnesota Press.

Sioui, G. (1992). *For an Amerindian autohistory: An essay on the foundations of a social ethic.* Montreal, QC: McGill-Queen's University Press.

St. Denis, V. (2007). Aboriginal education and anti-racist education: Building alliances across cultural and racial identity. *Canadian Journal of Education, 30*(4), 1068–1092.

Truth and Reconciliation Commission of Canada (TRC). (2015a). *Truth and Reconciliation Commission of Canada: Calls to Action.* Retrieved from http://trc.ca/assets/pdf/Calls_to_Action_English2.pdf

Truth and Reconciliation Commission of Canada (TRC). (2015b). *Canada's Residential Schools: Reconciliation. The final report of the Truth and Reconciliation Commission of Canada* (vol. 6). Retrieved from http://nctr.ca/assets/reports/Final%20Reports/Volume_6_Reconciliation_English_Web.pdf

Tuck, E., & Yang, K. W. (2012). Decolonization is not a metaphor. *Decolonization: Indigeneity, Education & Society, 1*(1), 1–40.

Veracini, L. (2010). *Settler colonialism: A theoretical overview.* New York, NY: Palgrave McMillian.

Veracini, L. (2015). *The settler colonial present.* New York, NY: Palgrave McMillian.

Wolfe, P. (2006). Settler colonialism and the elimination of the Native. *Journal of Genocide Research, 8*(4), 387–409.

Young, I. M. (1990). *Justice and the politics of difference.* Princeton, NJ: Princeton University Press.

Young, R. J. C. (2001). *Postcolonialism: An historical introduction.* Oxford, UK: Blackwell Publishing.

CHAPTER 9

Urban and Inner-City Studies: Decolonizing Ourselves and the University of Winnipeg

Chantal Fiola and Shauna MacKinnon

SITUATING OURSELVES

We, the authors, recognize the importance of introducing ourselves and highlighting our social locations and relationships to the issues at hand. We come from different cultures, **worldviews**, and experiences, which shape our understanding and efforts in relation to decolonizing the University of Winnipeg and the department we teach in, Urban and Inner-City Studies, which are situated on Treaty 1 territory and the homeland of the Métis Nation. We tell you about ourselves so you know where we come from and how we might relate to one another through place, culture, clan, experience; in this way, we honour Indigenous protocols around introductions.

Boozhoo nindinawaymaagunidoog! Zaagaatekwe ndizhinikaaz; biizhew nidoodem. Niin naawenaangweyaabe, bezhig Mide, onimu pahkosimowin. Michif ndaaw. Greetings my relatives! My spirit name is Sunrays Shining through the Clouds Woman (my French name is Chantal Fiola); I belong to the lynx clan. I am Two-Spirit, first-degree Midewiwin, and a Sundancer. I'm Michif (Red River Métis), with family from St. Laurent and Ste. Geneviève, Manitoba, and was born where the Red and Assiniboine Rivers converge (The Forks, St. Boniface). Since completing my PhD in Indigenous Studies (Trent University, 2012), I've been focusing on Métis cultural regeneration, especially via Métis participation in Indigenous ceremonies, and am writing a second book on that topic (Fiola, 2015). I joined the Department of Urban and Inner-City Studies (UIC) in 2016 at the rank of Assistant Professor and am responsible for teaching several **Indigenous Course Requirement (ICR)** courses. Through family and ceremony, I'm continually building and strengthening my relationships in Indigenous communities and, more recently, building inner-city community relationships by serving Indigenous community organizations catering to Indigenous women, children, and Two-Spirit people. I seek to remain accountable to my communities by, for example, working to ensure that UIC is contributing to bettering relationships between Indigenous and non-Indigenous peoples.

I, Shauna, am a second-generation White settler of Scottish and French descent. My commitment to social and economic justice is inspired by my mother. My father died from alcoholism when I was a teenager, leaving my mother, who had a Grade 9 education and earned minimum wage in the service industry, to raise four children on her own. Like many UIC students, I pursued my post-secondary school as a mature student, beginning university at the age of 28. I'm the only person in my family to attend university. I completed my PhD in 2011 and joined the University of Winnipeg Department of Urban and Inner-City Studies in 2013. I've been engaged in community development, social activism, and research in Winnipeg's inner city since the early 1990s. I have a particular interest in research and policy advocacy related to improving social and economic conditions for people living in poverty. In Canada, and more specifically in Winnipeg, colonial policies have ensured that Indigenous people remain overrepresented among those living in poverty. Central to my research and activism is walking beside Indigenous community partners to advocate for the **decolonization** of public policy toward inclusion.

THE URBAN AND INNER-CITY STUDIES DEPARTMENT

The University of Winnipeg's Department of Urban and Inner-City Studies (UIC) is intentionally located outside of the main campus in Winnipeg's North End, within the geographic boundaries defined by the City of Winnipeg as the "inner city." The inner city of Winnipeg is largely an Indigenous space but also home to a growing number of newcomers to Canada. Like the characteristics found in impoverished inner cities in other large urban centres, Winnipeg's inner city has a high incidence of racialized poverty, low education attainment, poor housing, poor health, weak labour market attachment, and a host of other challenges related to the deeply damaging effects of colonization (MacKinnon & Silver, 2017).

UIC continues to develop a unique pedagogical framework since relocating from the main campus to the North End in 2011. This framework is inspired by our understanding that colonization, including Eurocentric education, continues to fail Indigenous people (Battiste, 2013). Our research and practical experience have shown us that students who have had a negative experience with education typically find the conventional education trajectory overwhelming (MacKinnon, 2015; Silver, 2013). We believe in the importance of "small, safe" learning environments for students and especially for Indigenous students, who have been denied the opportunity to access education that is meaningful and respectful of Indigenous ways of knowing. We've learned that bringing students from diverse cultures and socio-economic backgrounds together to learn in small, safe spaces can be a useful way of "breaking barriers and building bridges" in what continues to be a city marred by racism (Canadian Centre for Policy Alternatives, 2013).

UIC is committed to decolonization. Our curriculum is rooted in critical social theories, including **critical race theory** (Delgado & Stefancic, 2012), feminist community research theories (Creese & Frisby, 2012), critical urban theories (Brenner, Marcuse, & Mayer, 2012), and **heterodox economic theories** (Lee, 2012). We integrate critical and decolonizing pedagogies building on the work of scholars including Freire (2006), Giroux (2011), Grande (2004), Haymes (1995), hooks (1994), and Smith (1999).

Our approach is also rooted in placed-based pedagogical theories, especially that of Haymes (1995), who calls for a "pedagogy of resistance" (p. ix) in the spirit of Frantz Fanon (1961). Urban spaces characterized by racialized, spatialized poverty can be sites to raise awareness of the sources of oppression (Freire 2006), and universities have an opportunity to engage in pedagogical methods to contribute to a process of decolonization and inspire reclamation of cultures and spaces. Aligned with Haymes's call for **pedagogy** of place to be linked to "black urban struggle," in the Winnipeg inner-city context, a pedagogy of place must be linked to Indigenous oppression, resistance, and cultural reclamation. As Giroux (1983) explains, **critical pedagogy** has "an important role in the struggle of oppressed groups to reclaim the ideological and material conditions for organizing their own experiences" (p. 237.)

The continued oppression of Indigenous people calls for a critical pedagogy that facilitates learning in safe spaces. We've seen how this can lead to personal transformation as students explore the historical and political context of their realities. This is particularly crucial for Indigenous students who have internalized colonization and have come to believe "that we are incapable of learning and that the colonizers' degrading images and beliefs about Aboriginal people and our ways of being are true" (Hart, 2002, p. 27). For non-Indigenous students, particularly those who benefit from the privilege of being White and middle class, learning in the inner city, with people who typically experience poverty and racism as an everyday experience, the true meaning of being an "ally" becomes more than a concept learned from a textbook. Our approach to education is rooted in decolonial reconciliation and the idea that White settlers need to do the heavy lifting to right past wrongs. Students learn that allies must walk beside and in support of Indigenous peoples—challenging the oppressive structures that perpetuate White supremacy and exclusion.

Expose, Propose, Politicize

While not always explicit in our curriculum, an overarching theme in UIC aligns with critical urban theories and the central concepts of the **Right to the City** (Brenner, Marcuse, & May, 2012; Lefevbre, 1968)—expose, propose, politicize. Indigenous leaders remind us that reconciliation as outlined by the Truth and Reconciliation Commission of Canada (TRC) requires understanding and acceptance of the truth about Canada's damaging colonial policies as the starting point that must lead to concrete action (Manuel & Derrickson, 2017; TRC, 2015b). Critical urban theories, and more specifically the "Right to the City," provide a framework and potential for **praxis** toward structural transformation (Freire 2006) aligned with the objectives of "reconciliation" and decolonizing education (Grande, 2004; MacKinnon, 2015).

Situated in a largely Indigenous space and challenged by intergenerational trauma caused by colonialism and reinforced by neoliberal capitalism (Grande, 2004), students from diverse backgrounds are inspired to learn "from, with, and in" the community and to be actively engaged in progressive social change. We take critical pedagogy out of the ivory tower, into the community, levelling the playing field for students to learn how the intersections of their experiences shape the way they view and experience the world. In the North End of Winnipeg, this often means White students with privilege stepping out of their comfort zones to study in a neighbourhood they have been taught to fear. It means learning that their classmates who have lived in poverty in the inner city, many who are Indigenous and have experienced the intergenerational trauma of colonization, have much to teach them. We've learned that bringing critical pedagogies into inner-city, colonized spaces can have a transformative impact on the lives of students from all walks of life.

Critical pedagogies make room for multiple ways of knowing. In addition to faculty and staff from diverse experiences, UIC engages Elders and long-time community practitioners and activists who have a wealth of experiential knowledge to share with students. Before discussing these and other efforts being undertaken by UIC, let us examine the concepts of decolonization, **indigenization**, and reconciliation as they relate to academia.

DECOLONIZATION, INDIGENIZATION, RECONCILIATION

Decolonization, *reconciliation*, and *indigenization* are not interchangeable, and there is no consensus on what they look like. There are many challenges and pitfalls when attempting to transform academia to better serve Indigenous people.

Decolonization

Decolonization identifies impacts of colonization, understands the resulting uneven distribution of power and oppression, dismantles colonial systems, and promotes Indigenous self-determination. Angela Wilson (Dakota) (2004) recalls Fanon's call to overturn the entire colonial structure if freedom from oppression is to be realized. Fanon explained the first step toward overthrowing colonial regimes is to decolonize the mind (Tuck & Yang, 2012). Winona Wheeler (Cree) explains, "Decolonization entails developing a critical consciousness about the cause(s) of our oppression, the distortion of history, our own collaboration, and the degree to which we have internalized colonialist ideas and practices" (as cited in Wilson, 2004, p. 71). Wilson identifies decolonial strategies for Indigenous empowerment, including reaffirming Indigenous epistemologies, ontologies, and traditional governance, and rebuilding communities. Eve Tuck (Unangax) and K. Wayne Yang (2012) observe, "Decolonization brings about the repatriation of Indigenous land and life" (p. 1)—"*all* land, and not just symbolically" (p. 7). They insist, "Decolonization eliminates settler property rights and settler sovereignty ... and upholds the sovereignty of Native land and people" (p. 26). This is the most difficult aspect of decolonization, yet fulsome decolonization requires it.

Reconciliation

The Truth and Reconciliation Commission (TRC) popularized the language of "reconciliation" (Gaudry & Lorenz, 2018; MacDonald, 2016). Arising from the 2007 Indian Residential Schools Settlement, the TRC spent six years travelling Canada. Commissioners listened to the stories of 6,000 witnesses and released the final report, including 94 Calls to Action, in 2015 (2015a). According to the TRC (2015b), "the Commission's focus on truth determination was intended to lay the foundation for the important question of reconciliation.... Reconciliation is not an Aboriginal problem; it is a Canadian one. Virtually all aspects of Canadian society may need to be reconsidered" (p. vi). Like decolonization, true reconciliation necessitates a complete restructuring of Canadian society.

Responding to the TRC, "universities vowed to undertake a concerted program of reconciliation, to correct the historical misuse of education in Canadian colonial endeavors" (Gaudry & Lorenz, 2018, p. 5).

Indigenization

According to Cree scholar Dr. Alex Wilson (2016), "the term *indigenization* has been linked historically to Christianization and was first used by the Catholic Church to indoctrinate Indigenous people so they would become good Catholics." It was later popularized in the 1990s as an "add [Indigenous to White settler frameworks] and stir" endeavour. In 2010, the Association of Canadian Deans of Education (ACDE) launched the *Accord on Indigenous Education* in hopes of "increasing Indigenous educational engagement, establishing partnerships with Indigenous organizations and communities, and using educational frameworks based on Indigenous knowledge" (p. 1). Together with the TRC's Calls to Action, universities now feel "pressured to indigenize their institutions" (Gaudry & Lorenz, 2018, p. 1).

In 2018, Adam Gaudry (Métis) and Danielle Lorenz (European ancestry) conducted an anonymous online survey of 25 scholars (mostly Indigenous academics and allies) and uncovered three distinct mobilizations of "indigenizing the academy":

- *Indigenous inclusion*—"A policy that aims to increase the number of Indigenous students, faculty, and staff ..." (p. 1);
- *Reconciliation indigenization*—"A vision that locates indigenization on common ground between Indigenous and Canadian ideals, creating a new, broader consensus on debates such as what counts as

knowledge ... and what types of relationships academic institutions should have with Indigenous communities" (pp. 1–2); and

- *Decolonial indigenization*—"The wholesale overhaul of the academy to fundamentally reorient knowledge production based on balancing power relations between Indigenous peoples and Canadians, transforming the academy into something dynamic and new" (p. 2).

Indigenization of the academy is often limited to "inclusion" through "cluster hiring" (Tuck, 2018). Several Indigenous faculty are hired over a short period of time; however, the colonial structures and practices of institutions remain intact. Reconciliation indigenization goes further by, for example, creating Indigenous advisory committees and Indigenous Course Requirements (ICRs), and considering power sharing in decision- and policy-making. Decolonial indigenization is the most radical form of indigenization. It requires dismantling settler colonialism entirely and promoting Indigenous resurgence (Gaudry & Lorenz, 2018). Gaudry and Lorenz conclude that "the Canadian academy still largely focuses on policies of inclusion" despite Indigenous faculty, staff, students, and allies desiring "a fundamental and decolonial shift" (p. 9).[1]

PITFALLS

Efforts to decolonize, reconcile, and indigenize are difficult and challenges abound. Tuck and Yang (2012) discuss the reduction of decolonization to a metaphor: "When metaphor invades decolonization, it kills the very possibility of decolonization; it re-centers whiteness, it resettles theory, it extends innocence to the settler, it entertains a settler future" (p. 3). Metaphorization, they argue, makes *settler moves to innocence* possible by "[relieving] the settler of feelings of guilt or responsibility without giving up land or power or privilege" (p. 10). One such move is *conscientization*—a "focus on decolonizing the mind ... as if it were the sole activity of decolonization; to allow *conscientization* to stand in for the more uncomfortable task of relinquishing stolen land" (p. 19). Another example is *at risk-ing/asterisk-ing Indigenous people*—ways that Indigenous peoples are "counted, codified, represented, and included/discluded" by researchers because it "conceals the erasure of Indigenous peoples within the settler colonial nation-state and moves Indigenous nations as 'populations' to the margins of public discourse" (p. 22). Academia often perpetuates settler moves to innocence.

Many Indigenous people are wary of claims to "decolonize," "reconcile," and "indigenize." Additional reasons for wariness include: racing past truth to "premature attempt[s] at reconciliation" (Tuck & Yang, 2012, p. 9), tokenism, and lip service, including territorial acknowledgements. Métis scholar Chelsea Vowel (2017) points out that territorial acknowledgements don't happen when farmers plow lands or when pipelines are laid; she also encourages they be followed by honest discussions on what it means to be a guest on Indigenous land and appropriate protocols. Some White settlers are immobile with fear of committing a faux pas; however, expecting Indigenous people to do all the work isn't fair either.

Anishinaabe scholar Andrea Landry (2018) argues that "the reigns of 'decolonization,' and 'indigenization' are being guided by colonialism. It has been co-opted so heavily that it is no longer an indigenous movement—but a colonial one." She encourages "no longer recognizing it as decolonization and indigenization.... [Instead,] becoming living examples of indigenous resurgence, revitalization through the recovery of our mother-tongues, kinship systems, healthy lifestyles, land-based practices, forgiveness processes, and traditional diets" (Landry, 2018). UIC, and the University of Winnipeg, is trying to heed these warnings, better Indigenous and non-Indigenous relationships, and promote Indigenous resurgence.

INDIGENIZATION AT THE UNIVERSITY OF WINNIPEG

Recently, the University of Winnipeg (UW) and Lakehead University became the first two Canadian universities to implement an Indigenous Course Requirement (ICR). The University of Winnipeg Students Association put forward an initial proposal that would enable every UW student to learn more about Indigenous peoples and realities. The UW Senate unanimously approved the ICR and, as of September 2016, all new UW students are expected to complete a minimum of one three-credit-hour, ICR-approved course during their degree to graduate. UW (2016a) explains that this "decision exemplifies the University's leadership in responding to the recommendations made in the final report of the Truth and Reconciliation Commission (TRC), while its spirit epitomizes the diversity-minded approach of the UWinnipeg community and its commitment to leading Indigenous inclusion."

The main criterion to obtain ICR approval is that the greater part of a course must contain local Indigenous content "based on analysis of the cultures, languages, history, ways of knowing or contemporary reality of the Indigenous peoples of North America (what is now called Canada and the USA)" (UW, 2016b). New course proposals are approved by the Department of Indigenous Studies Curriculum Committee and the Senate Curriculum Committee before receiving final approval from the Senate. Every department is encouraged to offer their students one or more ICR courses. This is a work in progress, with some departments not yet offering an ICR course, others offering a single course, and others offering several ICR courses (Indigenous Studies, Anthropology, History, Political Sciences, Religion, and Urban and Inner-City Studies). UW currently offers approximately 80 ICR courses university-wide, with several more undergoing the process for approval.

The University of Winnipeg recognizes that it sits on Treaty 1 territory in the homeland of the Métis Nation and sees the ICR as part of the university's larger efforts to decolonize our institution. Recently, UW's Board of Regents approved a new Strategic Direction for the university that highlights an "Indigenization strategy" as a response to the TRC's Calls to Action (2015a). An Indigenous Advisory Circle (IAC) has been formed to help this strategy take shape; membership in the IAC includes representation from urban, rural, and northern Indigenous peoples in Canada and abroad. More than just a commitment to increasing the number of Indigenous students, faculty, and staff, the IAC will help the university to ensure that Indigenous perspectives contribute to UW's governance, programs, and services, to identify and remove barriers for Indigenous students, and to improve access by advancing scholarships and bursaries.

UIC: A HISTORY OF DECOLONIAL EFFORTS

UIC's efforts to indigenize and decolonize predate the University of Winnipeg's mandate for indigenization. Department founder and longtime Chair Professor Jim Silver had a lengthy history conducting research on inner-city and Indigenous issues, with a particular focus on education. Locating UW's Department of Urban and Inner-City Studies in the neighbourhood was intended to complement other neighbourhood-based education initiatives, providing further opportunities for inner-city residents. Dr. Silver was inspired to establish the department and advocate for its location on Selkirk Avenue in the North End. Since then, faculty members, support staff, and contract academic staff have been carefully selected to ensure a diversity of experience and a commitment to decolonizing pedagogies and the broader social justice goals of the department.

Curriculum has been developed in line with our social justice goals, and the program has been strategically designed to ensure various entry points and opportunities for multi-barriered learners. For example, in addition to three- and four-year degree options, we have developed two certificate options for students, including a general certificate in UIC and a certificate specializing in community advocacy. Attaining a certificate typically takes a student two years to complete. Its purpose is three-fold. First, a certificate serves to recognize a student's achievement part-way through the program as a means of encouraging them to continue. Two, it provides those students who feel overwhelmed by the challenges of obtaining a degree with a concrete achievement that they can use to obtain employment in the community while also leaving open the possibility of returning to obtain a full degree. And three, it aligns with provincial social assistance policy that does not allow students to remain on government assistance while obtaining a degree. (Manitoba Employment and Income Assistance Policy typically limits EIA clients to a maximum two-year training program.)

Our interest in tackling racism, breaking barriers, and building bridges also predates UW's indigenization mandate. While this was not the initial intention of the program, it has become apparent to department faculty, staff, and contract instructors that something very special is happening in the classroom. Stereotypes are being challenged by bringing non-Indigenous (typically White and middle-class) students into the inner city to learn with Indigenous students and others from the inner city who face multiple barriers. Students who would otherwise not spend time in the inner city or with Indigenous people are learning a very different perspective, thereby challenging them to reflect on their worldviews. Indigenous students have found a space that honours Indigenous perspectives and validates their life experiences.

Because we are a department with a social justice mandate, with several courses integrating scholarly education with an activist edge, we tend to attract activist-oriented students. Others are drawn to social activism as a result of the critical pedagogy they are exposed to in our classrooms. Some students, especially those who have families to feed, remain focused on obtaining a degree so that they can find employment. While we encourage students to become actively engaged citizens, we do not pressure them to do so. Taking the time to participate in social activism and volunteerism is a privilege that many of our students feel they cannot financially afford. Indeed, the most activist students tend to be those who come from more privileged backgrounds. This complicates Freire's (2006) central thesis—that emancipation from oppression requires the oppressed to "become involved in the organized struggle for their liberation" (p. 65). While we agree that emancipation from oppression requires the oppressed to be actively engaged in changing the social and economic structures that serve to oppress, we also respect that many of our students may not be at this "place" in their lives.

Through a pedagogical approach designed to "expose, propose, politicize," leading to empowerment and mobilization, UIC provides students with the tools and space to move from reflection to action. What they choose to do with this knowledge is their choice. Empowerment comes from learning the truth about colonization and oppression, that they are not alone in their struggles, and that they can, if they choose, take agency toward change. Doing decolonial work like this requires support and resources. We now turn to a discussion on some of our successes and challenges.

REFLECTING ON CHALLENGES AND NEEDS MOVING FORWARD

When UIC moved to the North End in 2011, it occupied the basement of a building with a childcare centre on the main floor. For seven years, UIC faculty, staff, and students made the most of a small space with no natural light and the constant loud sounds of children playing overhead. In 2018, UIC moved into our current location. The building that UIC is currently housed in had a dubious past as the notorious Merchant's Hotel and Bar. It had the reputation of fuelling addiction and violence in the neighbourhood. Several community-based organizations and residents embarked on a long campaign to acquire the hotel and transform it into a community space. Community advocacy efforts eventually paid off with the provincial government acquiring the building and transferring ownership to the North End Community Renewal Corporation. After much fundraising and community effort, the Merchant's Hotel was converted into a gorgeous, modern building named Merchant's Corner. Comparing our old basement quarters to our new building, a student had this to say: "It's like going from an old, broken skateboard to a Mercedes Benz!"

Before our grand opening in April 2018, a respected local traditional knowledge holder conducted a sacred pipe ceremony in the new building to honour all those whose lives have been negatively impacted by the Merchant's Hotel, to cleanse the building of any lingering pain, and to bring blessings and guidance from Spirit for the work to be done by the new occupants in the building. UIC faculty, staff, and students, along with the Community Education Development Association (CEDA) staff and students, participated in the ceremony, which also brought us closer together.

UIC and CEDA are part of a growing community-based education hub located on Selkirk Avenue in the North End of Winnipeg. We continue to seek ways to collaborate with the Inner-City Social Work Program (University of Manitoba), Urban Circle Training Centre, and the Indigenous Education Directorate at the Murdo Scribe Centre, toward our shared goal of improving access to education and empowering inner-city (especially Indigenous and newcomer) residents. UIC actively pursues new ways to bring community into Merchant's Corner, as well as encouraging our students to experience community spaces and Indigenous communities inside and outside the city. One way of doing this is through ceremony. Traditional knowledge holders and Elders are often invited into our classrooms, and, when possible, students are taken to visit these knowledge keepers in community (sometimes on reserves). There are associated costs with adhering to Indigenous protocol: for example, tobacco, cloth, feast food, gifts, transportation, medicines, wood for sacred fires, and so on. UIC is a small department in a relatively small university, and our efforts are constrained by a very limited budget. We know all too well that "indigenization" requires sufficient funding to be effective.

One aspect of "indigenization" is increasing the number of Indigenous faculty and staff to teach from Indigenous worldviews so that Indigenous students can see themselves and their realities reflected. Currently, UIC has one Indigenous faculty member (out of four), and one Indigenous staff member (out of three). It is notable that the Indigenous faculty (Chantal) was initially hired on term contracts rather than directly into a tenure-track stream. Several UIC courses are taught by contract academic staff (CAS). Funding constraints have led to an increasing reliance on CAS at the University of Winnipeg. They are paid far less than regular academic staff (RAS), have no job security, and have few, if any, benefits. This is happening across Canadian universities, with implications for the hiring of Indigenous faculty. This exploitation risks worsening with pressures to teach ICR courses (Gaudry & Lorenz, 2019). One way to follow through with "indigenization" is to hire Indigenous faculty directly into the tenure-track stream. Senior administration often replies to this by saying "there's just not enough money." Yet decolonization requires making this a priority. Despite the emphasis on ICR

Chapter 9 | Urban and Inner-City Studies **167**

courses in recent years, of 59 faculty members hired at the University of Winnipeg since 2014, only five are Indigenous.

A related issue is the hiring of non-Indigenous faculty to teach ICR courses; while this can be appropriate in some circumstances, it is inappropriate when most ICR courses are taught by non-Indigenous faculty[2]—many of whom feel pressured to "indigenize" their courses. Indigenous faculty are often relied on to assist non-Indigenous faculty to "indigenize" their courses, guest lecture, and participate in virtually every university committee (i.e., service work) because of the pressure to "indigenize"; these pressures are compounded by the lack of Indigenous faculty in the first place. Considering the goal of tenure, new Indigenous faculty often feel unable to decline requests, despite feeling overworked and underappreciated. When seeking tenure, faculty are expected to spend most of their efforts teaching, publishing, and conducting research, with "service work" taking a backseat. However, for many Indigenous people, "service" or community work is a main priority for regeneration and resurgence of our communities. Commitments to community, including to ceremonies such as the Midewiwin and Sundance, require more time, energy, and effort than universities—which continue to be influenced by Eurocentric ways of knowing—understand. Commitments to Indigenous community involvement ensure our ceremonies and knowledge are passed down through the generations and are crucial in terms of self-determination. Involvement in ceremony typically takes us away from our scholarly work for several days four times a year to follow through with a single spiritual commitment. This leaves us open to criticism, having less time for teaching, research, and publishing. "Indigenization" and decolonization mean recognizing these commitments as equally important as teaching, research, and publishing. To correct this imbalance, Indigenous faculty with demonstrated commitments to community/ceremonial resurgence must be relieved of some of the pressure to "**publish or perish**" (Indigenous Advisory Councils can assist in determining what this might look like).

One additional challenge concerns resistance to the ICR. Some students—usually from privileged, White, settler backgrounds—say they feel "forced" to learn about Indigenous peoples. Considering that most courses are taught from a Western perspective (even if this remains unconscious and unmarked), three credit hours in an Indigenous-specific course isn't too much to ask! However, students may take their frustration out in their course evaluations, which can impact faculty performance and review when applying for tenure and promotion. UIC seems largely unaffected by such backlash—perhaps because of our unique situation and population as discussed above—but it occurs occasionally at the main campus. Indigenous faculty, especially women and Two-Spirit people, may suffer the brunt of this.[3] When considering tenure and promotion, backlash stemming from White supremacy should be taken into consideration and not inhibit upward mobility. These are just some of the issues that must be addressed by universities claiming to take "indigenization" seriously; none of them should result in paralysis and all can be worked through if decolonization is a priority.

The University of Winnipeg has taken an important step toward decolonizing the academy by introducing the ICR. However, there remains much to be done to ensure that this commitment is more than a token gesture. We believe that the Department of Urban and Inner-City Studies provides an example of how a small university department is integrating decolonization as an integral part of its social justice mandate. We too have more work to do, but we hope that the lessons that we have learned and shared herein might help others committed to decolonizing post-secondary education.

NOTES

1. For specific examples of indigenization in Canadian universities, see MacDonald (2006) and Pete (2016).

2. All ICR courses in UIC are taught by Indigenous faculty and contract academic staff.

3. Research shows that students evaluate professors occupying minority categories (female, people of colour, queer people, etc.) more harshly than those occupying privileged categories (straight, White, able-bodied males). See Huston (2006) and Lilienfeld (2016).

DISCUSSION QUESTIONS

1. What does it mean to "decolonize" post-secondary institutions?

2. What are some of the features of post-secondary education institutions that need to change if we are to effectively decolonize post-secondary institutions?

3. Is it possible to decolonize post-secondary institutions without a commitment to hiring Indigenous faculty members?

4. How can university teachers change their pedagogical practices to better align with university claims of decolonization and/or indigenization?

5. What are some of the challenges of implementing Indigenous Course Requirements? How can we address these challenges?

GLOSSARY

critical pedagogy: A pedagogical approach rooted in critical theories. Critical pedagogy incorporates a critical analysis of social and economic structures. It is committed to challenging oppressive symptoms, "empowering marginalized and economically disenfranchised students," and influencing "the development of a politically emancipatory and humanizing course of participation, voice and social action within the classroom" (Darder, Baltodano, & Torres, 2003, p. 11).

critical race theory: Rooted in legal scholarship, critical race theories examine social and economic structures as means of racial oppression and White supremacy.

decolonization: Actively countering/resisting colonization and the institutions that uphold it.

epistemology: The theory of knowledge; how we come to know. Tied to ontology and worldview; varies across cultures.

heterodox economic theories: The Association of Heterodox Economics defines them as "economic theories and communities of economists that are in various ways an alternative to mainstream economics. It is a multi-level term that refers to a body of economic theories developed by economists who hold an irreverent position vis-à-vis mainstream economics and are typically rejected out of hand by the latter; to a community of heterodox economists who identify themselves as such and embrace a pluralistic attitude towards heterodox theories without rejecting contestability and incommensurability among heterodox theories; and to the development of a coherent economic theory that draws upon various theoretical contributions by heterodox approaches which stand in contrast to mainstream theory" (Lee, 2008).

indigenization: Ensuring Indigenous perspectives, values, representation are included in, for example, courses, businesses, the justice system, and so on.

Indigenous Course Requirement (ICR): Mandatory number of credit hours in approved Indigenous-specific courses that must be taken to fulfill degree requirement.

pedagogy: Theories of practice of teaching.

praxis: The practical application of theory. Moving beyond research to action.

publish or perish: The pressure placed upon academics to constantly and quickly publish in order to maintain or further their career.

Right to the City: Aligned with critical urban theory, *Right to the City* is a term first coined by Henri Lefebvre (1968), calling for active participation of oppressed populations and their allies in demanding access to power and resources. Defined by Harvey (2008) as "a right to change ourselves by changing the city ... the freedom to make and remake our cities" (p. 23).

worldviews: Comprehensive understandings of the world from a particular standpoint; tied to culture.

FURTHER READINGS/WEBSITES

Adams, M., & Bell, L. B. (2016). *Teaching for diversity and social justice.* New York, NY: Routledge.

Association of Canadian Deans of Education (ACDE). (2010). *Accord on Indigenous education.* Retrieved from http://csse-scee.ca/acde/wp-content/uploads/sites/7/2017/08/Accord-on-Indigenous-Education.pdf

Battiste, M., & Henderson, S. (2016). *Indigenizing the academy: Indigenous perspectives and Eurocentric challenges* [Video]. Weweni Lecture Series, University of Winnipeg. Retrieved from https://www.youtube.com/watch?v=Hnw-G-D4wG8

Belzer, A. (2004). Blundering toward critical pedagogy: True tales from the adult literacy classroom. *New Directions for Adult and Continuing Education, 102,* 5–13.

Canadian Association of University Teachers. (2016). *Indigenizing the academy.* Retrieved from https://www.caut.ca/about-us/caut-policy/lists/caut-policy-statements/indigenizing-the-academy

Canadian Centre for Policy Alternatives. (n.d.). *Breaking barriers, building bridges* [Video]. Retrieved from https://www.youtube.com/watch?v=NIMrk8sE5tA

Cowden, S., & Singh, G. (2013). *Acts of knowing: Critical pedagogy in, against and beyond the university.* New York, NY: Bloomsbury.

Dudgeon, P., & & Fielder, J. (2006). Third spaces within tertiary places: Indigenous Australian studies. *Journal of Community and Applied Social Psychology, 16,* 396–409.

Gruenwald, D. A. (2003). The best of both worlds: A critical pedagogy of place. *Educational Researcher, 34*(4), 3–12.

Hyland-Russell, T., & Syrnyk, C. (2015). Challenging change: Transformative education for economically disadvantaged adult learners. *International Journal of Lifelong Education, 34*(5), 514–529.

Tejeda, C. (2008). Dancing with the dilemmas of a decolonizing pedagogy. *Radical History Review, 102*, 27–31.

REFERENCES

Association of Canadian Deans of Education (ACDE). (2010). *Accord on Indigenous education*. Retrieved from http://csse-scee.ca/acde/wp-content/uploads/sites/7/2017/08/Accord-on-Indigenous-Education.pdf

Battiste, M. (2013). *Decolonizing education: Nourishing the learning spirit*. Vancouver, BC: UBC Press.

Brenner, N., Marcuse, P., & Mayer, M. (Eds.). (2012). *Cities for people, not for profit: Critical urban theory and the right to the city*. New York, NY: Routledge.

Canadian Centre for Policy Alternatives. (2013). *Breaking barriers—Building bridges*. Winnipeg, MB: Author.

Creese, G., & Frisby, W. (2012). *Feminist community research: Case studies and methodologies*. Vancouver, BC: UBC Press.

Darder, A., Baltodano, M., & Torres, R. D. (Eds.). (2003). *The critical pedagogy reader*. New York, NY: Routledge-Falmer.

Delgado, R., & Stefancic, J. (2012). *Critical race theory: An introduction*. New York: New York University Press.

Fanon, F. (1961). *The wretched of the earth*. New York, NY: Grove Press.

Fiola, C. (2015). *Rekindling the sacred fire: Métis ancestry and Anishinaabe spirituality*. Winnipeg: University of Manitoba Press.

Freire, P. (2006). *Pedagogy of the oppressed*. New York, NY: Continuum. Original work published 1970.

Gaudry, A., & Lorenz, D. (2018). Indigenizing as inclusion, reconciliation, and decolonization: Navigating the different visions for indigenizing the Canadian academy. *AlterNative: An International Journal of Indigenous Peoples*, 1–10.

Gaudry, A., & Lorenz, D. (2019). Decolonization for the masses: Grappling with Indigenous course requirements in the changing Canadian post-secondary environment. In *Indigenous and decolonizing studies in education: Mapping the long view* (pp. 159–174). New York, NY: Routledge.

Giroux, H. (1983). *Theory and resistance in education: A pedagogy for the opposition*. South Hadley: Bergin and Garvey.

Giroux, H. (2011). *On critical pedagogy*. New York, NY: Continuum International Publishing.

Grande, S. (2004). *Red pedagogy: Native American social and political thought*. Lanham, MD: Rowman and Littlefield Publishers.

Harvey, D. (2008). *The right to the city*. New Left Review.

Hart, M. A. (2002). *Seeking mino-pimatisiwin: An Aboriginal approach to helping*. Halifax, NS: Fernwood Publishing.

Haymes, S. (1995). *Race, culture and the city: A pedagogy for Black urban struggle*. Albany: State University of New York Press.

hooks, b. (1994). *Teaching to transgress: Education as the practice of freedom*. New York, NY: Routledge.

Huston, T. (2006). Race and gender bias in higher education: Could faculty course evaluations impede further progress toward parity? *Seattle Journal for Social Justice, 4*(2), 591–611.

Landry, A. (2018, June 6). Decolonization and indigenization is the new reconciliation [blog]. *Indigenous Motherhood*. Retrieved from https://indigenousmotherhood .wordpress.com/2018/06/06/decolonization-and-indigenization-is-the-new-reconciliation/

Lee, F. S. (2008). Heterodox economics. In S. Durlauf & L. E. Blume (Eds.), *The new Palgrave dictionary of economics* (2nd ed.). UK: Palgrave Macmillan. Retrieved from https://hetecon.net/?page=about&side=heterodox_economics

Lee, F. S. (2012). Heterodox economics and its critics. *Review of Political Economy, 24*(2), 337–351.

Lefevbre, H. (1968). The right to the city. In E. Kofman & E. Lebas (Eds.), *Writings on cities* (pp. 63–184). London, UK: Blackwell.

Lilienfeld, E. (2016, June 10). How student evaluations are skewed against women and minority professors. The Century Foundation. Retrieved August 16, 2018, from https://tcf.org/content/commentary/student-evaluations-skewed-women-minority-professors/?agreed=1

MacDonald, M. (2016, April 6). Indigenizing the academy. *University Affairs*. Retrieved from https://www.universityaffairs.ca/features/feature-article/indigenizing-the-academy/

MacKinnon, S. (2015). *Decolonizing employment: Aboriginal inclusion in Canada's labour market*. Winnipeg: University of Manitoba Press.

MacKinnon, S., & Silver, J. (2017). Decolonizing for equity and inclusion. In F. Klodawsky, J. Siltanen, & C. Andrew (Eds.), *Toward equity and inclusion in Canadian cities: Lessons from critical praxis-oriented research*. Montreal, QC: McGill-Queen's University Press.

Manuel, A., & Derrickson, R. (2017). *The reconciliation manifesto: Recovering the land, rebuilding the economy*. Toronto, ON: James Lorimer and Company.

Pete, S. (2016). 100 ways to Indigenize and decolonize academic programs and courses. University of Regina. Retrieved August 17, 2018, from https://www.uregina.ca/president/assets/docs/president-docs/indigenization/indigenize-decolonize-university-courses.pdf

Silver, J. (Ed.). (2013). *Moving forward, giving back: Transforming Aboriginal adult education*. Winnipeg, MB: Fernwood Publishing.

Smith, L. T. (1999). *Decolonizing methodologies: Research and Indigenous peoples*. New York, NY: Zed Books.

Truth and Reconciliation Commission of Canada (TRC). (2015a). *Truth and Reconciliation Commission of Canada: Calls to Action*. Retrieved from http://trc.ca/assets/pdf/Calls_to_Action_English2.pdf

Truth and Reconciliation Commission of Canada (TRC). (2015b). *Honouring the truth, reconciling for the future: Summary of the final report of the Truth and Reconciliation Commission of Canada*. Retrieved from http://www.trc.ca/assets/pdf/Honouring_the_Truth_Reconciling_for_the_Future_July_23_2015.pdf

Tuck, E. (2018). "Universities don't become different just by wishing for it": Eve Tuck on the challenge of changing academia. *CBC Radio*. Retrieved from https://www.cbc.ca/radio/unreserved/decolonizing-the-classroom-is-there-space-for-indigenous-knowledge-in-academia-1.4544984/universities-don-t-become-different-just-by-wishing-for-it-eve-tuck-on-the-challenge-of-changing-academia-1.4547278

Tuck, E., & Yang, K. W. (2012). Decolonization is not a metaphor. *Decolonization: Indigeneity, Education & Society, 1*(1), 1–40.

University of Winnipeg (UW). (2016a). Background on Indigenous course requirement. Retrieved July 30, 2018, from https://www.uwinnipeg.ca/indigenous/indigenous-course-requirement/background.html

University of Winnipeg (UW). (2016b). Indigenous course requirement criteria. Retrieved July 30, 2018, from https://www.uwinnipeg.ca/indigenous/indigenous-course-requirement/ICR-criteria.pdf

Vowel, C. (2017, February 8). *Indigenization in the time of pipelines* [Video]. Weweni Indigenous Scholars Speaker Series. University of Winnipeg. Retrieved from https://www.youtube.com/watch?v=_h8ucu3J-tk

Wilson, A. (2016, December 6). Coming in to Indigenous sovereignty: Relationality and resurgence. Weweni Indigenous Lecture Series, University of Winnipeg. Retrieved August 17, 2018, from https://ro.uow.edu.au/jgi/vol2/iss2/2/

Wilson, A. (2004). Reclaiming our humanity: Decolonization and the recovery of Indigenous knowledge. In D. Mihesuah & A. Wilson (Eds.), *Indigenizing the academy: Transforming scholarship and empowering communities* (pp. 69–87). Lincoln: University of Nebraska Press.

CHAPTER 10

Speaking Back to the Institution: Teacher Education Programs as Sites of Possibility

Fiona Purton, Sandra Styres, and Arlo Kempf

INTRODUCTION

In this chapter, we share the findings of a preliminary study that followed a new mandatory Indigenous content course in a teacher preparation program at one university in Southern Ontario. The course was developed and adopted after the release of the Truth and Reconciliation Commission's (TRC; 2015) final report, which contained 94 Calls to Action. Many of the Calls to Action outlined in the report specifically called on educational policy-makers and institutions. The resulting pressure created a political push on governments, school boards, and education programs to better reflect the wider university commitment to respond to and address the TRC's Calls to Action. This created a moment in which the institution was ready and willing to change their teacher education program, and so a course was developed and implemented while there was receptivity. The course encourages new teachers to become familiar with the past and present consequences of racism and settler colonialism in policies, curricula, and teaching practices in public schooling in Canada.

Although the TRC has placed great hope in the arena of education as a site where positive changes can be made, the education system in Canada also trained teachers to work in Indian Residential Schools (IRS) and has perpetuated racism and violence against Indigenous peoples. So while the field of education is a site of possibility, it is also a site of contestation and violence for many Indigenous people, and as educators, we must be cognizant and accountable to this history. Faculties of education, teacher preparation programs, and mandatory courses are not yet creating the deep change envisioned. The data from this study suggests that such required courses are inadequate in the absence of more fundamental and far-reaching structural and cultural changes within higher education generally and teacher education programs specifically. This chapter addresses some of these proposed changes. First, we situate ourselves in relation to this work. We then move on to speak more broadly about the sociopolitical and institutional context in which this course takes place and further describe the research project. We then use theories of pedagogy to think through our data and conclude by offering some insights into what our findings mean for teacher education as a site of possibility.

SITUATING OURSELVES

Fiona Purton

I am a descendent of European ancestors from Scotland, France, and England who arrived on Turtle Island (North America) between 1700 and the early 1900s; this is where I was born and raised. As a child, I grew up on unceded Algonquin territory—a fact I only became aware of in recent years. Growing up, my formal and informal education did not include conversations about the history and original custodians of the land I lived in relation with. These experiences of silence and erasure are significant because they signal that I was not raised in a society or school system that fostered conscious awareness of the vibrancy and wisdom of Algonquin knowledge or worldviews, or the ways I was benefiting from Canada's settler colonial reality. I currently reside in Treaty 3 territory on the traditional lands of the Haudenosaunee Confederacy and Anishinaabe nations. My understanding of this history of this Land is evolving. This learning is mediated by my own colonial (dis) entanglements.

In my attempts to acknowledge the reverberations of the colonial realities of my ancestors and other settlers, I recognize that I have the privilege of doing so at my own pace—retreating when I need to, pausing, navigating if and how to move forward—as I move through moments of uncertainty and grief when faced with the reality of dispossession of Indigenous land, culture, and knowledges, which I am personally implicated in. While in agreement with Patai (1994) that "we do not escape from the consequences of our positions by talking about them endlessly," I also agree with Pillow (2003) that we should not stop talking about them; to know my positionality and how I sit in relation to the story of this Land is to know the place from which I speak and to continue the process of coming to understand my responsibly in this context.

Sandra Styres

I am Kanien'kehá:ka (Mohawk) and French on my father's side, and my mother's lineage connects me to my English and Welsh ancestors from Europe. I was born in Tiohtià:ke tsi ionhwéntsare (Montréal, Québec) but belong to the Six Nations of the Grand River community, which is made up of six culturally and linguistically distinct nations brought together by the Haudenosaunee Confederacy, whose traditional governance is united under the Kaianere'ko:wa (**Great Law of Peace**). I work in Tkaronto (Toronto) territory, which has a long and tangled history and carries the storied footprints of many nations, including the Ouendat (Wyandat/Wyandot-Huron), Chonnonton (Neutral), Onondowahgah (Seneca-Haudenosaunee), and Misi-zaagiing (Mississaugas-Anishinaabek) nations. Both Tiohtià:ke (Montréal) and Tkaronto (Toronto) are part of the **Dish with One Spoon** agreement to share the land between the Anishinaabek and the Haudenosaunee nations and their respective allies. The Dish with One Spoon agreement is a sovereign First Nation to First Nation agreement to share the hunting grounds of the vast territories covered by the agreement in peaceful coexistence. Tiohtià:ke and Tkaronto are also key sites on waterways that are important gateways into the north.

Locating oneself in relation to everything one does is one of the key foundational principles in Indigeneity. The only place from which any of us can write or speak with any degree of certainty is from the position of who we are in relation to what we know; in this way I am accountable for my own cultural location, which situates me in relation to my community at home and at large, as well as within this writing. Positioning and locating one's self culturally and geographically is a relational, respectful, and reciprocal process that is a key element of Indigenous philosophies. As an educator, I am always aware that I am intimately connected to the very systems I criticize. I am also always conscious of the fact that, within academia, as an Indigenous person of First Nations and mixed Euro ancestry, I must consistently embrace the messy fluidity of an insider/outsider perspective, and I am privileged and complicit in so many tangled ways, yet also simultaneously marginalized and erased within that very system in which I am intimately complicit. This necessitates that I participate in and negotiate multiple discourses that at times contradict, erase, or marginalize the *other* within myself, as well as challenging dichotomous lines of thought while opening up spaces of possibility.

Arlo Kempf

Acknowledging that where we come from informs where we are, Sandra, Fiona, and I are writing from different places. I am White settler Canadian. On my father's side, my ancestors came to North America from what is now Germany. On my mother's side, our people come from Oklahoma—after searching through a series of adoptions, stories, lies, and aspirations, as best I can tell my ancestors were likely Scottish and Cherokee; I'll never be sure and no one has made any claims or been claimed by one group or another. I was born on Kanien'kehá:ka (Mohawk) land in Tiohtià:ke (Montréal). My parents were recent immigrants from the United States. We later moved to Treaty 13 territory, and I grew up there, on the land of the Mississaugas of the New Credit in what is commonly known as Toronto, where I work and live today. Colonial momentum is a river into which Canadian settlers are born, or into which they migrate, and the TRC is not necessarily disruptive to this flow for many of us. Stepping out of the water requires first noticing its ceaseless movement—the way it flows around bends and breaks, over rocks and through low-hanging brush. If one is lucky enough to notice, it then takes some doing to get out of its rushing waters. I'm not there yet, but I work to find, at the very least, an eddy on the margins of the river from which to catch my breath and step out of the flow. In these moments, I more clearly see the colonial flow and recall that all that tides must eventually ebb. I write from this context of complication, privilege, and humility—a positionalty that informs my work as a scholar and my actions as a citizen, family member, descendant, and human.

THE CONTEXT AND THE COURSE

For generations, Indigenous communities and activists have been mobilizing, speaking out, and talking back to coloniality. They have resolutely refused to be silenced about the Canadian government's disregard for treaty relationships and rights, along with unjust, prejudiced, and genocidal policies that have profoundly impacted Indigenous peoples and their communities.

For decades, calls have also been made for Indigenous control over Indigenous education and for public education curricula to reflect the strength, vibrancy, and diversity of Indigenous communities.

Following the release of the TRC report in 2015, there has been considerable public and institutional mobilization around the 94 Calls to Action. This mobilization has resulted in a variety of Indigenous and non-Indigenous stakeholders once again echoing the need for students at the elementary, secondary, and tertiary levels to be taught the history and lived realities of Indigenous peoples of Turtle Island. In response, provincial and territorial governments are steadily working to expand curricula content on Indigenous perspectives and experiences (People for Education, 2015; Ontario Ministry of Education, 2007, 2014). Propelled by the widespread engagement around the TRC and bolstered by the Association of Canadian Deans of Education's (2010) *Accord on Indigenous Education*, many Canadian teacher preparation programs are implementing required courses that seek to provide teacher candidates with the knowledge and skills needed to respond to and address the persistence of colonial inequity as produced by and within K–12 education.

The course that is the subject of this chapter is one example, and although the impetus behind it was the TRC and the Calls to Action, the TRC came about because of dissatisfaction and inaction after the publication of the Royal Commission on Aboriginal Peoples (RCAP) report. The RCAP report, a 4,000-page document with 440 recommendations, was published in 1996 and it did not see the kind of widespread mobilization or political traction that has resulted from the TRC. Soon after RCAP, survivors of IRS brought the largest class-action lawsuit in Canadian history against the Canadian government, which resulted in a settlement agreement. One of the conditions of that agreement was the establishment of the TRC (TRC, 2012). The Calls to Action in the TRC are not dissimilar to the extensive recommendations outlined in RCAP and identified by activists and Indigenous groups before that.

RCAP called for a way to remedy the relationship between Canadians and Indigenous peoples and paid particular attention to the role of educational institutions (TRC, 2015). The final report of the TRC, almost 20 years later, explicitly noted the role teacher education programs played in contributing to residential schools, saying, "Educators told us about their growing awareness of the inadequate role that post-secondary institutions played in training the teachers who taught in the schools. They have pledged to change educational practices and curriculum to be more inclusive of Aboriginal knowledge and history" (p. 21). Beyond truth telling, it was necessary for the TRC to note that curriculum still needs to change because, in the two decades between RCAP and the TRC, the curricular changes that have been made have been, for the most part, superficial and not widespread across the curriculum. Although the response to the TRC has been more substantive than RCAP so far, we are mindful that there have been many other high-level directives that have occupied the political conversation around Indigeneity and settler/Indigenous relations that have accomplished little. Thus, we move forward cognizant that we have not yet come through to the other side, and the TRC may still meet the same fate as its predecessors and fail to create the change it seeks if there is not widespread, radical mobilization around the Calls to Action. In this sense, the jury is still out, and the outcome will be contingent upon the actions of Indigenous people and Canadians. It is within this moment that our work and this course take place.

THE RESEARCH PROJECT

This paper is based on research that uses discovery, reflection, and evidence-based methods to study effective teaching and student learning. The research was conducted on a single teacher education program and its new Indigenous content required course. The one-year ethnographic case study used pre- and post-diagnostic assessments, participant observations, and semi-structured focus groups.

Our findings are gathered from six initial lines of inquiry: (1) How do teacher educators understand the importance of the inclusion of this mandatory course in their program; (2) In what ways did the course impact/inform students during their practicum experiences; (3) How do teacher candidates understand the issues of pressing concern to Indigenous peoples and their communities prior to and again at the end of the course; (4) In what ways has their thinking shifted and changed as a result of the course, particularly in regard to their own lived experiences, other educational experiences, and other subjects they have taken in their program; (5) In what ways has the course met their goals and expectations, particularly as they relate to their goals as future educators; and (6) What can we do to improve the students' experience in the course? Data gathered was from students and instructors of a new required course in a teacher preparation program at one university in Southern Ontario.

EMERGING INSIGHTS

The majority of students enrolled in the course have been brought up and educated within a public Western education system. Hallmarks of this system include an emphasis on product over process, competition and competitive advantage, individualism, education for the labour market, global citizenship and education for democratic participation, and the promotion of a hegemonic narrative that denies the "equal dignity and essential worth" of Indigenous peoples (Battiste & Youngblood Henderson, 2000, p. 292). The course at the heart of this research, which provides the data, brings to the fore knowledge about Canada's shameful colonial relationship to Indigenous peoples. This includes knowledge about the enactment of racist, oppressive, and assimilationist legislation and political agendas. Additionally, the course pushes back against the notion that Indigenous sovereignty is a threat to Canadian sovereignty.

It can be difficult for students to have their cherished beliefs about "Canada the good and benevolent nation" disrupted and to be confronted with arguments suggesting the narratives that have shaped their worldviews are faulty. When students realize that they have been unknowingly complicit in the silencing and/or erasure of Indigenous experiences and worldviews, they often experience moments of dissonance. Further, the notion that this erasure has benefited them is a painful and difficult concept for many settler and non-Indigenous teacher candidates. Mackey (2016) refers to this unsettling as "settler anxiety" (p. 36). As Schick and St. Denis (2003) observe, "most students are unprepared for a social and political analysis in which they cannot stand outside and view themselves in a neutral and objective manner" (p. 4). Often the process of engaging with difficult or troubling knowledge is painful and unsettling because it shakes and rattles epistemological convictions and certainties and calls into question the foundational understandings that have shaped an individual's conception of the world and their place in it. Learners respond in different ways to their unsettling—some embrace it while others resist it, and many fall somewhere in between. Responses are unique to the individual and include a range of reactions throughout the learning journey as students negotiate and seek to make sense of the new knowledge and their relationship to it (Douglas, Purton, & Bascunan, forthcoming; Zinga & Styres, 2018).

We use the terms *settler*, *newcomer*, and *non-Indigenous* here to signal the nuanced and complex relationships individuals have to this land and their arrival stories. We recognize that some people find themselves here because of histories of enslavement and other forms of forced removal from their homelands, while others came to escape political and/or social strife. We also recognize that the privileges of settlerhood are inequitably distributed in terms of race, gender, income, immigration status, ability, sexuality, language, and other socio-identity pieces linked to material advantage and disadvantage. Nonetheless, all non-Indigenous people are located via the settler colonial project, and thus their presence on Turtle Island is an expression of the colonial project. In the remainder of this section, we consider the institutional context in which this work is taking place; share some of what we have learned from both the course instructors and the students; and reflect on theories of pedagogy that helped us make sense of our learnings.

Institutional Context

There is "a growing chorus of calls for mandatory courses on Indigenous issues in Canadian universities" (Kuokkanen, 2016, p. 1). Yet there are also a multitude of voices urging caution as these calls get taken up. Kuokkanen articulates a fear held by many, stating, "I fear we as Indigenous scholars and educators are selling ourselves short. Especially for universities that have not shown serious and long-standing commitments to Indigenous studies and scholarship, mandatory courses are an easy way out" (p. 1). Indeed, in the 20-plus years after RCAP, educational institutions did very little to take up the recommendations.

We now find ourselves in a moment when there is considerably more public pressure for institutions to respond to the 2015 TRC Calls to Action. Many would argue that institutions are using these mandatory courses simply to create the illusion of a commitment to Indigenous peoples by engaging in what Ahmed (2006) refers to as speech acts: acts (which can include a written policy) that publicly commit the institution to progressive actions. These speech acts are non-performative; they associate the institution with a particular policy or mandate but do not result in the deep structural and cultural change they name. In the context in which we are in now, these mandatory courses are presented as the institution's solution to the calls for all formal educational spaces to be safe, welcoming places for Indigenous peoples and their research, knowledge, and worldviews. What is not addressed is that these courses are developed primarily for settler and newcomer Canadians and not for Indigenous people. The intended purpose is the education of non-Indigenous people about the contexts of the colonial relationships between Canada and Indigenous peoples.

Our intention is not to be overly cynical; we recognize that many institutions are making sincere efforts to heed the calls of Indigenous educators, scholars, and communities, and they have been doing so since before the TRC. Yet, as our research demonstrates, the implementation of a course or the hiring of Indigenous staff is not enough if universities remain "contested site[s] where not only knowledge but also middle-class, Eurocentric, patriarchal and (neo) colonial values are produced and reproduced" (Kuokkanen, 2016, p. 2).

Instructors

In the data that emerged from the research, it became clear that the intention, relationship, and ethical imperative of pedagogy are mediated by the epistemological and philosophical orientations of the instructors (Castellano, Davis, & Lahache, 2000) and are influenced by the need to navigate institutional constraints and expectations. Our data suggests that for the instructors who taught this course (all of whom were Indigenous), the teaching of the course was always personal. One spoke about the Elder who had mentored him and taught him that work like that of the course was important and had urged him to devote himself to such projects. He also spoke about having family members who had experienced residential schools and how he wanted to bring those experiences to the students. Another spoke about coming to know who she is as an Indigenous person and her journey as someone who had been adopted and not raised with her culture. Because of experiences she had as a teacher, she wanted help others become aware of their Treaty obligations and felt that teaching teachers was a productive place to exert her energy. The third spoke about growing up and living on a reserve, about her experiences advocating for Indigenous education, and the importance of equipping teacher candidates with accurate knowledge so that they can be part of positive changes. These instructors brought with them an intention and purpose that were informed by their varied understandings of how to bring their epistemological certainties to life, and by their experiences and understandings of their community's needs and their vision of how to move into the future in a good way.

Students

When we looked at the student feedback of the course, some incongruences between the instructors' vision of the course's purpose and the students' expectations of the course became apparent. The students, although they felt the course was important and appreciated what they were learning, really struggled with the vulnerability or precariousness they felt. We contend that these feelings surfaced as a result of being asked to engage in a liminal space—in Grande's (2010) words, a space of "ambiguity, openness, and indeterminancy" (p. 203)—where the purpose was to disrupt hegemonic narratives, make settler colonial logic evident, and share the voices of Indigenous people speaking about their experiences.

The course was designed with the intention to have students think about the implications of what they were learning about Indigenous peoples extant, alongside the students' developing pedagogical commitments. In response to this, remarks such as the following were made: "I think I had much higher expectations and I felt disappointed at the end of the course. I hoped to gain a better understanding and by the end of course I felt like I had a small understanding of a few things and a lot of confusion about a lot of things" (student participant).

Many students desired a sense of accomplishment, a feeling of certainty about how to move forward (more will be said about this later). What many were left with was more questions than they had when they began and a feeling that there was so much left to learn.

Similar to their desire for closure and a sense that they now had answers, many students were disappointed that the course did not provide them with instruction on how to use an "Indigenous pedagogy." Common feedback from the students included statements such as "I thought we would be focused on more reading materials that focused on Indigenous pedagogical approaches, not Indigenous histories" or "[I wanted] more of this pedagogical approach and learning how as teachers we can actually use this in our class and stuff instead of just being a straight history class more or less" and "I wanted to learn about how to incorporate Indigenous pedagogies into my practice and classroom and how I can better support Indigenous students. That was my initial expectation." We did not see many instances of students pausing to question the schooling system they were being trained to work in. Rather than questioning the curriculum that they were being asked to teach, and the assumptions inherent within it, the students' dominant goal was to become skillful practitioners, able to apply Indigenous pedagogies in the classrooms they were entering. There was little evidence that the students understood that, to be effective in changing the conversations and experiences for Indigenous peoples, they needed to unpack their own lived experiences and prior knowledge, as well as their taken-for-granted biases and assumptions. Further, in the absence of this personal reflective work, the kind of change being called for by Indigenous activists, scholars, and communities will not be achieved.

The focus students had on acquiring practical skills is not surprising because, although their program encourages critical thinking and reflection in select ways, it is also explicitly intended to train them to teach the prescribed curriculum, to strictly adhere to Ministry of Education guidelines, and to advance ministry priority areas without critical engagement. This focus on applied teaching mandated curriculum leads to a preoccupation with technique and skills rather than critical consideration of the content and sociopolitical context in which schooling takes place. Many students struggled with the amount of reflecting they were being asked to do and with the amount of reading required (amounts typical in graduate work). They wanted answers, facts, more direct lectures, and fewer class discussions. They spoke about the utility of the course for their teaching practice and were dissatisfied when they personally felt that they did not get what they needed from the course; Mackey (2016) describes this as an "ontology of entitlement."

We share these examples not to depict the students as overly self-interested but rather to illustrate that they are products of a system and society that nurtures in them an expectation of entitlement to instant answers and quick fixes with minimal personal investment or risk, and a profession that puts a tremendous amount of responsibility on the role individual teachers play in the lives and well-being of their students. In this context, the tension manifests because what students are seeking is the opposite of what the course is designed to do—to help them to pause, unpack their assumptions, and think about the implications of the historical and contemporary events they are learning about for the first time, often from the voices of Indigenous peoples. This course was uncomfortable for some and others found that it did not meet their expectations. Overall, however, the students enthusiastically agreed that the course is not only needed but that it should continue to be a mandatory course offering. This indicates that even though students struggled to be comfortable in the liminal space the course created, they recognized the value it offered them.

PEDAGOGY

Aware that courses such as this one often create tension and dissonance, we turned to theories of pedagogy and relationality to gain insight into this uncomfortable phenomenon that occurs between those teaching and those

186 Decolonizing and Indigenizing Education in Canada

learning. There are many definitions of pedagogy; indeed, "the elusive question of what precisely is pedagogy has remained a moving target for education scholars" (Gaztambide-Fernández & Arráiz Matute, 2014, p. 52). Drawing from Gaztambide-Fernández and Arráiz Matute, we work with their theorization that

> pedagogy always implies a *relationship* that is driven by *intentions and desires* for particular kinds of shifts in subjectivity. We [Gaztambide-Fernández and Arráiz Matute] then make the case for the articulation of an *ethical imperative* that is always the premise of any discussion about pedagogy. (p. 53)

There was a difference in the students' orientation to and experience of the course and instructors' orientation to and experience of the course. The student/teacher interactions and engagement with course content were guided by the intentions and the shifts in subjectivities that both parties desired (or not). The course at the heart of this project does some of the preliminary work of shedding light on the gaps and taken-for-granted assumptions in the students' understanding of the current and historical coloniality for Indigenous people. The ethical imperative to learn how to move forward in a good way that motivated this course was one that both students and instructors agreed with.

Grande (2010) is also helpful to draw from when thinking through the relational and intentional aspects of pedagogy. As she says,

> Red Pedagogy, is, by definition, a space of engagement. It is the liminal and intellectual borderlands where Indigenous and non-Indigenous scholars encounter one another, working to remember, redefine, and reverse the devastation of the original colonialist "encounter." The main imperative before us as citizens is to reject capitalist forms of schooling and to acquire the grammar of empire as just *one* tool for unthinking our colonial roots. (p. 203)

The course was designed with an intentionality that is in keeping with Grande's articulation of Red Pedagogy. We understand Red Pedagogy to be, in part, about taking a step out of the fray. Grande (2010) urges those enacting Red Pedagogy to seek balance and "resistance of the new, fast, and sleek in favour of the smooth, traditional, and quiet. It's the replacement of 'to each his own,' and 'may the best man win,' with 'we are all related,' and 'all for one and one for all'" (p. 206). Although the course was fast-paced, it was designed to help students pause and take stock of the ways their thinking was shifting and how they were making sense of their new learning. The students were encouraged to work together and reflect in a collaborative learning environment. Therefore, spaces and assignments were purposefully set up to open opportunities for them to engage in this type of work. The course was about the big picture rather than the intricacies of teaching. The intention of the course was not to give students a how-to guide or toolbox for teaching Indigenous pedagogies. As we have said previously, despite the instructors being explicit at the beginning of the course about its purpose and pedagogy, the students wanted something different from the course and as such the course became a site of contestation.

As we move forward, we draw from Grande's (2010) encouragement to reject "pedagogies obsessed with measuring accountability, measured on one day by one test, through one means. Instead, we need to choose to embrace the long haul, the legacy, the big picture, the mountain, the generations, the ancestors, the whisper" (p. 206). As we navigate the terrain of the course and gain insights from applying Red Pedagogy in our particular context, we are also buoyed by Donald's (2016) provocation that challenges us to find "new ways of living together that are not fully circumscribed by colonial frontier logics" (p. 12). This work is not easy and can often be uncomfortable, but as Mayo (2002) asserts, "educational spaces engaging relations of difference will not be comforting but they may eventually be just" (p. 186). We contend that teacher education programs are spaces that have the potential to shift perceptions and understandings, and eventually foster new relationships to each other and to the places in which we live.

TEACHER EDUCATION AS A SITE OF POSSIBILITY

In a teacher education program that is enmeshed in Western (neo)colonial values and structures, it is too much to expect that one course would accomplish the heavy lifting of getting students to abandon their socialized beliefs related to what teacher education should be. The ways that students experienced the course are reflective of wider societal norms. As the data reveals, although students felt that the course was necessary in theory, in practice they struggled with the pedagogy and curriculum. Their discomfort was triggered when colonialism was decentred, commodification resisted, and Spirit included. Some students embraced the messy ambiguity of their discomfort, while others strongly resisted it. Indigenous experiences, pedagogies, perspectives, and resistance movements presented in the course prompted axiological disruptions to the status quo that undermined fixed narratives of education as a great equalizer and of teaching as inherently noble.

Courses such as the one at the centre of this research are often promoted as the panacea in efforts to change how settlers and non-Indigenous peoples in Canada see themselves in relation to Indigenous peoples, our places, and our shared colonial reality. We do not deny that, while these courses can be sites of possibility for change, they are also enmeshed within the larger societal ecosystem of coloniality. And as a result, these single courses cannot be expected to shoulder the weighty task of shifting understandings and creating change on their own. The data suggests that in moving forward, these courses cannot undertake the important work of truth telling while simultaneously equipping teacher candidates with the pedagogical knowledge and skills they so desperately seek. What the data does tell us is that there needs to be wider structural and cultural shifts across both teacher education programming and the wider institution as a whole. Only then will these mandatory courses truly be spaces where their possibility and potential can be fully realized.

DISCUSSION QUESTIONS

1. What are the challenges facing instructors of mandatory Indigenous education courses?

2. Who should be teaching these mandatory Indigenous education courses? Why?

3. How might who is teaching these mandatory Indigenous education courses be relevant and important for students' learning and their experience in these courses?

4. Discuss the relevance of students' previous educational and lived experiences in terms of their engagement with course content in the mandatory Indigenous education course.

5. Can the academy, widely recognized as a part of the EuroCanadian colonial project, ever be a site of true decolonization, indigenization, or reconciliation?

GLOSSARY

Dish with One Spoon: The Dish with One Spoon or One Dish One Spoon is a treaty agreement between the Anishinaabe, Mississauga, and Haudenosaunee nations and their allies to share the territory and protect the land.

Great Law of Peace: The pillar of governance and relationality for the Haudenosaunee Confederacy.

FURTHER READINGS/WEBSITES

Dion, S. D. (2007). Disrupting molded images: Identities, responsibilities and relationships—teachers and Indigenous subject material. *Teaching education, 18*(4), 329–342.

Dion, S. D. (2009). *Braiding histories: Learning from Aboriginal peoples' experiences and perspectives.* Vancouver, BC: UBC Press.

Gaudry, A., & Lorenz, D. (2018a). Indigenization as inclusion, reconciliation, and decolonization: Navigating the different visions for indigenizing the Canadian Academy. *AlterNative: An International Journal of Indigenous Peoples, 14*(3), 218–227. doi:10.1177/1177180118785382

Gaudry, A., & Lorenz, D. E. (2018b). Decolonization for the masses? Grappling with Indigenous content requirements in the changing Canadian post-secondary environment. In L. Tuhaiwai Smith, E. Tuck, & K. Yang (Eds.), *Indigenous and decolonizing studies in education: Mapping the long view* (pp. 159–173). New York, NY: Routledge.

Grande, S. (2015). *Red pedagogy: Native American social and political thought.* Lanham, MD: Rowman & Littlefield.

Kuokkanen, R. (2007). *Reshaping the university: Responsibility, Indigenous epistemes, and the logic of the gift.* Vancouver, BC: UBC Press.

Maracle, L. (2017). *My conversations with Canadians.* Toronto, ON: BookHug.

McNinch, J., & Spooner, M. (2018). *Dissident knowledge in higher education.* Regina, SK: University of Regina Press.

Regan, P. (2010). *Unsettling the settler within: Indian residential schools, truth telling, and reconciliation in Canada.* Vancouver, BC: UBC Press.

Styres, S. (2017). *Pathways for remembering and recognizing Indigenous thought in education: Philosophies of Iethi'nihsténha Ohwentsia'kékha (land).* Toronto, ON: University of Toronto Press.

Styres, S. (2019a). Literacies of land: Decolonizing narratives, storying & literature. In L. Tuhaiwai Smith, E. Tuck, & K. Yang (Eds.), *Indigenous and decolonizing studies in education: Mapping the long view* (pp. 24–37). New York, NY: Routledge.

Styres, S. (2019b). Reconceptualizing Indigenous education. In H. Jahnke, S. Styres, S. Lilley, & D. Zinga (Eds.), *Indigenous education: New directions in theory and practice*. Edmonton, AB: University of Alberta Press.

Tarc, A. M. (2013). "I just have to tell you": Pedagogical encounters into the emotional terrain of learning. *Pedagogy, Culture & Society, 21*(3), 383–402.

Tuck, E., & Gaztambide-Fernández, R. (2013). Curriculum, replacement, and settler futurity. *Journal of Curriculum Theorizing, 29*(1), 72–89.

Zinga, D., & Styres, S. (2018). Decolonizing curriculum: Student resistances to anti-oppressive pedagogy. *Power and Education,* 1–21. doi:10.1177/1757743818810565

REFERENCES

Ahmed, S. (2006). The non-performativity of anti-racism. *Borderlands, 5*(3).

Association of Canadian Deans of Education. (2010). *Accord on Indigenous education*. Ottawa, ON: Author.

Battiste, M., & Youngblood Henderson, J. (2000). *Protecting Indigenous knowledge and heritage: A global challenge*. Saskatoon, SK: Purich Press.

Castellano, M. B., Davis, L., & Lahache, L. (2000). *Aboriginal education: Fulfilling the promise*. Vancouver, BC: UBC Press.

Douglas, V., Purton, F., & Bascunan, D. (Forthcoming). What's so difficult about difficult knowledge? Unpacking K-12 classrooms as sites of possibility for teaching Indigenous knowledge. *Alberta Journal of Education Research,* Special issue: Teacher Education and Teaching.

Donald, D. (2016). From what does ethical relationality flow? An Indian act in three artifacts. In D. Jardine & J. Seidel (Eds.), *The ecological heart of teaching: Radical tales of refuge and renewal for classrooms and communities* (pp. 12–17). New York, NY: Peter Lang.

Gaztambide-Fernández, R., & Arráiz-Matute, A. (2014). Pushing against: Relationality, intentionally, and the ethical imperative of pedagogy. In J. Burdick, J. Sandlin, & M. O'Malley (Eds.), *Problematizing public pedagogy* (pp. 52–64). New York, NY: Routledge.

Grande, S. (2010). Red pedagogy. *Counterpoints,* 356, 199–207. Retrieved from http://www.jstor.org/stable/42980614

Kuokkanen, R. (2016). Reconciliation and mandatory Indigenous content courses: What are the university's responsibilities? *Decolonization*. Retrieved from https://decolonization.wordpress.com/2016/03/17/reconciliation-and-mandatory-indigenous-content-courses-what-are-the-universitys-responsibilities/

Mackey, E. (2016). *Unsettled expectations: Uncertainty, land and settler decolonization.* Winnipeg, MB: Fernwood Publishing.

Mayo, C. (2002). The binds that tie: Civility and social difference. *Educational Theory, 53*(2).

Ontario Ministry of Education. (2007). First Nation, Métis, Inuit education policy framework. Retrieved from http://www.edu.gov.on.ca/eng/aboriginal/fnmiFramework.pdf

Ontario Ministry of Education. (2014). First Nation, Métis, Inuit education policy framework implementation plan. Retrieved from http://www.edu.gov.on.ca/eng/aboriginal/OFNImplementationPlan.pdf

Patai, D. (1994). (Response). When method becomes power. In A. Gitlen (Ed.), *Power and method* (pp. 61–73). New York, NY: Routledge.

People for Education. (2015). *Ontario's schools: The gap between policy and reality (annual report on Ontario's publicly funded schools 2015).* Toronto, ON: Author.

Pillow, W. S. (2003). Confession, catharsis, or cure? Rethinking the uses of reflexivity as methodological power in qualitative research. *Qualitative Studies in Education, 16*(2), 175–196.

Royal Commission on Aboriginal Peoples (RCAP). (1996). *Bridging the cultural divide: A report on Aboriginal people and criminal justice in Canada.* Ottawa, ON: Author.

Schick, C., & St. Denis, V. (2003). What makes anti-racist pedagogy in teacher education difficult? Three popular ideological assumptions. *Alberta Journal of Educational Research, 49*(1).

Truth and Reconciliation Commission of Canada (TRC). (2012). *Truth and Reconciliation Commission of Canada: Interim report.* Retrieved from https://journalhosting.ucalgary.ca/index.php/ajer/article/view/54959

Truth and Reconciliation Commission of Canada (TRC). (2015). *Honouring the truth, reconciling for the future: Summary of the final report of the Truth and Reconciliation Commission of Canada.* Retrieved from http://nctr.ca/assets/reports/Final%20Reports/Executive_Summary_English_Web.pdf

Zinga, D., & Styres, S. (2018). Decolonizing curriculum: Student resistances to anti-oppressive pedagogy. *Power and Education,* 1–21. doi:10.1177/1757743818810565

CHAPTER 11

"If Not Here, Where?": Making Decolonization a Priority at an Undergraduate University

Mary Ellen Donnan, Avril Aitken, and Jean L. Manore

INTRODUCTION

Increased attention has been directed toward the role of institutions of higher education in addressing issues of disparity and racism brought to the forefront by the **Truth and Reconciliation Commission of Canada (TRC)**. While the TRC Calls to Action (2015b) direct universities to adjust selected programs, a comprehensive set of guidelines for increasing Indigenous student success in higher education was also put forward by **Universities Canada (UC)** within weeks of the release of the TRC reports (2015a; 2015b). The UC (2010) framework, *Principles on Indigenous Education*, was developed collaboratively by university leaders and Indigenous representatives and provides important points of departure for universities seeking to move forward with processes of **Indigenization**. This chapter looks at the case of one small institution of higher education where, within the political context of austerity in Québec (Graefe, 2016), professors from three departments (Sociology, History, and Education) designed a study to look at their university's potential to act upon the UC *Principles of Indigenous Education*. Given that existing university institutional structures for reflection and redesign tend to be compartmentalized, focused on neoliberal "efficiencies," and inclined toward maintaining the status quo or making—at most—minor reforms, we sought insight into the following questions: Is Indigenization an extended reach for our institution? And how might the existing institutional interest in disrupting colonial patterns and building less oppressive ones be transformed, so that actual changes are realized? In this chapter, we use the term *Indigenous* to refer to descendants of original peoples who inhabited the territory now known as Canada; this includes First Nations, Inuit, and Métis peoples. We draw on texts that use alternate terms circulating in the Canadian context, such as **Aboriginal**; it appears in documents such as the reports of the Truth and Reconciliation Commission (2015a; 2015b). We use the term **settler** to refer to those people who are not descended from Indigenous people in Canada. Settlers may be recent arrivals; however, their heritage may also be traced to much earlier arrivals.

SITUATING OURSELVES

Absolon and Willett (2005) call on researchers to relate their own history to the research focus as a means to resist colonial modes of writing. We three are settlers of European ancestry, who came to Bishop's via different paths, including working with First Nations youth and communities and researching our shared histories. In our post-secondary teaching, research, and community-based work, we have encountered the power and privilege related to our heritage, and national consciousness, that are invisible to many. We work toward reflexivity, learning, and unlearning, seeking to honour what we have learned from, and alongside, **Indigenous peoples**. Shelly Johnson (2016), Canada Research Chair in Indigenizing Higher Education, writes, "This process of Indigenizing post-secondary institutions will not be easy, but it is a necessary next step in reconciliation for all who live in Canada and have benefitted from the structures established and maintained by colonial acts" (p. 133). Johnson's words capture what has motivated the study described in this chapter.

Our university, Bishop's, is situated in traditional, unceded Abenaki and Wabenaki Confederacy territory. A small, primarily undergraduate institution, it offers a liberal education to just under 3,000 students. It is located southeast of Montréal, on the outskirts of the city of Sherbrooke, at the edge of farmland, forest, lakes, and the rolling peaks of the Appalachian mountains. The university's red-brick, Victorian-era buildings speak to the colonial vision and British roots that contributed to its founding in the 1830s. While the release of the TRC Calls to Action and UC's *Principles of Indigenous Education* led to new initiatives on campus, such as the creation of an Indigenous Student Support position in 2017 and planning for a redesign of a multi-dimensional building to serve Indigenous students, discussion among faculty and students began much earlier. A key moment was signalled by the formation of the student-run **Indigenous Cultural Alliance (ICA)** around the time of the emergence of the Idle No More movement. Through advocacy of the ICA leaders, formal self-identification became an option for Indigenous students on their application forms. Nonetheless, it is difficult to determine the numbers, as not all wish to identify. From what can be established, Indigenous students choosing Bishop's arrive from across the country and within Québec. They include students identifying as Algonquin, Cree, Inuk, Mohawk, Mi'kmaq, and Naskapi.

Currently, there are no Indigenous professors, instructors, staff, or Elders employed at the university. While a Minor in Indigenous Studies is offered, courses are taught by professors from diverse departments, whose research takes up related issues and histories. The absence of Indigenous faculty harkens to the question of what is, and what is not, Indigenization, and who should participate in Indigenizing processes (Bundale, 2018). A recent study shows that 1.4 percent of professors in Canada are Indigenous (Smith & Bray, 2018); significantly, as Altamirano-Jiménez (2014) points out, "universities have relied heavily on Indigenous students' and faculty's work to support new [Indigenization] initiatives because of the minimal funding involved" (p. 37). Lori Campbell (2018), a director of Indigenous Initiatives at a college of the University of Waterloo, writes, "Indigenization occurs with Indigenous bodies. Indigenous bodies bring Indigeneity, which brings Indigenization." She goes on to comment on the role for non-Indigenous actors: "Everything else [beyond hiring Indigenous people] is simply correcting Euro-centrism in academia so more accurate knowledge & learning are available to students." She is not alone in signalling the intersection of Indigenization and actions that challenge **Eurocentrism**. In a recent lecture, Marie Battiste (2018) distinguishes between—but also links—Indigenization and decolonization, indicating the interdependence of actions that need to be taken for change to occur.

In a typology of representations of perspectives on decolonization in higher education, Andreotti, Stein, Ahenakew, and Hunt (2015) propose four "spaces of enunciation." Between the two extremes are the spaces of "soft reform" and "radical reform" (p. 31), each of which has different commitments and perspectives of analysis. **Soft reform** focuses on increasing access and success for Indigenous students, as exemplified by the UC *Principles*.

However, Wilson and Battiste (2011) write that such institutional changes are inadequate unless there is a plan in place to challenge colonial structures and address "the systemic barriers and cultural discrimination within the education systems" (p. 15). **Radical reform**, on the other hand, targets the entire university community and beyond, as it involves recognition of **settler privilege** and universities' role in neocolonial systems of oppression, which are embedded in university culture, curricula, and research (Cupples, 2015; thedisorderofthings, 2016). Such spaces attend to Indigenous "representation, redistribution, voice and reconciliation" (Andreotti et al., 2015, p. 31).

While the typology of decolonization is an attempt to sort and compare different perspectives, the actual state of practices in Canadian universities reveals the blurring of the lines between soft and radical reforms. Uncertainty surrounds the challenge of decolonization work in higher education (Altamirano-Jiménez, 2014). In the inaugural issue of *Decolonization: Indigeneity, Education and Society*, Sium, Desai, and Ritskes ask, "Is it possible to decolonize institutions of colonial power (such as the academy, government, etc.), but, further, is it possible to decolonize *through* them?" (2012, p. iv). As Darlaston-Jones and colleagues (2014) suggest, if Indigenous voices and knowledge are to be authentically represented in institutions of higher education, then we have to figure out how to disrupt the colonial structures of power and privilege in the university. What follows is our analysis of Bishop's University's preparedness to attempt such work.

FINDINGS AND DISCUSSION

Our study of views and aspirations at Bishop's concerning Indigenization and decolonization undertaken in Spring 2016 reveals diverging opinions, including not only soft reform and radical reform perspectives but also an element of resistance to reform. Online surveys solicited reactions to a variety of ideas from across the spectrum of ideologies-for-change, such as those identified by Andreotti and colleagues (2015), and of various models for better serving Indigenous students (Wilson & Battiste, 2011).

The research approach taken in our study was exploratory and qualitative, so rather than testing a model, it allowed a nuanced reading of the terrain of the partially formed, ideological, and paradoxical views about responsibilities for Indigenous education. Surveys were designed with closed-ended questions, Likert-scale rankings, and open-ended questions to provide descriptive data about views of Bishop's faculty, administrators, and managers from which we could begin to hypothesize relationships between concepts (Neuman & Robinson, 2015). Faculty participation rates were satisfactory, at 27.6 percent. The number of faculty members invited to participate included all active professors and totalled 185. The administrators and managers participation rate was just sufficient, at 25.6 percent. A focus-group process, participant observation, and reports of the ICA were sources of data on the views of Indigenous students. The focus group included all interested Indigenous students at Bishop's in a two-hour dialogue about their experiences at university, changes they would like to see, and priorities for those improvements. There were seven participants. Additionally, participant observations occurred at the university over more than five years, including professors working closely with the leadership of the ICA in internships; a *Principles* talking circle on reconciliation, which included Indigenous students as well as interested professors and community members; observations of Indigenous and settler students in classrooms and hallways; as well as participation in Indigenous Cultural Alliance events and meetings.

Perspectives at Bishop's about decolonization cluster in three groups, representing a variety of the educational models discussed by Wilson and Battiste (2011). For clarity, the positions can be described as: (1) keepers of the status quo, (2) limited reformers, and (3) relational reformers. Those we might see as keepers of the status quo express satisfaction with what Wilson and Battiste describe (2011) as the assimilationist model of Aboriginal education. Such views tend to create and reinforce barriers to change, so in the upcoming analysis, barriers to Bishop's decolonization are included in the "status quo" section. The second category, that of "limited reformers," captures a more contemporary critical perspective of Indigenous education but imagines the changes as happening within the existing frameworks of the university's programs and conceptualizations of education. Relational reformers are invested in active learning with Indigenous people and are more profoundly critical of the colonial culture shaping universities, and the "colonial frontier logics" (Donald, 2012, p. 335) that tend to be present in Canadian institutions.

RESISTANCE TO CHANGE AND OTHER BARRIERS

The momentum for decolonization at Bishop's is constrained by the attitudes of some members of the university population, as well as by fiscal restraints. To begin, the evidence indicates some people lack awareness of Indigenous rights and educational concerns. Depending on the specific issue, between 25 and 30 percent of those surveyed still endorse aspects of the assimilationist model of Indigenous education, with an expectation that Indigenous people themselves are responsible for making any changes or improvements in opportunity via their individualized choices within the existing systems. About 30 percent of participants in the surveys fundamentally disagreed with the Truth and Reconciliation Commission's views on education. Of faculty respondents 10 percent disagreed and of administrators and managers 22 percent disagreed that Bishop's has responsibilities in relation to reconciliation. Similarly, when asked if Bishop's is a place for decolonization to occur, among faculty 10 percent said no, while 20 percent gave no answer, and 70 percent said yes. In the administrators/managers' responses for the same question, 30 percent said no, while 70 percent said yes. About 30 percent of faculty and of the combined group of administrators and managers reject both provision of any supports for Indigenous students and expansion of culturally relevant or appropriate curricula.

That pattern of assimilationist views also shows up in individual comments to open-ended questions. Comments reveal the way some professors fail to recognize that their own knowledge frameworks and assumptions are colonial. One professor made a suggestion that the "best way to integrate *Indigenous students* is to provide them [with] good support outside the classroom, the *same support* that is offered to all students with difficulties" (emphasis added). Another felt that giving some privileges to Indigenous students based on the "Indigenous" criterion is racism, and one professor defended their indifference with the belief that "I teach science, which is neutral." While these troubling comments came from individuals, when taken alongside the status-quo preferences of a significant minority, widespread need for education within the institution is evident.

Individual perspectives rooted uncritically in settler privilege are a barrier to decolonization, but there are also barriers at institutional levels. If the goal is Indigenization as imagined by Campbell (2018), then the settler-identities of professors who have taken the initiative to participate in the **Indigenous Studies Minor (ISM)** are among the barriers, as are the neoliberal funding patterns of Canadian and Québec governments. Professors of Indigenous identities have been hired a few times on contract to teach courses while full-time professors took leave. Professors offering courses within the ISM work in four different departments (History, Sociology, Education, English), each of which has experienced reductions in course offerings, in course replacements by contract faculty, and in numbers of full-time positions (mainly with non-replacement of retiring faculty) in recent years. As Bishop's collective awareness of the importance of Indigenous concerns has been growing, neoliberal ideologies have been reducing the priority on education for Québec and Canadian governments.

There is an uncomfortably eerie familiarity to Québec's austerity context for university budgets. Under settler-colonialism, government refusal to spend equitably was and is used to justify innumerable decisions that work violently against Indigenous peoples. **Colonial logics** (Donald, 2012) are also present in negotiations between governments and universities. Negotiation decisions are justified almost entirely by measures of productivity and profitability, rather than primacy being given to long-term questions of human well-being, preservation of cultural integrity, or planetary interests.

Additionally, the absence of Indigenous faculty and managers at Bishop's leaves serious limitations in knowledge, which dramatically slows momentum toward decolonization. Among professors, 23.5 percent indicated some cultural knowledge relevant to Indigenous cultures and communities, and 27.4 percent had direct experience living in or working with an Indigenous community or communities, but the self-assessed depth of knowledge is shallow, with 86 percent claiming "a little" cultural knowledge or less. None of the professors are fluent in any Indigenous language.

Currently, the limitations based on who we are—and what we can offer—could have serious consequences for Indigenous students. With Indigenous scholars testifying to experiences of racism as part of higher education (Battiste, 2018; Cote-Meek, 2014), and echoes of that sentiment expressed by Indigenous students at Bishop's, our data also supports the understanding that universities need to respond to the colonial mentalities present in university contexts if further harm is to be avoided. Nearly 16 percent of faculty respondents were not confident in their ability to recognize and respond constructively to racism or gave no answer to this question. Additionally, 40 percent of the administrators and managers lacked confidence that their staff would be able to recognize racist remarks and respond effectively without further training, whereas 40 percent believed responses would be appropriate and 20 percent did not answer that question. One administrator or manager who participated in the survey had experience with best educational practices for supporting people with **intergenerational trauma**.

LIMITED REFORM

The second category of views on decolonization and reconciliation at Bishop's critically recognizes the history of colonialism (if not the contemporary experiences of it) and the necessity, in fairness, of providing supports in order to help compensate for that legacy. There are some drivers of change evident in views expressed within this interpretation of reforms, as well as from the relational perspective. This perspective is strong enough that a unified and specific effort from key students, staff, faculty, and administrators resulted in the creation of a new position and hiring of an Indigenous Student Support and Community Liaison Officer for the first time beginning in Fall 2017.

It is in this range of expectations that we find the voices of Indigenous students expressed most persistently and tenaciously. Leaders among Indigenous students at Bishop's have advocated since 2012 for three things: (1) dedicated space, (2) a support person, and (3) access to an Elder. Focus group discussions revealed that numerous other ideas and hopes (some of which are more radical) follow these, but efforts and attention of ICA members are quite concentrated on these three as first priorities.

Space issues have been particularly contentious on this campus, with renovations making several buildings currently inaccessible and one building threatened with demolition. Enrollments have been increasing without corresponding increases in classroom space. Despite these challenges, the university administration has made significant progress in creating an Indigenous gathering and cross-cultural learning space on campus in response to the desires of the ICA. More than a majority of faculty, administrators, and managers do want changes made so that Indigenous students can fully enjoy what is marketed as "the Bishop's experience." The surveys indicate that 70 percent of participating administrators and managers perceive that the university should provide designated space for Indigenous students. Faculty support for this idea was a little more tepid at 59 percent.

Much of the Bishop's community agreed with providing services other schools have already. Survey responses indicate that 60 percent of administrators and managers, plus 71–72 percent of faculty, were in favour of providing all of the following: designated support staff for Indigenous students; creation of a new coordinator position to oversee strategies for Indigenous student success; cultural bridging programs and academic support programs to smooth the transitions into undergraduate education; and creation of scholarships.

Faculty were asked some questions about possible adjustments to pedagogy and evaluation strategies in response to Indigenous students' needs. Some willingness to make adjustments and some resistance to change are again evident. Over 70 percent expressed willingness to participate in workshops that would enhance their abilities to teach Indigenous students effectively, and the same proportion would participate in organizing mentorship or peer-support for Indigenous students. A smaller proportion supported making individual exceptions for Indigenous students: 39 percent would be tolerant of more absences from class and 45 percent said they would allow extensions on student work deadlines. It might be useful for faculty of all departments to be made more aware of the unique characteristics of Indigenous students, such as the greater likelihood of First Nations students than non-Indigenous students to be carrying family and/or community responsibilities while pursuing post-secondary education, and the colonially created financial challenges some contend with (Malatest & Associates Ltd., 2002; Cote-Meek, 2014).

Professors other than those who teach in the ISM and/or participate in the **Indigeneity and Race Research Axis (IRRA)** express interest in learning more about Indigenous cultures and issues. On the Likert scale, 64 percent described themselves as fairly or very interested in increasing their knowledge of Indigenous cultures and issues, while if the "somewhat interested" category is included, then the percentage rises to 86 percent. This paper represents only a small portion of the research done and presented internally at Bishop's University. In response to the evidence, an Ad Hoc Committee of Senate was formed in November 2018 to coordinate and continue decolonization and reconciliation efforts at the university.

There is interest in expanding the Indigenous Studies curriculum but not yet an evident strategy. Languages are crucial subjects but their importance is not reflected under Québec cost/benefit formulas, and they have not been especially popular in recent years. In this context, Bishop's faculty are almost perfectly divided on the necessity and importance of adding courses in an Indigenous language. For faculty, 49 percent said an Indigenous language should be taught, 47 percent said no, and 3 percent did not respond to this question. Faculty opinion showed some polarization around religion, and stronger support for almost all other Indigenous topics of study that were proposed, as described in Table 11.1.

Table 11.1: Faculty Agreement with Offering Courses in Indigenous Study Subject Areas

	DISAGREE/ STRONGLY DISAGREE (%)	SOMEWHAT AGREE (%)	MOSTLY AGREE/ STRONGLY AGREE (%)	NEITHER AGREE NOR DISAGREE (%)
Religion	12	24	62	2
Systems of Governance	8	27	55	10
Ontology/ Philosophy	6	28	60	6
Science/ Traditional Ecological Knowledge	8	30	58	4
Epistemology	8	32	48	12

For administrators and managers, 70 percent indicated the belief that the university has a responsibility to offer curricula relevant to Indigenous students.

One of the models for reform involves providing Indigenous educational opportunities closer to Indigenous people's homes (Wilson & Battiste, 2011). Offering relevant programs in remote communities and/or scheduling patterns that work in relation to traditional cultural practices would be a significant step toward equalizing the opportunities for higher education between Indigenous and non-Indigenous people. Of participating faculty, 67 percent, and 50 percent of administrators/managers, agreed with the idea of teaching an entire course in a remote community, while 47 percent of faculty supported the idea of teaching a segment of a course in a remote community.

RELATIONAL REFORM

In a 2018 lecture, Marie Battiste spoke of experiencing higher education in terms of both victimization and as a beneficiary because she had gained a job that provided a good living for a long time, but it also felt like she had been "marinated in Eurocentrism" (see also Cote-Meek, 2014, pp. 11, 87–112; Allan & Smylie, 2018; Monture-Angus, 1999). The research conducted so far at Bishop's has limited measures for assessing the extent of interest in the kind of reform that could fully make space for culturally profound practices of Indigenous knowledge-development and achievement. Since Bishop's currently is staffed by settlers, the starting points for finding appropriate roles in relation to decolonization is in developing awareness of settler privilege and informing ourselves about Indigenous cultures through relationship-building with Indigenous people. There are some indications of a small core group at Bishop's University recognizing that systemic change is required for decolonization and for Indigenization of the academy. For a few among Bishop's faculty and management, fascination with, and respect for, Indigenous knowledge has become a learning process spanning decades and scholarly work has been published. Mohawk, Métis, and Mi'kmaq students have contributed to decolonizing Bishop's through the work of the ICA, and they have been supported in their efforts by members of IRRA, and, at community levels, dialogues representing systemic change are at the beginning.

One way to increase community dialogues and relationships is through establishing partnerships with Indigenous leaders and communities. Ideas of developing new partnerships with Indigenous communities were well received by BU professors participating in the survey: 82 percent of faculty respondents supported the pursuit of a long-term relational education process with an Indigenous community. Bishop's School of Education and Naskapi Nation of Kawawachikamach (NNK) have had a partnership since 2010, in which the NNK community school began covering all expenses, yearly, for two School of Education students seeking a practicum experience in their territory; this allows the community school to vet future employees. A similar partnership with the Cree School Board also exists. Furthermore, there is Bishop's involvement with proximate Indigenous communities. Within the last two years, particular effort has been made to include Abenaki leaders and Elders in discussions of relationship-building and in conferences dedicated to social and environmental justice. Ceremonies commemorating residential school victims and survivors, territorial acknowledgement, and the welcoming of Indigenous leaders and artists to various classrooms to share knowledge have taken place on campus.

Working with and learning from Indigenous communities is essential if institutions staffed and managed by settlers within settler-developed systems are to move forward in a less-colonial way. Bishop's efforts to develop better awareness and to deepen relationships with Québec First Nations, as referred to above, are a step in the right direction. Additional dialogues about a variety of projects are underway involving Indigenous leaders, faculty researchers, and senior university administrators. These efforts are fairly new and overdue.

CONCLUSION

Our research shows that the Indigenization and decolonization of Bishop's University are a long way off; yet there is significant, but not universal, support for engaging in action, per the UC *Principles* and the TRC Calls to Action. Survey respondents indicated an interest in limited reforms, such as learning about Indigenous peoples and about their specific situations relating to post-secondary education, and in providing appropriate services and support to aid them in achieving academic success. The survey also indicated that there was considerable support for more relational reform through developing long-term partnerships with Indigenous communities and leaders for the purposes of sharing knowledge, meeting Indigenous students' needs, and assisting in community capacity building.

Whether all these expressions of interest will transform into action remains uncertain. The current members of the Bishop's community who have been engaged in processes of decolonization, reconciliation, and relationship-building are sincere, but relatively few. As Bopp, Brown, and Robb (2017) argue, these small-scale efforts, while worthwhile, are rarely sustainable and do little to address the dominant approaches to knowledge, learning, and dissemination. If Bishop's is to succeed in honouring the UC *Principles of Indigenous Education* and the TRC's Calls to Action, and if it is to attempt to decolonize and/or Indigenize, then it must transform its thinking and embrace change. This includes: (1) accepting other learning paradigms and knowledge systems, and the individuals who have them, with respect and humility; (2) making efforts to close the capacity gaps that exist within the university knowledge, leadership, and services structures with trained people who can guide and support the university through its transformation from a colonial institution to one of reconciliation; and (3) seeking and sustaining partnerships, with Indigenous knowledge-keepers, leaders, Elders, and communities. For Bishop's, as represented by the survey results, while changes are starting, it would appear, given various factors, that the best method of advancing Indigenization, at least for now, is through pursuing the last of the three processes listed above. Efforts to form partnerships have increased over the past few years, and it is through this process of relationship-building that Bishop's might undergo significant change, provided the partnerships are truly collaborative efforts based on mutual need, benefit, and responsibility.

Given the resistance that exists within Bishop's toward fundamental reform, current faculty and administrators and managers who support Indigenization can only move incrementally toward this goal. Increasing the numbers of the Indigenous faculty, staff, and administrators on campus, for example, as other universities have done, is not something that is currently supported across the institution; working with Indigenous communities and individuals through partnerships is a way to attempt a process of Indigenizing at Bishop's that gives voice to Indigenous ways of teaching, learning, and being in the existing world of academia. The School of Education and other individual faculty are developing and expanding partnerships with the Naskapi, Abenaki, and Cree First Nations. The administration is working with Indigenous students and communities to provide a gathering space for Indigenous students, Elders, and cross-cultural learning, and an Indigenous Student Support and Liaison Community Officer is again funded. These small but important steps can serve as the building blocks for greater Indigenous community and student engagement. It is through this process of partnership-building that Bishop's can start to pursue its commitments to the *Principles of Indigenous Education* and the TRC's Calls to Action, as well as move toward the further Indigenization of the campus and all that goes on within.

DISCUSSION QUESTIONS

1. Is settler privilege evident in the courses you have been taking or the program in which you are studying, and if so where do you see it?

2. Do you think universities have the potential to be decolonizing institutions? Why or why not? If not, what obstacles do you see in your university becoming decolonized?

3. What steps toward decolonization or Indigenization are evident where you go to school? Would you characterize these as soft reforms, radical reforms, or something else?

4. Why are focus groups a good way to learn about student experiences and perceptions? Do you see limitations or weaknesses in this methodological approach?

5. Have you experienced or witnessed anti-Indigenous racism in your time as a higher education student within your institution? What response did you have to that incident? What would help you to respond in the way you would have liked to should such a moment occur again?

GLOSSARY

Aboriginal: A term previously used by the Canadian government in reference to First Nations peoples, and in documents such as the reports of the Truth and Reconciliation Commission.

colonial logics: In universities, logics represented by government funding models that favour productivity and profitability, rather than long-term questions of human well-being, preservation of cultural integrity, or planetary interests. They also discriminate against Indigenous students because they do not fund such students equitably vis-á-vis settler students.

Eurocentrism: A term used to describe a worldview that privileges or is biased toward Western civilization. In universities and other educational institutions, Eurocentrism is evident in pedagogical approaches, course content, and homogenous standards for entrance, participation, and success.

Indigeneity and Race Research Axis (IRRA): A member organization of professors of Bishop's University with interests in research that fall loosely under the study of Indigenous and/or race-related issues.

Indigenization: A process that occurs through the presence and participation of Indigenous people in all areas of the university, including teaching, learning, research, and administration.

Indigenous Cultural Alliance (ICA): A member organization of students of Bishop's University, founded by the Indigenous students attending Bishop's in 2012.

Indigenous peoples: Descendants of original peoples who inhabited the territory now known as Canada; this includes First Nations, Inuit, and Métis peoples.

Indigenous Studies Minor (ISM): An interdisciplinary minor offered at Bishop's University, comprised of 24 credits drawn from the departments of Sociology, History, English, Education, Political Science, Environmental Studies and Geography, Religion, and Classics.

intergenerational trauma: The transmission of historical oppression and its negative consequences across generations. Used often in the context of the legacy of residential schools, it should also be noted that intergenerational trauma is more broadly a product of colonialism and can therefore affect not only survivors of the schools and their families but any member of Indigenous societies.

radical reform: Reforms that target the entire university community and beyond. It seeks to recognize and address settler privilege, as well as examine and overcome the effects of universities' roles in neocolonialism.

settler: A person who is not descended from Indigenous peoples in Canada. Settlers may be recent arrivals; however, their heritage may also be traced back to much earlier arrivals.

settler privilege: Includes the idea of Eurocentrism but also the economic, social, and political advantages that members of the dominant society have when gaining access to universities and achieving success within those institutions.

soft reform: In universities, focuses on increasing access and success for Indigenous students through providing specific staff and other resources for Indigenous students without fundamentally changing the Eurocentric practices of the institution.

Truth and Reconciliation Commission of Canada (TRC): A commission formed as a result of the largest class-action lawsuit in Canada, which resulted in the Indian Residential Schools Settlement Agreement. The TRC's role was to document the experiences of survivors in a process of truth telling.

Universities Canada (UC): A membership organization representing the 96 Canadian universities, providing a voice on issues in higher education, research, and innovation.

FURTHER READINGS/WEBSITES

Association of Canadian Deans of Education. (2010). *Accord on Indigenous education.* Retrieved from http://csse-scee.ca/acde/publications-2/#indigenous

Cote-Meek, S. (2018, November 6). Making a long-term commitment to Indigenous education. *University Affairs.* Retrieved from https://www.universityaffairs.ca/opinion/from-the-admin-chair/making-a-long-term-commitment-to-indigenous-education/

Gaudry, A., & Lorenz, D. E. (2018). Decolonization for the masses? Grappling with Indigenous content requirements in the changing Canadian post-secondary environment. In L. Tuhiwai Smith, E. Tuck, & K. W. Yang (Eds.), *Indigenous and decolonizing studies in education* (pp. 182–197). New York, NY: Routledge.

208 Decolonizing and Indigenizing Education in Canada

Green, J. (2014). *Indivisible: Indigenous human rights*. Halifax, NS: Fernwood Publishing.

MacDonald, M. (2016, April 6). Indigenizing the academy. *University Affairs*. Retrieved from http://www.universityaffairs.ca/features/feature-article/indigenizing-the-academy/

Truth and Reconciliation Commission of Canada. (n.d.). Retrieved from http://nctr.ca/reports2.php

Wabanaki and Their Territory

Musée des Abénakis. https://museeabenakis.ca/en/

Obomsawin, A. (Director). (2006). *Waban-Aki: People from where the sun rises* [Documentary]. Ottawa, ON: National Film Board of Canada. Retrieved from https://www.nfb.ca/film/waban-aki_en/

Wabanki Collection. (n.d.). A new dawn. https://www.wabanakicollection.com/videos/wabanaki-a-new-dawn/

Indigenous Language Learning

Newhouse, D., Orr, J., & the Atlantic Aboriginal Economic Development Integrated Research Program. (Eds.). (2013). *Aboriginal knowledge for economic development*. Halifax, NS: Fernwood Publishing.

Niimkii Aazhabikong. (2018). http://onamancollective.com/research/

REFERENCES

Absolon, K., & Willett, C. (2005). Putting ourselves forward: Location in Aboriginal research. In L. Brown & S. Strega (Eds.), *Research as resistance: Critical, Indigenous and anti-oppressive approaches* (pp. 97–126). Toronto, ON: Canadian Scholars' Press.

Allan, B., & Smylie, J. (2018). The role of racism in the health and well-being of Indigenous peoples in Canada. In M. J. Cannon & L. Sunseri (Eds.), *Racism, colonialism, and Indigeneity in Canada: A reader* (pp. 214–228). Don Mills, ON: Oxford University Press.

Altamirano-Jiménez, I. (2014). Neo-liberal education, Indigenizing universities? *Canadian Journal of Native Education, 37*(1), 28–45.

Andreotti, V., Stein, S., Ahenakew, C., & Hunt, D. (2015). Mapping interpretations of decolonization in the context of higher education. *Decolonization: Indigeneity, Education & Society, 4*(1), 21–40.

Battiste, M. (2018, May 27). *Decolonizing and Indigenizing the academy: Achieving cognitive justice* [Video]. Canadian Society for the Study of Education 2018 Plenary Lecture. Retrieved from https://www.youtube.com/watch?v=XKQyvcOvAPI

Bopp, M., Brown, L., & Robb, J. (2017). Reconciliation within the academy: Why is Indigenization so difficult? Four Worlds Centre for Development Learning. Retrieved from http://www.fourworlds.ca/pdf_downloads/Reconciliation_within_the_Academy_Final.pdf

Bundale, B. (2018, May 13). University under fire over residential schools course taught by white prof: "Part of reconciliation is making space for Indigenous faculty members at universities." *Canadian Press*. Retrieved from https://www.cbc.ca/news/canada/nova-scotia/university-under-fire-over-residential-schools-course-taught-by-white-prof-1.4660716

Campbell, L. [campbelllor]. (2018, July 11). Indigenization occurs with Indigenous bodies. Indigenous bodies bring Indigeneity, which brings Indigenization. Everything else is simply correcting Eurocentrism in academia so more accurate knowledge & learning opportunities are available for students. [Tweet]. Retrieved from https://twitter.com/campbelllor/status/1017255320236814336

Cote-Meek, S. (2014). *Colonized classrooms: Racism, trauma and resistance in post-secondary education*. Winnipeg, MB: Fernwood Publishing.

Cupples, J. (2015). Decolonizing the academy [blog]. Retrieved from https://juliecupples.wordpress.com/2015/10/

Darlaston-Jones, D., Herbert, J., Ryan, K., Darleston-Jones, W., Harris, J., & Dudgeon, P. (2014). Are we asking the right questions? Why we should have a decolonizing discourse based on conscientization rather than Indigenizing the curriculum. *Canadian Journal of Native Education, 37*(1), 86–104.

Thedisorderofthings (2016). The dissonance of things #5: Decolonising the academy. Retrieved from https://thedisorderofthings.com/2016/02/08/decolonising-the-academy/

Donald, D. (2012). Indigenous Métissage: A decolonizing research sensibility. *International Journal of Qualitative Studies in Education, 25*(5), 533–555.

Graefe, P. (2016). *Austerity in Quebec: Neither romance nor despair*. Retrieved from https://socialsciences.mcmaster.ca/austerity-and-its-alternatives/documents/w5-aug-1-2017-peter-graefe-austerity-in-quebec.pdf

Johnson, S. (2016). Indigenizing higher education and the Calls to Action: Awakening to personal, political, and academic responsibilities. *Canadian Social Work Review, 33*(1), 133–139.

Malatest, R. A., & Associates Ltd. (2002). Best practices in increasing Aboriginal postsecondary enrolment rates. Council of Ministers of Education Canada.

Monture-Angus, P. (1999). *Journeying forward: Dreaming First Nations independence.* Winnipeg, MB: Fernwood Publishing.

Neuman, W. L., & Robinson, K. (2015). *Basics of social research: Qualitative and quantitative approaches.* Toronto, ON: Pearson.

Sium, A., Desai, C., & Ritskes, E. (2012). Towards the "tangible unknown": Decolonization and the Indigenous future. *Decolonization: Indigeneity, Education & Society, 1*(1), i–xiii.

Smith, M. S., & Bray, N. (2018). Equity at Canadian universities: National, disaggregated and intersectional data. Academic Women's Association, University of Alberta. Retrieved from https://uofaawa.wordpress.com/awa-diversity-gap-campaign/equity-at-canadian-universities-national-disaggregated-and-intersectional-data/

Truth and Reconciliation Commission of Canada (TRC). (2015a). *Honouring the truth, reconciling for the future: Summary of the final report of the Truth and Reconciliation Commission of Canada.* Ottawa, ON: Author.

Truth and Reconciliation Commission of Canada (TRC). (2015b). *Truth and Reconciliation Commission of Canada: Calls to Action.* Retrieved from http://nctr.ca/assets/reports/Calls_to_Action_English2.pdf

Universities Canada. (2015). *Universities Canada principles on Indigenous education.* Retrieved from http://www.univcan.ca/media-room/media-releases/universities-canada-principles-on-indigenous-education/

Wilson, A., & Battiste, M. (2011). *Environmental scan of educational models supporting Aboriginal post-secondary education.* Saskatoon, SK: University of Saskatchewan Aboriginal Education Research Center. Retrieved from https://docs.education.gov.au/system/files/doc/other/wilson_and_battiste_2011.doc

CHAPTER 12

Reconciliation Rainbows and the Promise of Education: Teaching Truth and Redress in Neocolonial Canada

Michelle Coupal

SITUATING SELF

I am Algonquin/French and a member of the Bonnechere Algonquin First Nation. Like many Algonquins, my family was displaced from our traditional homelands and our traditions more broadly. The legacies of colonial violence that pervaded my family inform my scholarship and are one of the main reasons why I work in the area of Indigenous literary studies, trauma studies, Indian residential school literature, and, importantly, truth and reconciliation.

INTRODUCTION

That there is a critical need to decolonize the ways in which truth and reconciliation are being mobilized in public discourse speaks to ongoing, largely unstated **neocolonial** resistance to Indigenous sovereignty—the heart of true reconciliation. Reconciliation has become enmeshed in troubling discourses of closure and settler innocence that seek to avoid truth issues—unsettled land claims, dishonoured Treaties, resource extraction from Indigenous lands without permission or compensation, boil water advisories, murdered and missing Indigenous women and girls, and a disproportionate number of Indigenous children in the child foster care system, to name but some of the deep concerns facing our communities. There is an under-articulated chasm between the ways in which Indigenous peoples discuss reconciliation and the ways in which many settler peoples do. Indigenous peoples have been involved in the project of reconciliation for many years now through resistance and resurgence initiatives aimed at restoring their Treaty and human rights. At the same time, public discursive practices about reconciliation are focused on fostering harmony, understanding, and the nationalist project of bringing our country together. For Indigenous peoples, sovereignty is what is required to establish the nation-to-nation relationships enshrined in our constitution.

In *The Inconvenient Indian*, King (2012) reworks Sigmund Freud's famous question and asks, "What do Indians want?" (p. 215). It is a great question, says King, but not the right question. A better question according to King is "What do Whites want?" (p. 216). The answer? "Land. Whites want land" (p. 216). King's polemical assertion risks alienating non-Indigenous Canadians, yet the appropriation of Indigenous lands and resources is what has always defined settlement on Turtle Island. Land rights and resource extraction remain central to the neocolonial project of protecting and enriching non-Indigenous peoples and governments. In this era of truth and reconciliation, land has become the elephant in the room that no one wants to talk about. It should not be easier to discuss Indian residential schooling than it is to discuss land rights. Yet it is. Non-Indigenous peoples can feel sorry that children were taken away from their parents and raised in loveless, abusive institutions. With land rights, there is more at stake than feelings of sorrow and sympathy.

Ironically, Treaties are also easier to discuss than outstanding land issues. In Saskatchewan, for example, Treaty education is mandatory for K–12 students. While Treaty education is a necessary addition to the curriculum, it can serve settler agendas by reinforcing a false view of harmony created by Treaties—that is, "we are all Treaty people." We are not all Treaty people. The Métis, for example, were not part of Treaty-making in this country. The only Indigenous groups who were part of historical Treaty-making in Canada are status First Nations under the Indian Act. The rest of us are in a legislative void. From an Indigenous perspective, the original reconciliatory spirit of the Treaties has not been respected. In fact, because of the intersection of the Treaties with the Indian Act, there has been an elision of the crucial issue of who has legitimate claim to the lands and resources of this country. Like Treaties, talking about reconciliation seems to be easier than talking about the truth, which continues to go missing in numerous

Chapter 12 | Reconciliation Rainbows and the Promise of Education   213

discursive arenas (corporations, governments, education systems). We need to spend much more time talking about truth matters before we make the pre-emptive leap to talk of reconciliation. Between truth and reconciliation is a gap that can only be overcome by cultural and judicial **redress**.

This chapter argues that *redress* is the missing word between truth and reconciliation in Canada. Without redress, reconciliation will remain a vague, imagined ideal of an inclusive country where "sharing" means that nothing changes for either Indigenous peoples or non-Indigenous Canadians. Teaching truth and reconciliation requires a focused approach on truth and redress. Arguing that the allocation of a paltry 0.2 percent of Canada's land base to Indigenous peoples by way of the reserve system for First Nations has created systemic impoverishment, Manuel (2017) cautions, "You cannot have reconciliation under the colonial 0.2 per cent Indian Reserve System. It is impossible. Nothing can justify that kind of human degradation. The land issue must be addressed before reconciliation can begin" (n.p.). Given, then, that 99.8 percent of Canada's land mass is owned by the settler/newcomer nation-state, this injustice, along with all the inequities and discriminatory policies and practices faced by Indigenous peoples across the country, needs to be fully accounted and compensated for before reconciliation should even be considered.

As educators across the country are beginning the work of responding to the educative Calls to Action of the Truth and Reconciliation Commission (TRC), I argue that it is imperative that they do so under the umbrella of the *United Nations Declaration on the Rights of Indigenous Peoples* (UNDRIP; United Nations, 2007) rather than under the umbrella of reconciliation.[1] UNDRIP clarifies the need for redress and compensation for the many forms of colonial violence suffered by Indigenous peoples across the world. The TRC's ten principles of reconciliation are all grounded in its first principle: that the "*United Nations Declaration on the Rights of Indigenous Peoples* (2007) is the framework for reconciliation at all levels and across all sectors of Canadian society" (2015b, p. 3). Canada officially adopted this declaration "without qualification" in May 2016. Following this, in November 2016, in direct contradiction to the articles in UNDRIP, Justin Trudeau's government approved Kinder Morgan's Trans Mountain Pipeline and Enbridge's Line 3. Indigenous protestors called this the "Standing Rock of the North." The proposed and legally contested Kinder Morgan Trans Mountain Pipeline expansion, if eventually reapproved, would slither its way through 518 kilometres of Secwepemc territory. That Secwepemc lands are unceded adds to the violence of the pipeline a very real land rights issue.

214 Decolonizing and Indigenizing Education in Canada

I hear the *United Nations Declaration on the Rights of Indigenous Peoples* mentioned in a variety of speech acts, official and unofficial, without ever hearing what the declaration declares. I would like to draw attention to a few of the articles in the declaration, which get to the heart of what is required of Canada and Canadians to redress the wrongs perpetrated on Indigenous peoples:

Article 8.2: States shall provide effective mechanisms for prevention of, and redress for: (a) any action which has the aim or effect of depriving [Indigenous peoples] of their integrity as distinct peoples, or of their cultural values or ethnic identities; (b) Any action which has the aim or effect of dispossessing them of their lands, territories or resources; (c) Any form of forced population transfer which has the aim or effect of violating or undermining any of their rights; (d) Any form of forced assimilation or integration.

Article 26.1: Indigenous peoples have the right to the lands, territories and resources which they have traditionally owned, occupied or otherwise used or acquired.

Article 26.2: Indigenous peoples have the right to own, use, develop and control the lands, territories and resources that they possess by reason of traditional ownership or other traditional occupation or use, as well as those which they have otherwise acquired.

Article 28.1: Indigenous peoples have the right to redress, by means that can include restitution or, when this is not possible, just, fair and equitable compensation, for the lands, territories and resources which they have traditionally owned or otherwise occupied or used, and which have been confiscated, taken, occupied, used or damaged without their free, prior and informed consent.

Article 28.2: Unless otherwise freely agreed upon by the peoples concerned, compensation shall take the form of lands, territories and resources equal in quality, size and legal status or of monetary compensation or other appropriate redress.

If we are serious about reconciliation, teaching truth and reconciliation, and including language about reconciliation in strategic plans of universities

Chapter 12 | Reconciliation Rainbows and the Promise of Education **215**

and school boards across the country, I echo the TRC and suggest that the UNDRIP articles need to be our guiding principles. These articles provide a framework for reconciliation grounded in truth, as opposed to the rhetorical and imaginary ways the term *reconciliation* is often deployed.

TRUTH TROUBLES

The *Oxford English Dictionary* (OED) defines *truth* as that which adheres to reality: "conformity with fact; agreement with reality; accuracy or correctness in a statement, thought, etc." (truth, n.d.). Legal definitions of truth are more restrictive. To speak "the truth, the whole truth, and nothing but the truth" is to speak "the absolute truth; esp. used to emphasize that something, esp. a statement, is or should be true in every particular, with no facts omitted or untrue elements added" (truth, n.d.). To be successful in the courtroom, Indian residential school survivor testimonies of abuse must conform to this strict legal definition of truth.

Yet, as I reflect on this definition from the OED, I realize how un-Indigenous it is. Stories are also true. Even though the facts may move around or take different shape in different tellings of a story, the connections between elements tend to remain the same. For Indigenous peoples, truth is connected not only to honesty, but also to embedded relationships between land, water, animals, humans, and the spirit world. Truth is relational, reciprocal, and connected to memory, history, and story—which is *not* to say that truth is subjective. On the contrary, the multiplicity of Indigenous understandings of truth provide a comprehensive objectivity outside of Western conceptions of truth. In Anishnawbemowin, the word for truth is *debwewin*. Simpson (2011) explains that Elder Jim Dumont taught students and community members at Trent University that if you place the letter "o" in front of debwewin, "the first component of the word is 'ode' which means heart. The component 'we' means sound of. So (o)debwewin is 'the sound of the heart'" (p. 59). My own community emphasizes that Anishnabe philosophy asks us to listen to our hearts and to listen to teachings, as truth can be found in both. I have been taught that truth is found in more than one direction, which I partially take to mean that there are different kinds of truth, all of which need to be respected. Truth, in all its forms, matters. We are at a moment in time when the truth about colonization in Canada requires the attention of the nation and will continue to require that attention until the fullness of our history is meaningfully, deeply understood.

The Truth and Reconciliation Commission of Canada collected "truths," facts and stories, histories and memories, of survivors across the country. In her preamble to her collection of poetry *Burning in This Midnight Dream* (2016), Cree writer and residential school survivor Louise Bernice Halfe Sky Dancer responds to the TRC's collection of stories/truths, which she participated in: "The Truth and Reconciliation process opened the door to sharing that dark history. Truth is hard to find however. Hard to share, hard to hear" (p. ix). The poems in this collection, says Halfe, "are intended to share yet more of that truth" (p. ix). Notice her reticence and caution about the word truth in the context of public testimonials. Indeed, through the poems in the collection, Sky Dancer, in what she calls her "backward walk," expresses deep ambivalence about truth-telling and not truth-telling, which is not to say that she does not know what her truth is. Indigenous speech acts of disclosure of colonial violences are shaped by memories, time, and the act of narrativizing past lived experiences. Gaertner (2016) cautions that in the context of the TRC, these public testimonials risk "exposing [survivors] to a scopophilic gaze driven by the colonial desire to know and own" (p. 143). Indigenous testimonial reticence is a panacea to tortured public testimonies that under a Western gaze can render an Indian residential school survivor, in the words of Hall (1997), a "spectacle of the 'other'" (p. 223). Truth for Indigenous peoples of Turtle Island is, as Tanana Athabascan scholar Million (2009) theorizes, "felt knowledge: colonialism as it is *felt* by those who experience it" (p. 58). This felt knowledge is not legible to settler Canadians. The nation needs to wake up to the truths Indigenous peoples choose to share, not to feel those truths or pity those survivors, but to *do* something with this sharing. We need action. We need the political will of our government to make change real. Education is critical to this process.

RECONCILIATION IS A METAPHOR

I would like to spend a few moments discussing the meanings of the word *reconciliation*, because its multiple meanings can create conceptual slippages. Reconciliation, according to the OED, is the action of "bringing a thing or things to agreement, concord, or harmony" (reconciliation, n.d.). Ironically (given the culpability of Christianity in the imperial project of claiming what is now Canada), the word *reconciliation* also has biblical connotations: in the Christian faith, "the action of restoring humanity to God's favour, esp. as through the sacrifice of Christ" (reconciliation, n.d.). It can mean a reconciliation with God; or, in the Roman Catholic church, a sacrament of reconciliation with confession, penance, and absolution. It also means "the purification or reconsecration of a desecrated church or holy place" (reconciliation, n.d.). In bookkeeping, reconciliation is the "action or practice of rendering one account consistent with another by balancing apparent discrepancies" (reconciliation, n.d.). Christie (2012) cautions that because the term *reconciliation* is used in different contexts, there can be shifts in meaning, which complicate singular idealizations of what reconciliation means. However, the definition that is most widely understood as pertaining to truth and reconciliation commissions is "the action of restoring estranged peoples or parties to friendship" (reconciliation, n.d.). This definition is broad and therefore open to different interpretations. Australian scholars Mackinlay and Barney (2014) suggest that loose definitions of reconciliation can be mobilized in the service of settler society. They say,

> We frequently use words like "reconciliation," "hope," "action," and "social justice" as panaceas to the ongoing impact of colonialism on the daily lives of Indigenous peoples and our knowing collusion in it. We have felt comfortable using these words as non-Indigenous people working in Indigenous Australian Studies and education because they provide us with a place of belonging—a place where the performance of our identities as White settler colonials has value, worth, authority, and power. (p. 57)

Empowering and feel-good terms like "reconciliation" and "hope for a better future" risk dilution into a Canadian nation-state pool of neocolonial "inclusion" and "diversity," which undermines what could be a radical reconciliation, that is, one that both reconciles *and* makes redress for the long history of assimilative and genocidal practices in Canada.

Partly at issue is what I see as a conceptual bundling of truth with reconciliation through former TRCs (for example, in South Africa). Truth does not necessarily or inevitably lead to reconciliation. This semantic entanglement has led to an it-goes-without-saying, naturalized entwining of truth with reconciliation, as if truth guarantees reconciliation. "Truth and reconciliation" slide off one's tongue so easily that the terms can stand in for each other. They have become interchangeable in speech acts. We are not done with truth-telling in this country, and yet we seem to be moving away from it, as if we are (innocently and conveniently) at the stage of reconciliation. Reconciliation is now a government and media buzzword, while truth continues to go missing. If Canada ever hopes to begin the long road toward reconciliation, it needs to put truth first and linger on it until the fullness of its history and present-day colonial practices are understood and, importantly, taught to learners across the country.

I would here add to Tuck's and Yang's (2012) seminal statement—"decolonization is not a metaphor"—that reconciliation has become a metaphor (p. 3). While masked in terms of restoring relationships through consultation, reconciliation is now a metaphor for ongoing settler domination through so-called renewed understandings between Indigenous and non-Indigenous peoples. Reconciliation has exceeded its meaning to become a discursive weapon of governments, university administrations, and corporations to quell the insurgence of Indigenous voices decrying the neocolonial machine. It is as if repeating the word "reconciliation" in strategic plans, government initiatives, and corporate visioning statements somehow makes it real, while the systemic discriminatory practices that have always kept Indigenous people in relative positions of weakness continue. As Nagy (2012) argues, "with respect to reconciliation, there are disturbing similarities in settler and White denial in Canada and South Africa as seen in the desire to enact reconciliation so it maintains the status quo" (p. 364). To become a real word, reconciliation needs to be buttressed by scholarship and practical tools grounded in the view that Indigenous peoples in Canada are self-determining with human and constitutional rights that need to be foregrounded.

The work of Wakeham (2012) is an important contribution to the idea that reconciliation often becomes performative, rather than leading to substantive structural changes in settler-colonial authority. The idea of a reconciliatory imaginary without any transformation relating to Indigenous sovereignty and reparations for wrongs against Indigenous nations is echoed by numerous scholars from around the world. Indeed, a considerable body of international work on truth and reconciliation has emerged, for example, from South Africa, Australia, and New Zealand. Although the colonial context is different, particularly in post-apartheid South Africa, there is much to be learned from the experiences of other countries grappling with issues of judicial reform, redress, and education.[2] In discussing reconciliation in post-apartheid South Africa, Christie (2012) argues that the process of reconciliation has been slow because the term has been deployed as an impossible imaginary that in seeking transformation becomes repeatedly deferred (p. 34). Short (2003) contends that the Australian government tied reconciliation to its nation-building effort by employing a rhetoric of reconciliation as "a United Australia" (p. 496). Furthermore, former Prime Minister John

Howard's "practical reconciliation initiative" effectively curtailed discourses of self-determination and land rights for Australia's Aboriginal peoples (p. 503). Short (2012) disrupts an easy acceptance of the reconciliatory process by asserting its futility within the colonial contemporary political climate in which acts of acknowledgement of past injustices are made.

Unity, harmony, and diversity have become what "reconciliation" metaphorically connotes. As Carastathis (2013) asserts, "when multicultural tolerance is reinvented as reconciliation, conflict is repressed in the name of a harmonious resolution" (p. 240). Carastathis ultimately suggests that the blurring of reconciliation with harmonization omits concrete definitions and thereby creates a slippage in how the public understands reconciliation as a practice. Reconciliation can thus become entwined with hegemonic discursive practices that place reconciliation within a frame of inclusivity and multiculturalism as a way to move past present inequities. In the rush to move from truth to reconciliation, then, truth is forestalled, and reconciliation becomes a starry-eyed, imagined postcolonial Canadian nation-state. In this way, as Christie (2012) asserts, "unease remains that the 'truth' has been 'commissioned' and the past 'managed'" (p. 35). Or, in the words of James (2013), "framings of multiculturalism that present Canada monophonically as a 'land of immigrants' finding 'unity in diversity' efface the country's ongoing nature as a project of settler colonialism resting on Indigenous dispossession" (p. 33). The term "reconciliation" needs to not only be troubled and scrutinized; it also needs to be decolonized.

Truth and Reconciliation in the Classroom

There is a growing body of scholarly work arising from faculties of education across the country in response to the Calls to Action of the TRC. This work marks a significant starting point in addressing the many issues swirling around the incorporation of Indigenous texts and knowledges in the classroom. Dion (2016), for example, is "concerned with the voices of Indigenous youth who express what they need and what they want from education and the voices of teachers and teacher candidates who express fear and trepidation about their capacities to integrate Indigenous content in their classrooms" (p. 468). The "fear and trepidation" voiced by teacher candidates can be addressed, at least in part, through the inclusion of extensive, in-depth pre-service teacher training. Dion (2009) articulates concern that teachers describe themselves as "perfect stranger[s] to Indigenous people" (p. 178). Her apprehension involves the potential for teachers to deploy terms of unfamiliarity as a way of exculpating their responsibility to teach Indigenous content to which they are often resistive. In addition to addressing resistive teachers, there needs to be more discussion about hands-on strategies to deal with student opposition to Indigenous content. During a presentation I recently gave, a Regina teacher voiced her concern that students are pushing back against Indigenous content, saying, "Do we have to discuss this again?" The simple answer is "yes, we do." Nurturing students beyond resistance to understanding of and engagement with Indigenous issues takes time, patience, and no small amount of work.

Fears of inaccuracies, errors, appropriation, and disturbing hegemonic narratives of Canadian nationhood can problematically conspire with a spectrum of racist responses and a reluctance to confront one's own privilege and complicity in colonial Canada. And yet teaching the history and legacies of colonial violence against Indigenous peoples, as uncomfortable as it can be, needs to be foregrounded in pre- and in-service teacher education. Tupper (2014) contributes to discussions of mandatory Treaty education in Saskatchewan, in part, by querying the disjuncture between the numbered Treaties and the Indian Act when it comes to on-reserve education. She argues that a local initiative, Project of Heart,

> helped many of the teacher candidates to understand that the topic of residential schools—and by extension, Treaty education—meant encountering and teaching through colonial tensions and resistances, engaging in dialogue on (previously submerged) sensitive conflictual issues, and being attentive to their own and their students' ignorance and gaps in knowledge, respectfully and with humility. (pp. 482–483)

Respect and humility are two of the core teachings of the Seven Grandfathers. Both can present challenges to Western conceptions of pride. Respect and humility require understanding the gifts we have been given, that no one is better or worse than anyone else, and that we are required to be gentle and calm with whomever we encounter. Bringing Elder knowledges into the classroom for basic teachings such as these is integral to overcoming obstacles to Indigenous curricula.

This said, Simon (2013) cautions that teachers need to move beyond curriculum as a singular response to ensure that the addition of education on Indian residential schooling or Treaties does not become simply a symbolic gesture that unwittingly perpetuates the neoliberal state. In "Towards a Hopeful Practice of Worrying," Roger Simon articulates concerns about the educational mandate recommended by the TRC, and questions whether listening with *"an open heart and mind* to the stories of what happened in the past" will move beyond empathy and critique of history to changes in thinking that can lead to the much more difficult work of reconciliation (p. 131; emphasis in original). Simon's main argument is that more than an affective response is required to instigate meaningful change in the path to reconciliation: "A public memory of residential schooling that heavily relies on pathos to achieve its effect risks diverting attention away from the nexus of government and institutional policies and practices that enacted and subsequently implemented residential school legislation" (p. 133). Simon further suggests that the **"too bad, so sad" syndrome** has problematic implications:

> One implication of this syndrome is that it feeds the commodification of stories of suffering. Essentially this means that when non-Aboriginal Canadians express sorrow and sympathy as a response to the anguished testimony of former residential school students, they also confirm their "own humanitarian characters" and consequently end up feeling good about feeling bad. (p. 133)

CONCLUSION: TOWARD A PEDAGOGY OF WITNESS

Feeling good about feeling bad might be recontextualized in the classroom through a discussion of pity versus witness. Teachers and students may not fully understand the power imbalance embedded in pitying, say, an Indian residential school survivor or a fictionalized character who is experiencing the legacies of residential school. To objectify Indigenous peoples as victims denies their subjectivity and thus their agency. Allowing and then moving beyond feelings of sorrow, sympathy, or pity in the classroom are crucial to work toward what I see as a necessary **pedagogy of witness**. To be meaningful and healing to the survivor, testimony requires ethical witness. I have argued elsewhere (2016) that "Indigenous fictional testimony is literature that gives evidence to the experiences of individuals or communities, often with pedagogical, therapeutic, or activist impulses" (p. 477). Teaching Indigenous literatures from a relational perspective that invites students to take on the role of witness can foster a deeper connection to the material and to one's implicit mandate to act upon the knowledge bestowed by the text/writer.

222 Decolonizing and Indigenizing Education in Canada

Following Indigenous protocols of the West Coast, honorary witnesses were invited to all of the TRC's events:

> Witnesses are asked to store and care for the history they witness and to share it with their own people when they return home. For Aboriginal peoples, the act of witnessing these events comes with a great responsibility to remember all the details and be able to recount them accurately as the foundation of oral histories. (Truth and Reconciliation Commission of Canada, 2015a, p. 442)

Following this protocol, to become ethical witnesses to stories and histories of Indigenous lives thus requires students and teachers to listen actively, to remember the story, and to share what they have learned with family, friends, colleagues, other students, local politicians, and members of parliament.

To be an ethical witness to the lives of Indigenous peoples is to be an active witness—to *do* something with what one has learned. It is not enough to be passive consumers or voyeurs of Indigenous stories of colonial violence. To begin the process of discursively shifting the word "reconciliation" from a metaphor of harmony to an equitable restoration of Indigenous and settler/newcomer relationships, there needs to be action. There needs to be redress. Henderson (2013) contends that true reconciliation will only come through constitutional reconciliation: "literally, the reconciling of Canadian law with the Aboriginal and Treaty rights entrenched within it" (p. 115). It is not enough for educators to teach, as the TRC suggests, the history and legacies of residential schooling, Treaties, and Indigenous contributions to Canada. Educators need to teach the global human rights of Indigenous peoples by way of the United Nations Declaration on their rights. Indigenous peoples already know and understand what truth and reconciliation are. Education is the key to bringing the rest of the country into understanding the meaning of truth and reconciliation, so that we might effect real change.

NOTES

1. At this time, Ontario is a sad example of government delay tactics when it comes to education. In July 2018, the Ontario government cancelled work already underway to accomplish much-needed revisions to Ontario's school curricula in response to the Calls to Action of the Truth and Reconciliation Commission of Canada. The Ontario Conservative government led by Doug Ford may be successful in endlessly deferring

Chapter 12 | Reconciliation Rainbows and the Promise of Education **223**

curriculum revision. This comes at a time when Indigenization and responding to the calls pertaining to education should be matters of fact rather than points of contention.

2. Relevant work from Australia and New Zealand includes (but is not limited to): Rosanne Kennedy's work on the Sorry Books Campaign and the pedagogy of compassion (2011); Megan Davis's claim that Australia may never achieve substantive change in its treatment of Aboriginal Peoples because, she says, it is the least progressive country in terms of "structural accommodation of their first peoples" (2014, p. 56); Matalena Tofa's work critiquing the settling of grievances between the New Zealand state and Māori peoples as reinstatements of Crown authority (2014); Rosemary Nagy's argument that comparisons between Canada's and South Africa's TRCs are too loose, while offering up a more precise analogy that suggests that what needs to be learned from the South African situation is that a lack of truth and ongoing violence lead to shallow understandings of reconciliation (2012); Rosemarie Buikema's parsing of the important role of the arts in shaping post-apartheid South Africa (2012); and the many scholarly contributions of Yusef Waghid on cultivating justice through classroom teachings that engender responsiveness, democratic citizenship, and compassion (2005, 2009, 2015).

DISCUSSION QUESTIONS

1. Is reconciliation a desirable or even tenable goal for Canadians? Why or why not?

2. If reconciliation is desirable and/or tenable, then what does it really mean? That is, what would a reconciled Canada look like for Indigenous peoples? For settlers/newcomers? For the Canadian government (including its jurisdiction over First Nations by way of the Indian Act)?

3. What would need to happen to achieve decolonization in Canada?

GLOSSARY

neocolonial: In the Canadian context, this term refers to the political, capitalist, and social systems that subjugate Indigenous peoples in the present day. In other words, Canada is not a postcolonial country, but rather a country that harbours the illusion that colonialism is in the past, while at the same time upholding colonial practices that govern Indigenous identities and land rights and, through the reserve, penitentiary, and child-welfare systems (to name a few), work to keep Indigenous peoples in a relative state of systemic impoverishment.

pedagogy of witness: In *Witnessing* (2001), Kelly Oliver theorizes the "address-ability and response-ability" that should undergird the process of witnessing the pain of others (p. 17). She asks, "how can we witness and bear witness to oppression, domination, subordination, enslavement, and torture in ways that open up the possibility of a more humane and ethical future?" (p. 18). Building on Oliver's work on ethical witnessing, what I am calling a *pedagogy of witness* means a pedagogical approach to Indigenous stories of colonial violence that nurtures students to be ethical witnesses to what they are hearing and learning—to take responsibility for this knowledge and *do* something with it.

redress: The reparation and/or compensation for an injustice. Redress seeks to remedy and rectify past wrongs.

"too bad, so sad" syndrome: *Too bad, so sad* is a mock expression of sympathy. Roger Simon (2013) uses to argue that such sympathy can serve colonial interests by recognizing injury, while "'splitting off' of any responsibility for the injury or the injured. This 'splitting off' then creates the conditions that enable a justified refusal to give up any of the structural privileges accumulated over the last 250 years" (p. 133).

FURTHER READINGS/WEBSITES

Ahluwalia, P., Atkinson, S., Bishop, P., Christie, P., Hattam, R., & Matthews, J. (Eds.). (2012). *Reconciliation and pedagogy.* New York, NY: Routledge.

Henderson, J. S. Y. (2008). *Indigenous diplomacy and the rights of Peoples: Achieving UN recognition.* Saskatoon, SK: Purich Publishing.

Hill, G. L., & McCall, S. (Eds.). (2015). *The land we are: Artists & writers unsettle the politics of reconciliation.* Winnipeg, MB: ARP Books.

Manuel, A., & Derrickson, R. (2017). *The reconciliation manifesto: Recovering the land and rebuilding the economy.* Toronto, ON: James Lorimer and Company.

Robinson, D., & Martin, K. (Eds.). (2016). *Arts of engagement: Taking aesthetic action in and beyond the Truth and Reconciliation Commission of Canada.* Waterloo, ON: Wilfrid Laurier University Press.

Simpson, L. B. (2017). *As we have always done: Indigenous freedom through radical resistance.* Minneapolis: University of Minnesota Press.

Wakeham, P., & Henderson, J. (Eds.). *Reconciling Canada: Critical perspectives on the culture of redress.* Toronto, ON: University of Toronto Press.

REFERENCES

Buikema, R. (2012). Performing dialogical truth and transitional justice: The role of art in the becoming post-apartheid of South Africa. *Memory Studies, 5*(3), 282–292.

Carastathis, A. (2013). The nonperformativity of reconciliation: The case of "reasonable accommodation" in Quebec. In P. Wakeham & J. Henderson (Eds.), *Reconciling Canada: Critical perspectives on the culture of redress* (pp. 236–260). Toronto, ON: University of Toronto Press.

Christie, P. (2012). Beyond reconciliation: Reflections on South Africa's Truth and Reconciliation Commission and its implications for ethical pedagogy. In P. Ahluwalia, S. Atkinson, P. Bishop, P. Christie, R. Hattam, & J. Matthews (Eds.), *Reconciliation and pedagogy* (pp. 29–44). New York, NY: Routledge.

Coupal, M. (2016). *Teaching Indigenous literature as testimony: Porcupines and china dolls and the testimonial imaginary.* In D. Reder & L. M. Morra (Eds.), *Learn, teach, challenge: Approaching Indigenous literatures* (pp. 477–486). Waterloo, ON: Wilfrid Laurier University Press.

Davis, M. (2014). Australia's reconciliation process in its international context: Recognition and the health and wellbeing of Australia's Aboriginal and Torres Strait Islander Peoples. *Australian Indigenous Law Review, 18*(2), 56-66.

Dion, S. (2009). *Braiding histories: Learning from Aboriginal people's experiences and perspectives.* Vancouver, BC: UBC Press.

Dion, S. (2016). Mediating the space between: Voices of Indigenous youth and voices of educators in service of reconciliation. *Canadian Review of Sociology, 53*(4), 468–473. doi:10.1111/cars.12128.

Gaertner, D. (2016). "Aboriginal principles of witnessing" and the Truth and Reconciliation Commission of Canada. In D. Robinson & K. Martin (Eds.), *Arts of engagement: Taking aesthetic action in and beyond the Truth and Reconciliation Commission of Canada* (pp. 135–155). Waterloo, ON: Wilfrid Laurier University Press.

Halfe, L. B. (2016). *Burning in this midnight dream.* Regina, SK: Coteau Books.

Hall, S. (1997). *Representation: Cultural representations and signifying practices.* London, UK: Open University.

Henderson, J. Y. (2013). Incomprehensible Canada. In P. Wakeham & J. Henderson (Eds.), *Reconciling Canada: Critical perspectives on the culture of redress* (pp. 115–126). Toronto, ON: University of Toronto Press.

James, M. (2013). Neoliberal heritage redress. In P. Wakeham & J. Henderson (Eds.), *Reconciling Canada: Critical perspectives on the culture of redress* (pp. 31–46). Toronto, ON: University of Toronto Press.

Kennedy, R. (2011). An Australian archive of feelings: The Sorry Books Campaign and the pedagogy of compassion. *Australian Feminist Studies, 26*(69), 257–279. doi: 10.1080/08164649.2011.606603

King, T. (2012). *The inconvenient Indian: A curious account of Native people in North America*. Toronto, ON: Doubleday Canada.

Mackinlay, E., & Barney, K. (2014). Unknown and unknowing possibilities: Transformative learning, social justice, and decolonising pedagogy in Indigenous Australian Studies. *Journal of Transformative Education, 12*(1), 54–73. doi:10.1177/1541344614541170

Manuel, A. (2017, January 18). Until Canada gives Indigenous people their land back, there can never be reconciliation. *Rabble.ca*. Retrieved from http://rabble.ca/blogs/bloggers/views-expressed/2017/01/until-canada-gives-indigenous-people-their-land-back-there-ca

Million, D. (2009). Felt theory: An Indigenous feminist approach to affect and history. *Wicazo Sa Review, 24*(2), 53–76. Retrieved from http://www.jstor.org/stable/40587781

Nagy, R. (2012). Truth, reconciliation and settler denial: Specifying the Canada-South Africa analogy. *Human Rights Review, 13*(3), 349–367. doi:10.1007/s12142-012-0224-4

Oliver, K. (2001). *Witnessing: Beyond recognition*. Minneapolis: University of Minnesota Press.

reconciliation. (n.d.). In *Oxford English dictionary*.

Short, D. (2003). Reconciliation, assimilation, and the Indigenous peoples of Australia. *International Political Science Review / Revue internationale de science politique, 24*(4), 491–513. doi:10.1177/01925121030244005

Short, D. (2012). When sorry isn't good enough: Official remembrance and reconciliation in Australia. *Memory Studies, 5*(3), 293–304. doi:10.1177/1750698012443886

Simon, R. I. (2013). Towards a hopeful practice of worrying: The problematics of listening and the educative responsibilities of Canada's Truth and Reconciliation Commission. In P. Wakeham & J. Henderson (Eds.), *Reconciling Canada: Critical perspectives on the culture of redress* (pp. 129–142). Toronto, ON: University of Toronto Press.

Simpson, L. B. (2011). *Dancing on our turtle's back: Stories of Nishnaabeg re-creation, resurgence and new emergence*. Winnipeg, MB: Arbeiter Ring Publishing Books.

Tofa, M. (2014). Incomplete reconciliations: A history of settling grievances in Taranaki, New Zealand. *Journal of Historical Geography, 46*, 26-35. doi:10.1016/j.jhg.2014.05.027

truth. (n.d.). In *Oxford English dictionary*.

Truth and Reconciliation Commission of Canada (TRC). (2015a). *Final report of the Truth and Reconciliation Commission of Canada: Honouring the truth, Reconciling the future*, vol. 1, *Summary*. Toronto, ON: Lorimer.

Truth and Reconciliation Commission of Canada (TRC). (2015b). *What we have learned: Principles of truth and reconciliation*.

Tuck, E., & Yang, K. W. (2012). Decolonization is not a metaphor. *Decolonization: Indigeneity, Education & Society, 1*(1), 1–40.

Tupper, J. A. (2014). The possibilities for reconciliation through difficult dialogues: Treaty education as peacebuilding. *Curriculum Inquiry, 44*(4), 469–488. doi:10.1111/curi.12060

United Nations. (2007). *United Nations Declaration on the Rights of Indigenous Peoples*. Retrieved from https://www.un.org/development/desa/ indigenouspeoples/wp-content/uploads/sites/19/2018/11/UNDRIP_E_web.pdf

Waghid, Y. (2005). Action as an educational virtue: Toward a different understanding of democratic citizenship education. *Educational Theory, 55*(3), 323–342. doi: 10.1111/j.1741-5446.2005.00006.x

Waghid, Y. (2009). Patriotism and democratic citizenship education in South Africa: On the (im)possibility of reconciliation and nation building. *Educational Philosophy and Theory, 41*(4), 399–409. doi: 10.1111/j.1469-5812.2008.00436.x

Waghid, Y. (2015). Cultivating responsibility and humanity in public schools through democratic citizenship education. *Africa Education Review, 12*(2), 253–265. doi: 10.1080/18146627.2015.1108003

Wakeham, P. (2012). Reconciling "terror": Managing Indigenous resistance in the age of apology. *American Indian Quarterly, 36*(1), 1–33.

CHAPTER 13

Decolonizing Non-Indigenous Faculty and Students: Beyond Comfortable Diversity

Linda Pardy and Brett Pardy

INTRODUCTION AND SITUATING OURSELVES

Universities across the country, in response to the Calls to Action outlined in the Truth and Reconciliation Commission of Canada (TRC) report (2015), are offering Indigenous events, such as art exhibits, Elders-in-residence programs, name-place tours, and collaborative readings of the TRC report. There are ongoing professional development opportunities, publications, and resources available to help faculty "indigenize" their practice and, in turn, educate students. The K–12 system is slowly starting to reframe what and how students learn about Canada's Indigenous peoples, but these students are not yet on our campuses. And while it is encouraging to see intentional work being done, we, along with other scholars, have come to question the academy's level of transformational change, the effectiveness of reconciliation efforts, and our role as non-Indigenous educators in supporting decolonization (e.g., Clark, Maddison, & de Costa, 2016; den Heyer, 2015; Ladner & Tait, 2017; Pidgeon, Archibald, & Hawkey, 2014). Efforts to support unlearning and provide faculty and students with Indigenous pedagogies are essential, but in our work with non-Indigenous faculty and students, we have identified a significant developmental gap in their ability to decolonize.

This gap results from trying to get non-Indigenous faculty and students to take on the responsibility for their own development and to acknowledge the racialized lens they most often don't recognize in their approach to education. While we recognize that not all non-Indigenous people are white, we found DiAngelo's (2011) work on **white fragility** helpful. As a result, where she refers to **whiteness**, we view her work as applied to the whiteness of the academy's dominant epistemology. DiAngelo suggests that white people often sit back and wait for the Other to give them their knowledge—rarely are they self-directed in doing the needed self-development work. We frequently witness non-Indigenous faculty and students waiting for an invitation from an Indigenous instructor or an Elder to educate them using techniques that only require them to passively participate. However, transformational change requires individuals to participate in radical openness, an engaged process of critical reflection, an acknowledgement of oneself, an awareness of the social constructs of power, and an accountability for one's actions. hooks (1994) outlines that faculty must be self-actualized if they are to empower students, and they must embrace an engaged pedagogy if education is going to play a role in learning how to live in the world.

We deeply appreciate living, working, and playing on the traditional unceded Territory of the Sto:lo Nation. We are non-Indigenous educators who are continuously learning about and questioning our role in efforts to decolonize. We are thankful to the many Indigenous artists, mentors, and Elders that open their hearts to us, provide guidance, teach us, and set us back on the right path when we make mistakes. We are two educators with different backgrounds. I (Linda) have worked my entire career in the transformational learning space. My research and teaching are grounded in critical pedagogies, as well as adult learning and student development theory. I have years of experience working with students the academy often deems at-risk, which commonly include mislabelled Indigenous students. Over the years, I have facilitated, alongside Elders, a variety of workshops for faculty on the topic of decolonization.

Brett's background is in history, communication, media, and cultural studies. His research explores the affective potential of film's ability, when combined with a setting inductive of **transformative learning**, to engage non-Indigenous people in discussing difficult issues around decolonization and Canadian racism. As a doctoral candidate, he has been fortunate to teach in a variety of different courses and learning spaces where diversity and racism are central to the core content. The experience of facilitating difficult discussions and witnessing student reactions, along with his background in critical theory, has provided him with valuable learning and research opportunities.

We are also mother and son, and because of this, our time engaged in informal dialogue while hiking together has served as a significant transformational learning opportunity. Our discussions started when trying to describe the reactions of the participants we were facilitating and recognizing how puzzling the stories were. We truly understand each other's level of discomfort or puzzlement—more so than when debriefing with a colleague. Our reactions to the stories led to ongoing inquiry and moved us to critical reflection and the literature to better understand what we were witnessing.

Often in our busy lives we don't stop to reflect on the lessons randomly presented to us. We just push through and try to address the uncomfortableness by focusing on programmatic changes. However, we find that taking this approach rarely results in transformational change. Deconstructing uncomfortable is where we realized the complexities of decolonization and the various developmental stages non-Indigenous faculty and students need to pass through before they are ready to embrace decolonization. We are writing this chapter using a narrative inquiry methodology and drawing on the insights we have gained through this critically reflective work. We hope that by sharing our stories and outlining ways we have found to participate in decolonization without engaging in cultural appropriation, we can motivate the academy to move beyond comfortable diversity in their "indigenization" efforts.

The aim of this chapter is to draw on examples from having facilitated a number of "indigenization" initiatives to first demonstrate that, even though the non-Indigenous people we have worked with are well meaning, there is a gap in their learning process and development that often results in either **symbolic change** at best or complete pushback at worst. We place "indigenization" in quotations because while it is the official language of the university's initiatives, their use of the term does not accurately reflect the academic understanding of the term. The Canadian institutional preference for "indigenizing" is rooted in Len Findlay's (2000) work, which Elina Hill (2012) critiques as a misreading of Linda Tuhwai Smith's (2012) work on decolonizing methodologies. Smith (2012) argues indigenizing is an Indigenous project, not, as Findlay writes, something "to direct the efforts of non-Indigenous colleagues" (p. 309). Smith instead emphasizes decolonization, with indigenizing being one of many projects working toward this. Non-Indigenous people can contribute by respecting Indigenous thought, but cannot be active agents in indigenizing. Because of this, the university's "indigenizing workshops" for non-Indigenous faculty is inappropriate terminology, and we use the term in quotations where it refers to policy. We use decolonization in our recommendations for what we as white educators can participate in, particularly in anti-racist pedagogies. We follow Smith's (2012) definition of decolonization as "a long-term process involving the bureaucratic, cultural, linguistic and psychological divesting of colonial power" (p. 98) while also keeping in mind Tuck and Yang's (2012) emphasis that decolonization is not a metaphor for improvement, but must ultimately work toward material change.

Secondly, we hope to open a dialogue that motivates the academy's "indigenization" initiatives to do more than support comfortable diversity. We define comfortable diversity as the embrace of "diversity" as surface-level symbolic initiatives that are added in addition to, rather than in place of, existing power structures. Razack (2001) describes education's approach toward multiculturalism as the "management of diversity" (p. 9), through which symbols such as the talking stick or healing circles are appropriated. This form of learning "produces a refined catalogue of cultural differences" that allows cultural differences to remain "merely different" (p. 8) rather than recognizing the systems of domination at play in their relationships. By incorporating the trappings of "diversity," people and institutions believe they now "own" diversity as a skill or ability. In this way, decolonization is itself colonized as a resource to be extracted for the faculty's own gain as a "good person" (Heron, 2007) who has "indigenized."

This is comfortable because it does not involve having to question their own epistemology as to what it means to be an educator in an education system built over centuries to centre Western colonialism as the norm. Instead, diversity is consumed into this system where symbolism masks the lack of change in how power operates. Universities in particular are spaces that too often focus on the symbolic level of change rather than challenge dominant power structures. Bannerji (2000) emphasizes that symbolic diversity creates the ahistorical notion that cultures float equally among each other rather than within relations of power. Difference is emptied of any political or true cultural content. However, comfortable diversity is easy to mandate through policy and institution-wide "indigenization" initiatives. Ahmed (2012) further demonstrates how empty diversity initiatives are when framed by hollow policies and a lack of actualization. To move beyond this, faculty will need support and encouragement to engage in a critical pedagogy, and the academy will need to argue for the emancipatory potential of democratic learning to better the situation for disenfranchised groups (Berila, 2016).

Louie, Pratt, Hanson, and Ottmann (2017) point out that "a common frustration voiced by non-Indigenous scholars is a lack of knowledge, training,

Chapter 13 | Decolonizing Non-Indigenous Faculty and Students 233

or confidence to incorporate Indigenous knowledge or methods of education in their classrooms" (p. 22). They also describe how Smith's (2012) decolonizing methodologies and 25 guiding principles can serve as an effective framework for teaching and learning. We agree these principles are essential. However, the assumption is that training in Indigenous knowledge or methodologies is a straightforward learning process and that faculty's assumptions and knowledge are starting from an unbiased beginning. Comfortable diversity is what happens when institutes add on to faculty's base knowledge rather than shift the foundation of this knowledge base. The challenge remains that the majority of university leaders and faculty have never engaged personally in a critical or transformational reflective practice. They have no formal academic training or experience engaging in critical, anti-oppression, or anti-racist pedagogies. For the most part, the academy's response is still essentially rooted in Western colonial epistemologies and not able to move beyond its institutional history, which devalues Indigenous ways of knowing (Battiste, 2013). Consequently, often those invested in taking on a leadership role to decolonize have a steep learning curve and as a result find themselves drawn to what Bolman and Deal (2014) outline as the symbolic approach to problem solving.

How we frame our teaching practice has significant epistemological and ontological dimensions that impact power dynamics and what is recognized as student success. It was only through what Brookfield (1995) and Palmer (1998) describe as deep self-reflection, and learning from critical incidents, that we have come to appreciate how racialized the academy is and how unprepared most faculty are to engage in the deep self-reflective work needed to transform the learning space, bring about meaningful change, influence students, and bridge the gap between the academy and Indigenous peoples.

This chapter uses stories to illustrate the knowledge gap and set the stage for discussing the impact of rethinking "indigenization" framed on a symbolic level of change, and unpacks the racialized tensions commonly embedded in curriculum and teaching practices. The chapter closes by proposing key considerations to address the gap and bring about authentic change.

IT IS NICE TO BE SEEN: REFRAMING SYMBOLIC CHANGE

I (Linda) had the honour of teaching in a program that enabled a group of Indigenous students to complete a bachelor's degree using a condensed format. The students were from Indigenous ancestry and had indirect or direct experience with residential schools and damaged communities. They shared learner characteristics similar to what Lange and colleagues (2015) call "wounded" students, in that their experiences with school are easily framed in terms of conflict and violence. They had experienced marginalization in various areas of their lives, yet they remained passionate about education and wanted to take on leadership roles in their communities.

I was the cohort's first non-Indigenous instructor and scheduled to teach a course on group dynamics and facilitation skills early in the schedule. I believe the non-Indigenous program coordinators went into the planning process trying to balance explicit program learning outcomes while at the same time demonstrating to their Indigenous counterparts their ability to "indigenize." To this end, they established explicit protocols that were to be followed and set the learning outcomes in stone. I was told the students were a cohesive group with identical learning preferences and that the program organizers, both non-Indigenous and Indigenous, agreed that each morning would start with a smudging ceremony and close with a circle, and all students would be evaluated using prescribed assessment tools.

The first time I met the students, I thought I would practise what Bennett (2003) and Derrida (2000) describe as a pedagogy of hospitality, so I arranged to introduce myself before they actually had to meet me on the first day of class. When I arrived, the program coordinators immediately organized me into the morning smudging ceremony. I was very unsure of myself in this situation and realize now I experienced what George (2017) describes as a heightened form of performative morality whereby accommodation of Indigenous cultural practices is used. "This method of reconciliation and recognition serves as a settler move to innocence in which Canadians are not required to make substantial structural change, or to question their continued benefit in the colonial project" (p. 53). For the very reason I was uncomfortable, mandated smudging can be comfortable diversity.

The students had hesitant looks on their faces. I came away from this first meeting realizing there were many culturally sensitive elements, as well as teaching practices, that needed resolving. In consultation with and under the guidance of Elders, I prepared to create what I thought would be an excellent experience. However, I was not prepared for the underlying tensions that became apparent on the first day. I discovered the students had been putting up a brave front to appear cohesive in order to fit into the university. In reality, there were deep-rooted group dynamic challenges. With this being a course on group dynamics, it was impossible to ignore the tension in the room.

There were participants from a variety of Nations who expressed discomfort with being grouped as all the same. Some expressed feeling more marginalized than others in the class. Adding to the tension was the fact that some thought it was great I was not Indigenous, while others thought it was completely inappropriate. There was tension across ages, genders, and Nations, and between those sponsored by their bands and those paying their own tuition. There was anxiety around the APA essay assignment as a colonial requirement. The learning space was uncomfortable.

I left the first day with my head spinning as I tried to figure out how to balance my university's directive with the students' needs. I knew if we were truly going to explore facilitation, then I needed to first facilitate the group's ability to achieve a peaceful learning experience. There was a need to build community, and I knew I would need to embrace what Tanaka (2016) and Butterwick and Selman (2012) stress as a dangerous or risky pedagogy and revise the course using critical and transformative pedagogies that include embodied learning activities to "contribute to a remembering and naming of oppression but also to how these processes may be facilitated in such a way as to generate new knowledge that leads to enfranchisement and action" (p. 62). And most significantly, I had to try to infuse my practice with teachings from the work of Indigenous educators (e.g., Battiste, 2013; Cote-Meek, 2014; Goulet & Goulet, 2014; Smith, 2012).

I boldly revised "on the fly" and switched the focus from facilitation skills to understanding diversity when facilitating. I immediately contacted Theresa Neil-Kumiga, an Elder-in-residence whom I had worked with for many years, and explained the situation. She graciously agreed to join me and to guide my work in trying to shift the dynamic in class. She agreed to attend the class. The next morning, she and I opened the class with a quote from the textbook:

> Any time a person seeks truth over comfort, that person will be perceived as a threat to others around the individual. Consequently, those people who make up the various systems (co-workers, family members or friends) will try, either through seduction or sabotage, to get that person hooked back into being dependent on the system. It is often easier to just go along than to do the right thing. (Robinson and Rose, 2007, p. 3)

Everyone immediately responded to this quote. I had read it many times, but this time I really heard it. We explored what it meant and felt like.

Everyone participated, talked, and shared. It was an emotional, passionate, and charged learning space that bonded the group.

We learned that the deep-rooted source of the various tensions was coming from the course delivery protocols. I had misread the looks on the students' faces the first day. They were not hesitant; they were frustrated and hurt. They had perceived my participation in the smudging ceremony as just another disingenuous symbolic or token effort, and they had no faith I, as a non-Indigenous instructor, would be of any use to them. Beyond questioning cultural appropriation, there was disappointment around the university's assumption that all Indigenous peoples share the same values and practices. There was no consideration as to whether everyone should be required to participate in smudging ceremonies or not, even if it was not part of their own cultural practice. There was a profound sense of distrust among the students for the program's ability to embrace "indigenization."

In consultation with Theresa, I revamped the skills component of the course into learning activities that challenged Otherness. I created an opportunity for those that wanted to participate in smudging ceremonies to do so. But I also provided an opportunity for those that did not want to participate to remain respected for their personal choice. Together we (Theresa, the students, and myself) established our own protocols for the opening and closing of the day.

The climate in the room changed. I was teaching in the moment, student-centred, and from a place of heart. Open, honest dialogue and problem solving became the focus. As a group, we laughed, cried, expressed frustration, learned from each other, practised authentic feedback, and honoured each other's knowledge practices. And oh yes—we met the prescribed learning outcomes but perhaps not in the exact way the coordinators had envisioned.

Changing the morning smudging ceremony is only one example of rethinking a symbolic or performative response to decolonization. It challenged the dominant power structures of the academy and its overall contribution to explicitly meeting the learning outcomes is difficult to measure. But should these be reasons for not having taken the risk when the impact for the students was profound? Is questioning and/or shifting power not an essential element toward decolonization?

After the course was over, I attended other events with the students. I have a common practice of greeting people with "it is nice to see you!" and generally people respond, "It is nice to see you too." But instead, one of the students would respond with "it is nice to be seen." At first, I did not pay too much attention, but then I grew curious. I finally asked him about it and he told me that for many years he had felt completely insignificant and invisible—especially in a learning environment. He mentioned that during our time together he felt seen and heard—and this was a first. He felt respected for his Indigenous ways of knowing, as his Nation did not smudge, and that by changing the smudging ceremony expectations I demonstrated that he mattered. He commented that seeing me learning from Theresa was empowering. His response "it is nice to be seen" was his way of recognizing and giving thanks for being acknowledged as a knower. To me this is, in a small way, an example of decolonization in action.

I HAVE INDIGENIZED. I TELL STORIES: UNPACKING THE RACIALIZED LENS

"White fragility" is defined by DiAngelo (2011) as "even a minimum amount of racial stress becom[ing] intolerable, triggering a range of defensive moves" (p. 57), such as positioning white opinions as merely rational, unemotional, and unideological, while racialized identities' opinions are somehow biased. White fragility disrupts any movement toward decolonization because it centres the conversation upon making white people feel better about themselves rather than placing whiteness as an aspect that affects relationships between people and groups. The following short examples are designed to stimulate a much-needed discussion around white fragility and the need to help shift the lens through which non-Indigenous faculty and students approach decolonization and knowledge creation.

"I have indigenized already—I tell stories to my students all the time." This is a comment I get more times than I (Linda) can count. When I push back and gently ask if they have considered the power around *I tell* or *my students*, I get a puzzled look. When I ask them to explain their understanding of story as an Indigenous pedagogy, they often get a blank look and say, "Indigenous students like stories, so I try to tell one or two." There is rarely any acknowledgement that storytelling is about using individual and shared perspectives to represent, remember, understand, and connect to collective and expressed knowing. There is also little or no awareness for the shared emphasis on telling and listening as a respectful relationship.

"I am attending this workshop because my department has to indigenize. We don't have a lot of time so can you give me a few strategies that are easy to implement." It never fails that there are faculty in the room with their laptops open, ready to receive the tips. Sometimes, for sport, I say, "Okay, be

238 Decolonizing and Indigenizing Education in Canada

sure to include a territorial welcome, have Indigenous artwork in your office, find one reading by an Indigenous scholar or talk about the medicine wheel, sit in a circle at least once, and accept late assignments." What amazes me is that they type away and actually start to look relaxed, as if they now have the solution. This is their dream of comfortable diversity, a simple checklist that requires a bit of symbolic change and no epistemological change. But then when I say, "If you think this is what you need to indigenize, then this is the wrong workshop for you," and explain what we will be doing, I can see complete confusion and discomfort come over them.

"Well, it is okay to indigenize in some areas, but when you have essential content to cover like forest fire science you cannot. They need to learn proper techniques." These faculty were teaching non-Indigenous and Indigenous students in northern BC and assumed the Indigenous communities knew nothing about forest fires. This is a particularly egregious example, as many Indigenous Nations had firekeepers to burn underbrush and create natural fire barriers to prevent mega-fires. Such practices were banned in the 1930s and their absence is believed to create the conditions for today's mega-fires (Brend, 2017). This comment becomes deeply troubling because not only is there no deficit in what is considered "essential," Indigenous knowledge is completely devalued and the faculty involved could not see the racialized tension underlying their practice or the missed learning opportunity for all the students. This example emphasizes how who has the knowledge is always an important consideration, because it influences which knowledges are dismissed and which are considered "objective, proper" techniques. When I suggested they may want to draw on the knowledge the learners already had and start by having them compare techniques used over generations as a way to infuse ways of knowing, they grew very defensive. And sadly, this example is typical of most content-focused faculty.

"I am not racist. I just had nothing to do with residential schools so there is nothing I can do to fix it." Much like the faculty, the students that I (Brett) witnessed struggled, particularly when coming out of high school, where they had learned a view of history that centres Western European history. There was pushback that to (even partially) reframe history around the experiences of colonization upon the land's original inhabitants was simply "political correctness" because it was changing the way history had been "set in stone" for decades. In reality, the teaching of history has always been politically correct—in the sense of not upsetting white fragility by suggesting that the history of Western colonialism was not a linear progression toward

Chapter 13 | Decolonizing Non-Indigenous Faculty and Students **239**

increased justice, but about invasion and genocide in the name of resource extraction. As DiAngelo (2012) identifies, "the ideology of Individualism is one of the primary barriers to well meaning (and other) white people understanding racism," that "as long as I don't see myself as personally engaged in acts of racism, I am against it" (p. 168). As the popular conception of history is understood from an individual point of view, white faculty and students often come to decolonizing as if they are an innocent individual in a meritocratic system rather than aided by historical circumstances. Part of unlearning is to see the world not as isolated individuals but to attune ourselves to the relationships we have with the people and environment around us.

These comments are only four examples, from many, that reflect the dominant racialized lens and the colonial framing of power dynamics living in our learning spaces and influencing the legitimization of what counts as knowledge.

When I (Linda) first started doing workshops, they were built on transformative and critical pedagogies, where non-Indigenous faculty shared with other non-Indigenous faculty and, when ready, sought the expertise and teachings from Indigenous educators and Elders. Time was spent facilitating sensitive discussions needed to introduce faculty to critical reflection. These early workshops were successful. Deep transformational learning occurred, and faculty left equipped to challenge their own assumptions, to seek mentorship from Elders, to engage in readings from Indigenous scholars, and to remain open to reframing and decolonizing their view of education and knowledge. They left able to see that their ultimate goal should be framed as a responsibility to first decolonize by changing their practice to include sharing power, and infusing curriculum, learning activities, and assessments with Indigenous ways of knowing and doing. I was hopeful, under the guidance of Elders, they could develop an appreciation for methodologies such as Smith's (2012) framework as instrumental in shifting the lens they view research and teaching through.

Unfortunately, success was short lived. As the university placed more strategic emphasis on indigenization, the demand for faculty training grew. The name of the workshop was changed to "Indigenizing the Curriculum," and faculty came from a variety of disciplines (e.g., biology, psychology, political science, math, business, trades, and technology). Most were recommended to attend by their deans. Few had experience with reflective practice or had taken the time to unlearn their conception of a sanitized "history"—let alone question colonial practices. Many came reluctant, and some were even hostile.

After running several of the workshops, I was exhausted beyond exhausted. I was very shocked by the racialized tensions that continuously needed addressing. My heart knew this was not my place or my work, and I realized how truly ineffective the workshops were in addressing "indigenization." Sure, the university could report the number of faculty that had been trained to "indigenize," but I knew, other than perhaps one or two people in each workshop, their numbers were completely misleading. I stopped doing the workshops and have been trying to engage the university in a mindful discussion about how best to engage faculty in anti-racist education and critical reflection instead of settling for workshops focused on symbolic change.

This is an ongoing, challenging discussion, because comfortable diversity never allows for this step. As Razack (2001) writes, "cultural diversity too often descends, in a multicultural spiral, to a superficial reading of differences that makes power relations invisible and keeps dominant cultural norms in place" (p. 9). Trying to help non-Indigenous people learn to dismantle the hierarchy is difficult due to how "helping" is part of being the good, middle-class, liberal, white, Canadian subject. Non-Indigenous subjects can imagine themselves as good precisely for recognizing that acknowledging the humanity of the Other is a choice they have to extend. Indeed, Ahmed (2004) suggests this "may even provide the conditions for a new discourse of white pride" (p. 184) around declarations of goodness that stand in for any actual action. But all this accomplishes is creating what Thobani (2007) calls the "suffocating blanket of compassion imposed by nationals upon Aboriginal peoples and immigrants" (p. 252). The crucial step for white people is to realize that we are already in relationships with the Other, be it as ally or complicit in systems of oppression rather than either in a helping relationship or being completely autonomous.

However, as a result of our experiences, we have learned—as Ahmed (2004), DiAngelo (2011), Dion (2009), and Razack (2001) suggest—that non-Indigenous people often have difficulties exploring anti-racism because it challenges their positive construct of what a "good person" who helps others is. And, as Schick and St. Denis (2003) remind us, even if the conversation is started, it is often silenced because it is not considered "polite."

This is where our role as non-Indigenous educators is necessary—to prepare faculty members to be open to deeper senses of diversity. We can help Indigenous educators by sharing the workload and ensuring there is more than one token Indigenous voice at the planning table. Often, non-Indigenous people will demand Indigenous people educate them. Hytten and Warren (2003)

Chapter 13 | Decolonizing Non-Indigenous Faculty and Students 241

stress these demands absolve people from doing the hard work of learning, and contributing to answers is draining on the racialized community by asking them to bear the burden of education. DiAngelo (2011) emphasizes such a request repeats unequal power relations in four ways: it makes it seem racism is not perpetrated by anyone; asks racialized people to do all the work; assumes that white people are innocent and do not already know; and ignores the numerous racialized people who have repeatedly tried to tell their stories, only to be dismissed through phrases like "playing the race card" (p. 212) or, as we often hear, "they should get over it and move on."

As non-Indigenous educators, the first step to move beyond comfortable diversity is to acknowledge that training or resources framed as the solution will not achieve decolonization alone. Instead, we need to commit to anti-racist education and self-engaged transformation first, which can be accomplished in several ways. We need to draw on our expertise with critical pedagogies and advocate relentlessly for their application in the academy's approach to decolonization (e.g., Cote-Meek, 2014; Freire, 1970; Giroux, 1992; hooks, 1994; Mohanty, 2003; Tuck & Yang, 2012). Using these strategies, we boldly create opportunities to engage other non-Indigenous faculty and students in uncomfortable discussions and help them to unpack their assumptions. This work is not to be taken lightly; as Butterwick and Selman (2012) stress when working in the transformative space "the potential for surprise and danger needs to be recognized and anticipated to avoid overwhelming individuals ... these experiences must be embraced and turned into positive outcomes" (p. 62). This takes skill, but each university has people with this expertise. Faculty and students need mentors and university systems that celebrate the use of critical pedagogies and that support risk taking. We can share our moments of uncomfortableness and questioning, and provide spaces for people to challenge themselves without the fear of negative evaluations/grades. We can use films and literature as proxies for other people's stories, not because they diversify the syllabi, but because they can open the dialogue that creates conditions for transformational learning.

By doing this, we would resist the cultural appropriation of symbolic diversity and instead infuse anti-oppression pedagogies into our teaching and into our interactions with colleagues, no matter the subject. This shift would put an end to communicating "indigenization" in the academy as a strategic goal to be accomplished within unrealistically short timelines. As Indigenous educators emphasize, decolonization will require time and respect for generational healing (e.g., Battiste, 2013; Stonechild, 2006; Wilson, 2008).

Universities need to let go of their expectation to showcase results that, when unpacked, are simply symbolic. For non-Indigenous faculty and students, decolonization should be framed as a journey of first self-exploration and unlearning, followed by new learning and new practices in a continuous cycle of critical reflection. Instead of aiming for quick and comfortable change, we must turn our full attention to being accountable for our actions and the messages we are passing on to the faculty and students coming behind us.

DISCUSSION QUESTIONS

1. What opportunities are made available at your university to engage in challenging or uncomfortable dialogue with others?

2. What elements of your university's indigenization initiative(s) fall into symbolic change?

3. What evaluation measures could your university use to determine if faculty and students are exploring and open to transforming the racialized tensions in our classrooms?

GLOSSARY

symbolic change: The small, visual representations of minority groups without changing how these groups are received within the institution.

transformative learning: Learning that does not just provide new facts but changes understanding of the world.

white fragility: White defensiveness in response to discussions of race.

whiteness: The invisible, default standard of norms in a Western, colonial society.

FURTHER READINGS/WEBSITES

Chabot Davis, K. (2014). *Beyond the white negro: Empathy and anti-racist reading.* Urbana: University of Illinois Press.

Obomsawin, A. (Producer & Director). (2017). *Our people will be healed* [Motion picture]. Canada: National Film Board of Canada.

Wilmot, S. (2005). *Taking responsibility, taking direction: White anti-racism in Canada.* Winnipeg, MB: Arbeiter Ring Publishing.

REFERENCES

Ahmed, S. (2004). *The cultural politics of emotion*. New York, NY: Routledge.

Ahmed, S. (2012). *On being included: Racism and diversity in institutional life*. Durham, NC: Duke University Press.

Bannerji, H. (2000). *Dark side of the nation: Essays on multiculturalism, nationalism, and gender*. Toronto, ON: Canadian Scholars' Press.

Battiste, M. (2013). *Decolonizing education: Nourishing the learning spirit*. Saskatoon, SK: Purich Publishing.

Bennett, J. B. (2003). Constructing academic community: Power, relationality, hospitality, and conversation. *Interchange, 34*(1), 51–61. doi:10.1023/A:1024510618699

Berila, B. (2016). *Integrating mindfulness into anti-oppression pedagogy: Social justice in higher education*. New York, NY: Routledge.

Bolman, L. G., & Deal, T. E. (2014). *How great leaders think: The art of reframing*. San Francisco, CA: Jossey-Bass.

Brend, Y. (2017, July 15). Forget Smokey the Bear: How First Nation fire wisdom is key to mega-fire prevention. *CBC News*. Retrieved from https://www.cbc.ca/news/canada/british -columbia/fire-fighting-first-nations-firekeepers-annie-kruger-penticton-bc-wildfire-mega-fire-1.4205506

Brookfield, S. D. (1995). *Becoming a critically reflective teacher*. San Francisco, CA: Jossey-Bass.

Butterwick, S., & Selman, J. (2012). Embodied knowledge and decolonization: Walking with theater's powerful and risky pedagogy. *New Directions for Adult and Continuing Education,* (134), 61–70. doi:10.1002/ace.20018

Clark, T., Maddison, S., & de Costa, R. (2016). Non-Indigenous people and the limits of settler colonial reconciliation. In S. Maddison, T. Clark, & R. de Costa (Eds.), *The limits of settler colonial reconciliation: Non-Indigenous people and the responsibility to engage* (pp. 1–12). Singapore: Springer.

Cote-Meek, S. (2014). *Colonized classrooms: Racism, trauma, and resistance in post-secondary Education*. Halifax, NS: Fernwood Publishing.

den Heyer, K. (2015). An analysis of aims and the education "event." *Canadian Journal of Education, 38*(1), 1–27.

Derrida, J. (2000). *Of hospitality*. Stanford, CA: Stanford University Press.

DiAngelo, R. (2011). White fragility. *The International Journal of Critical Pedagogy, 3*(3), 55–70.

DiAngelo, R. (2012). *What does it mean to be white?: Developing white racial literacy*. New York, NY: Peter Lang.

Dion, S. (2009). *Braiding histories: Learning from Aboriginal peoples' experiences and perspectives*. Vancouver, BC: UBC Press.

Findlay, L. (2000). Always Indigenize! The radical humanities in the postcolonial Canadian university. *Ariel, 31*, 307–328.

Freire, P. (1970). *Pedagogy of the oppressed*. New York, NY: Seabury.

George, R. Y. (2017). Inclusion is just the Canadian word for assimilation. In K. L. Ladner & M. J. Tait, (Eds.), *Surviving Canada: Indigenous peoples celebrate 150 years of betrayal* (pp. 49–62). Winnipeg, MB: ARP Books.

Giroux, H. (1992). *Border crossings: Cultural workers and the politics of education*. New York, NY: Routledge, Chapman, and Hall.

Goulet, L. M., & Goulet, K. N. (2014). *Teaching each other: Nehinuw concepts & Indigenous pedagogies*. Vancouver, BC: UBC Press.

Heron, B. (2007). *Desire for development: Whiteness, gender, and the helping imperative*. Waterloo, ON: Wilfrid Laurier University Press.

Hill, E. (2012). A critique of the call to "Always Indigenize!" *Peninsula: A Journal of Relational Politics, 2*(1). Retrieved from https://journals.uvic.ca/index.php/peninsula/article/view/11513/3212

hooks, b. (1994). *Teaching to transgress*. New York, NY: Routledge Press.

Hytten, K., & Warren, J. (2003). Engaging whiteness: How racial power gets reified in education. *International Journal of Qualitative Studies in Education, 16*(1), 65–89.

Ladner, K. L., & Tait, M. J. (Eds.). (2017). *Surviving Canada: Indigenous peoples celebrate 150 years of betrayal*. Winnipeg, MB: ARP Books.

Lange, E., Chovanec, D., Cardinal, T., Kajner, T., & Smith Acuña, N. (2015). Wounded learners failed by schooling: Symbolic violence and re-engaging low income adults. *Canadian Journal for the Study of Adult Education, 27*(3), 83–104.

Louie, D. W., Pratt, Y. P., Hanson, A. J., & Ottmann, J. (2017). Applying Indigenizing principles of decolonizing methodologies in university classrooms. *Canadian Journal of Higher Education, 47*(3), 16–33.

Mohanty, C. T. (2003). *Feminism without borders: Decolonizing theory, practicing, and solidarity*. Durham, NC: Duke University Press.

Palmer, P. (1998). *The courage to teach*. San Francisco, CA: Jossey-Bass.

Pidgeon, M., Archibald, J-A., & Hawkey, C. (2014). Relationships matter: Supporting Aboriginal graduate students in British Columbia, Canada. *Canadian Journal of Higher Education, 44*(1), 1–21.

Razack, S. (2001). *Looking white people in the eye: Gender, race, and culture in courtrooms and classrooms*. Toronto, ON: University of Toronto Press.

Robinson, G., & Rose, M. (2007). *Teams for a new generation: A facilitator's field guide*. Bloomington, IN: Author House.

Schick, C., & St. Denis, V. (2003). What makes anti-racist pedagogy in teacher education difficult? Three popular ideological assumptions. *Alberta Journal of Educational Research, 49*(1), 55–59.

Smith, L. T. (2012). *Decolonizing methodologies: Research and Indigenous peoples* (2nd ed.). New York, NY: Zed Books.

Stonechild, B. (2006). *The new buffalo: The struggle of Aboriginal post-secondary education in Canada*. Winnipeg: University of Manitoba.

Tanaka, M. (2016). *Learning & teaching together: Weaving indigenous ways of knowing into education*. Vancouver, BC: UBC Press.

Thobani, S. (2007). *Exalted subjects: Studies in the making of race and nation in Canada*. Toronto, ON: University of Toronto Press.

Truth and Reconciliation Commission of Canada (TRC). (2015). *Final report of the Truth and Reconciliation Commission of Canada* (vols. 1–6). Montreal, QC: McGill-Queen's University Press.

Tuck, E., & Yang, K. W. (2012). Decolonization is not a metaphor. *Decolonization: Indigeneity, Education & Society, 1*(1), 1–40.

Wilson, S. (2008). *Research is ceremony: Indigenous research methods*. Halifax, NS: Fernwood Publishing.

CHAPTER 14

Reframing Reconciliation: Turning Our Back or Turning Back?

Keri Cheechoo

Leave

Squaw, they said
Sit down
Shut up.

Colonial rule
Are you cold?
Take this blanket.

Your child
Let us have it
It's still Indian.

We'll create
Children
In God's image.

Mind you,
They will lose
Sanity and souls.

Your business
Is ours
Your ovaries, too.

Shush
Don't speak
Unless you're spoken to.

You can't
Eat or sit here
Leave.

Leave your ancestors.
Leave your home.
Leave your land.
(Cheechoo, 2017c)

~

SITUATING SELF

Wachiye. I am a Cree woman. My community is Long Lake #58 First Nation. I am daughter, mother, sister, grandmother, wife, auntie, cousin, and niece. These are my relations, they hold my history and are my memory anchors (Gadgil, Berkes, & Folke, 1993; Mitchell, 2013). As a published poet, I use poetic inquiry (an arts-based methodology) in my doctoral work in a way that connects my spiritual aptitude for writing with educational research. I use my poetry to make space for Indigenous voice by interrupting and subverting Western constructs of academic writing. I also share narratives that speak to my lived experiences because it is necessary that we create community, dear reader. It is critical that I position myself because I am daughter to people who have experienced the horror and atrocities of Indian Residential Schools (IRS). My father subsisted through his childhood in IRS, and my mother is daughter to survivors of IRS. They both live what they know. The **intergenerational trauma** I experienced as a child contributed to my becoming well educated in the poetics of marginalization, silence, and speech as a theme of subjugation vis-à-vis colonialism pervades my work. I began writing when I was six years of age and continued writing

Chapter 14 | Reframing Reconciliation **249**

lyrical poetry into adulthood to depict my journey from an oppressed, sub-jugated child to a strong and free woman.

With "Reframing Reconciliation: Turning Our Back or Turning Back?" as its impetus, this chapter explores the complexities of reconciliation. Residential schools continue to impact every life they have touched. The poem "I'll (Not) Be Home for Christmas" was created for *The Fulcrum* (an English-language student newspaper at the University of Ottawa) and is a direct juxtaposition of Indigenous and settler children's lives. In the 1870s, Indigenous children began to be apprehended from their families and were forced into violently oppressive assimilation. In contrast, in the 1870s, settler children indulged in the delights of Christmas and the creation of Santa Claus without being forced to leave their homes or families. I have intentionally placed impacting snippets of Christmas carol lyrics throughout the poem to create cognitive dissonance.

~

I'll (Not) Be Home for Christmas

In our Winter Solstice
We celebrated the sun
And each other

Through the long day
We feasted
We visited

(Baby, it's cold outside)

Until
Until we were
Banished

Banished into the spaces
Of neither here
And neither there

(Better watch out, … you'd better not cry)

We were in between
Their Church
And our Land

In the 1870s
Indigenous children
Celebrated escape

Escaped into the cold
Before The Longest Day
And visits from priests
(... I've gotta get home ...
              ... but baby, you'll freeze out there ...)
(Cheechoo, 2016)

~

Way back in 1996, the *Report of the Royal Commission on Aboriginal Peoples*, or RCAP, was published. The report proposed that "the relationship between Aboriginal and non-Aboriginal people in Canada be restructured fundamentally and grounded in ethical principles to which all participants subscribe freely" (RCAP, 1993, p. 12). And in 2015, the Truth and Reconciliation Commission (TRC) published a report that advised that reconciliation must

> support Aboriginal peoples as they heal from the destructive legacies of colonization that have wreaked such havoc in their lives. But it must do even more. Reconciliation must inspire Aboriginal and non-Aboriginal peoples to transform Canadian society so that our children and grandchildren can live together in dignity, peace, and prosperity on these lands we now share. (p. 8)

The report contains a stark reminder that "survivors [of residential schools, intergenerational violence survivors] are more than just victims of violence. They are also holders of Treaty, constitutional, and human rights ... they are women and men who have resilience, courage, and vision" (TRC, 2015, p. 207). Both the RCAP and the TRC use very plain language indicating a need to engage learning about and in reconciling truths about Canada. Yet that is easier said than done.

I am a mom, kookum (grandmother), PhD candidate, and part-time professor who resists daily the systemic and institutional racism that is deeply embedded within society and higher education. I am my lived experiences. The following narratives edge the very fabric of my personalized grasp of reconciliation. Through each event, I have struggled to maintain agency but have also experienced a severe bifurcation of self, due to intergenerational and contemporary impacts of such colonial violence, or "ethnostress" (LaDuke, 2005). "Ethnostress" embodies the accrual of the effects of oppression and violence that have been conferred by colonial culture. As I have mentioned, my parents are Indian Residential School survivors. They did not possess nurturing instincts, realize the necessity of engagement as a family unit, or know how to foster love through hugs. I grew up in a stilted manner, and was due to have my first child at 18. It was then that I realized that my body was the epitome of asylum. I held medicine to protect this new ancestor that I was carrying. My agency resurged through all of my being, and I began to love my body in a way that created much-needed space for decolonization. Acknowledging that the childhood I suffered through did not have to cycle again, I decided to become the parent I should have known. Regrettably, my beautiful, brown, expectant body was considered offensive and in dire need of regulation. School administrators insisted that I abandon high school while I was in Grade 12. Silenced, I became an unwilling statistic. I am a high school dropout.

My academic journey had to begin in a Native Access Program (NAP) at Lakehead University, because I could not fulfill the expected criteria of being a high school graduate. My projected trajectory insisted that I complete both the NAP and Honours Bachelors of Arts program in five years, but I successfully navigated both programs in four years. I attempted a Bachelor of Education (BEd) program, but the prerequisite of passing a mandatory math exam led to me facing adversity, and I was unable to access the degree. While in my Master of Arts (MA) in English program, I wanted to know why I had this apparent inability to "do" math. After hours of formalized testing, I learned that my *in*ability was instead a *dis*ability. After completing the MA program, I re-applied to a different concentration of the BEd program and gained both the BEd degree and certification with the Ontario College of Teachers. My learning disability is called dyscalculia, and I now do the hard work of breaking down barriers and stigma surrounding learning disabilities. There are many Indigenous children and adults alike who struggle in Western educational institutions with learning disabilities, so I try to use my lived experiences to demonstrate perseverance and accessible success.

The next story from my early life holds the space where I emerge as a Cree scholar in higher education. My brother and myself were adopted. With our adoptions came a violent researcher who shadowed us and subjected us to frequent intrusive interviews. Though we have questioned who the researcher was and what the research was about, we have *never* received any authentic information as to why data was being extracted from us. My parents do not even know, which is not surprising; Indian Residential Schools ensured that my parents never questioned authority again. My journey as an experiment ended in a confrontation when I was 21 years old. I still have no actual knowledge about the researcher, the project itself, or even *who I was* in relation to this experiment I had become. I have come full circle, and I am reconciling that I am now in the role of researcher. I share these narratives with you because all past, present, and future generations require that I interrogate who I am, how I got to be here, and how to ensure that I do not harm others as I do my own research.

Drawing on poetic inquiry and an Indigenous conversation research methodology (Kovach, 2009), I am proposing to address existing missing histories of the dehumanizing, state-sponsored policy of forcing sterilization on Indigenous women as part of my commitment toward educational mandates of the Truth and Reconciliation Commission. My doctoral research seeks to enact transformative Canadian and First Nation, Métis, and Inuit (FNMI) relationships that speak in turn to the educational and reconciliation processes of Indigenizing school curriculum (Smith, Ng-A-Fook, Berry, & Spence, 2011). Settler colonialism remains omnipresent; seeking to invade, conquer, and claim people, time, and space. I am guided by Simpson's (2000) seven principles of Indigenous worldviews. She indicates that there are many truths, and that these truths are dependent upon individual experiences. For instance, existing literature points to the higher likelihood of Indigenous women being victimized by sterilization than their non-Indigenous counterparts, who instead had to fight for the ability to have access to voluntary sterilization (Barker-Benfield, 1977; Cairney, 1996; Carey, 1998; Caulfield & Robertson, 1996; Grossboll, 1980; Littlewood, 1977; Ralstin-Lewis, 2005). In Canada, there are thousands of cases of forced or coerced sterilization. This is the space where my research comes in. Ultimately, I seek to educate the Canadian public while creating a space for long-missing historical and contemporary narratives belonging to objectified Indigenous women. I am working to re-centre the voices of women who have experienced the state-sponsored violence of reproductive injustice. It is my hope that my research assists in developing curricular strategies to educate the Canadian public about these women's missing narratives.

You should know that there are well over 4,000 missing and murdered Indigenous women and girls in Canada (Radek, 2011). Officially, the Government of Canada launched an independent national inquiry into these missing and murdered Indigenous women and girls in early 2016. The commission is tasked with examining

> practices, policies and institutions such as policing, child welfare, coroners and other government policies/practices or social/economic conditions … commissioners have been mandated to examine the underlying historical, social, economic, institutional and cultural factors that contribute to the violence. (Indigenous and Northern Affairs Canada, 2016)

Indigenous women are inherently positioned to be a threat to settler colonialism because our bodies create a counternarrative to resource extraction/depletion and land possession (Anderson, 2011). The case involving accused murderer Bradley Barton and his victim Cindy Gladue has been in and out of the courts since 2011. Barton was acquitted of Gladue's death and continues to maintain his innocence, indicating that he had not realized that she had perished during the night. The linkage between Indigenous women's bodies and land becomes apparent "[when] gender violence [is used] to remove Indigenous peoples and their descendants from the land, [removing] agency" (Simpson, 2014, p. 4). Cindy Gladue was an Indigenous woman whose very agency and existence maintained a bodily and ancestral connection to the land. That connection vanished with her.

I struggle with compartmentalizing the epistemological violences that FNMI Peoples face daily, just so I can function. "Systemic Squaw" springs from my frustration of being a targeted, oppressed, and marginalized Cree woman.

~

Systemic Squaw

Eternally bronze
Exotic cheekbones
Bursting lips
Opaque eyes

Basic attributes
Shared by countless
Women
Pocahontas-complex

Western eyes
Mold us
Molest us
We're fetishized

Western hands
Crave our hair
Touching it
Petting us

Western ears
Ignore our dialogue
Pleas
Please, just stop

Just stop
Your excuses
Stereotypes
Phony ideologies

Just stop
Your righteousness
Privileged
Entitled-ness

Halt
Your denials
Pernicious
Deprivation

Cease
Your altruism
Third world
Exists *here*

Desist
Your attempts
Extermination
Genocide
(Cheechoo, 2017d)

~

I will be frank about what reconciliation means to me. Initially, I was on board with reconciling Canada's difficult past and learning to move through it with healing strategies. But then I began to see different things on social media and began to hear bizarre things on the news. Small, tokenistic changes were beginning to filter through, serving as a means of reconciliation. A street name was changed there, a statue was removed here, but all the while, there was no real interaction or evidence of ethical relationality (leaning on human relationality or a reciprocity with one another (Donald, 2009; Tupper, 2012) taking place. With each shift came unequivocal resistance. Reconciliation began to resemble political posturing, but still I clung to this idealized notion of reconciliation in the hopes of a better Canada. I deserve to sleep though a night without "ethnostress" (LaDuke, 2005) slinking into bed with me. Triggered by vicarious trauma, I began to turn this idea over in my mind that the ideology and intent of reconciliation was meaningless, and that the *application of reconciliation* was deliberately out of reach for FNMI Peoples.

As I was working through the complexities of reconciliation, the terrible and untimely deaths of Tina Fontaine and Colten Boushie occurred. If I had thought of reconciliation as being on shaky ground before, well—I felt sick knowing that reconciliation had completely failed them. On February 23rd, the day after Cormier was acquitted for Tina Fontaine's death, I was scheduled to teach. I was furious, triggered, and terrified for my children, my grandchildren, and myself. I went to the university but I brought my youngest daughter with me because I was broken, and I needed to be able to physically see her. That was a difficult day. I did my best to teach about injustice while I was being simultaneously shattered by injustice. The violence that Fontaine and Boushie experienced both inside and outside of the courtroom is appalling, and that very day became my tipping point. I became fixed on turning my back on reconciliation.

As I had mentioned earlier, intergenerational trauma governed my childhood. While my parents were still suffering from the effects of Indian

256 Decolonizing and Indigenizing Education in Canada

Residential Schools, my brother and I were adopted from different places and different spaces. The poem "Feral" provides a snapshot of my life back then. We were reminded frequently that we were unnatural to the extended families we were incorporated into, and consequently, every thread of my childhood has contributed to the tapestry of who I continue to be.

~

Feral

Adopted kids
Those adopted kids
Or them
That's what they called us

People were gruff
Didn't realize
Care
We were children

With feelings
For awhile
We were hurt
Toughened up

After the fact
Our parents
Began oddly
Parenting

Drove us
To parks
Gave me a bat
Jeff got a ball

Told to play
Play what?
They always drove away
Left us there

Instead
We smoked
Watched and waited
Wild
(Cheechoo, 2017b)

~

Three years after the TRC put forth the 94 Calls to Action, Canada continues to fail in redressing the "problems inherent in state-dominated reconciliation forums for [I]ndigenous communities ... and fails to promote a necessary balance between restitution and reconciliation strategies" (Corntassel & Holder, 2008, p. 466). Although educators and stakeholders in Canada's educational sector continue to verbally support calls for creating ethical and relational spaces of reconciliation, we continue to fail for the most part in doing so. The creation of the TRC is an attempt, in my opinion, to navigate the constructs of a shared Indigenous memory, but within a Westernized framework, and move to renegotiate that memory. There are countless settlers who inhabit Indigenous spaces in Indigenous organizations, the academy, and especially within the education field. I have watched and listened as settler teachers have taught "Indigenous curriculum" within a First Nation school and then have turned around and ridiculed the exact same curriculum in the teachers' staff room. I have been supervised by settlers with less education but more clout and bluster, and I have watched programming meant specifically for Indigenous Peoples become so whitewashed, deplorably unusable, and yet somehow more palatable.

Some pieces of the TRC report resonate within me, especially the final line of this quote: "Survivors of residential schools, intergenerational violence survivors are more than just victims of violence. They are also holders of Treaty, constitutional, and human rights ... they are women and men who have resilience, courage, and vision" (TRC, 2015, p. 207). Despite severe assimilative policies, I remain here, demonstrating "resilience, courage, and vision" for our future ancestors.

Next, I would like to move into sharing a narrative about a foundational course I have taught as a part-time professor. To provide context, the course introduces concepts, narratives, curriculum policies, and pedagogies that address some FNMI historical experiences and contemporary perspectives, and works to engage one another in ethically relational discussions about

258 Decolonizing and Indigenizing Education in Canada

possibilities and limitations of reconciliation. Essentially, I have instructed teacher candidates who could be potential teachers in our FNMI communities. The teacher candidates I have interacted with are asked to re-imagine education. They are tasked with learning about how to teach without contravening boundaries. Canada needs future teachers to be in a good space where they can teach accurate historical narratives, while reconciling their own discomfort with the things they read, watch, or hear. It can be difficult for them because they are decolonizing while they are learning, and they are being asked to do it in a compressed time frame.

I have taught this course twice. In the first year, I was naively set on creating community in the classroom and really worked at creating pockets of "safe spaces," and honestly, that blew up in my face. I was met with violence and resistance. I had a student who expressed that if the space was authentically safe, then the door should be open widely enough for them to speak freely, thus enabling them to bring hate speech into our shared space. This was incredibly disconcerting to me not only as an educator, but also as a marginalized woman. Many of the teacher candidates did not want to be in this class because they could not link Indigenous perspectives with their own teaching philosophies. In some instances, there was stark refusal on their part to engage with course texts or class discussions, which sometimes became combative. After the course, I received many disparaging evaluations, and the trauma of reading these evaluations triggered me to reconsider teaching.

Fast forward to January 2018—I taught the course again, but completely revamped it. I used my initial experience as a teachable moment for myself. I have come to think that safe spaces cannot really exist. After some discussion with colleagues and friends, I learned more about ethical spaces and ethical relationality. From my understanding, Dwayne Donald (2009) says that ethical space is a space of possibility that can only be created when we are dealing with two different worldviews or knowledge systems. Ethical relationality does not deny difference, but instead seeks to more deeply understand how our different histories and experiences position us in relation to each other. In other words, engaging in ethical relationality means recognizing that you are in a space with people who are unlike than you and respecting those dissimilarities enough to meet halfway, and learn from each other in the space where you meet.

During my first class with this year's cohort, we spoke openly about safe spaces and then about ethical relationality. We agreed to be responsible for the different energies we bring into the classroom and to maintain a level of respect that maintained all of our dignity. The course ended in April, and I am happy to report it was a good space to be in. The teacher candidates were able to think critically about what they were learning, reading, and hearing. It was heartening to hear that instead of reproducing the superficial or false knowledge they had previously learned about Indigenous Peoples, they would instead consciously consider using ethical relationality to make choices about how they will deliver content in their own future classrooms. I have recently received my course evaluations, and I am over the moon to know that the teacher candidates felt comfortable with the course content and that they loved the class (yay!).

Before I was teaching in a post-secondary setting, I was the literacy resource teacher/librarian at a K–12 school in a First Nation community. Despite being bandied about in the mouths of politicians, tangible reconciliation efforts have not reached most FNMI communities. I became re-acquainted with epistemological violence that encouraged an "us versus them" mentality during my time at the school. I was forced to remind unqualified, settler teachers of the school's policies, and that student safety and wellness were the number one priority. I never understood why I was met with derision and ire when I provided fresh fruit to students I interacted with daily, and it still boggles my mind.

Because I interacted with students from kindergarten to Grade 12 daily, I became heartbreakingly familiar with the effects of intergenerational trauma. Frequently, I set aside who I was as a literacy teacher, and I just sat and listened. I listened to narratives from students in Grade 2 who spoke about their overwhelming sadness and confusion after learning about a familial suicide. I listened to students in Grade 7 who worried about having no food at home because their parents or guardians were absent or had spent money on negative coping strategies instead. I have let students nap during our time together because sometimes they felt safer at school, and their little bodies could not stay awake any longer. I have learned that compassion and empathy go a long way in helping students heal or feel validated. Please note that not all of my time at this school was negative; in fact, I count the experience as one of the absolute best of my life. Despite the hardships students endured, they still radiated the purely good energy that only children can.

I want to backtrack, somewhat. After the Boushie verdict in February 2019, I ended up having a very significant dream. Mitchell (2013) speaks about engaging in mindfulness:

When my grandmother used to tell me stories, I would close my eyes and I would feel as if I were walking through that time. I could just imagine everything the way that it looked, the tools that people used, what kind of clothing they wore, how the weather felt, what people were feeling; it all came alive to me! It is as if I was right there at the time. (p. 55)

I apply mindfulness to re-engage with this dream; I can close my eyes and see the dream live again. In it, I was out on the land. I can still see a tree line, the bruised lavender of the sky at dusk, and I can see and smell smoke from a crackling and soaring campfire. I remember going out into the bush and collecting medicines like cedar and just being. Being still, listening and feeling the quiet. In the dream I was leading my family, elders, and people I do not even know yet to the fire, and we sat there. Feeling connected, I experienced a genuinely peaceful sense of community. When I opened my eyes the next morning, I felt resurgence sweep through my spirit and I knew my ancestors had provided healing throughout the night. The ensuing poem "Agency" emerged while I was writing my MA final project. "Agency" speaks to my journey of healing and resilience.

~

Agency

Shoved down
Apprehended
I experienced life
On society's terms
Enforced.

Indigenous Woman
I swam beneath the surface
Of society
I spoke and my words
Evaporated.

I examined those around me
I spoke distinctly
But vacant eyes barely met mine
Eyes downcast, I stopped speaking
Muted.

Shuffling through existence
I swallowed discourse
Both society's and mine
My narrative left untold
Absent.

Watched my peers
Laugh off cruel pranks
Watched my father
Slog through life
Defeated.

Residential school
Devoured his self-esteem
Made him pay
For being himself
Oppressed.

Soundless, I noted
Despair and loss
Shadowing us, me
Wherever we went
Malignant.

Until one day
I walked into a store
Heard a commotion
Firm, Female, Feminist
Voice.

I overheard Her
Defend Her right
To walk freely
That She was a paying customer
Censured.

Surprised, I heard my voice
Join hers
Righteous and resilient

Dissipating
Injustice.

Defiant, I strode
Into my life
Reclaimed what was mine
Advocated for the voiceless
Ally.

I lent my daughters
My backbone
And my shoulders
Made them strong
Women.

Society created monsters
Stereotypes reigned
I took my rightful place
Eyes clear and back straight
Valiant.

I stood
And I spoke
Shattered a fallacy
Me, I have agency
Emancipation
(Cheechoo, 2017a)

~

On turning back to reconciliation: I am obligated to return again and again to the concept of reconciliation. I turn back to reconciliation because my parents are survivors of IRS. My spirit reminds me about my responsibilities to every survivor and the collective pain they share due to Indian Residential Schools. Reconciling trauma is a difficult space to toil in because the potential for triggering or re-victimizing people is very real.

I am still working with reframing reconciliation. As Wilson (2008) reminds me, I am answerable to all of my past, present, and future relations.

Ethical relationality, or the act of being responsible for what we bring into any space with us, is critical. It is also critical to remember that as educators we have agency to leave life's stressors at the school doors, but our students cannot help but carry their traumas into classrooms with them. It is my hope that by sharing my lived experiences and poetry, I have (re)ignited readers' personalized decolonization. *Meegwetch*.

DISCUSSION QUESTIONS

1. Does this chapter challenge you to view or speak to reconciliation through different lenses?

2. What have you taken up to support the ongoing process of reconciliation?

GLOSSARY

intergenerational trauma: "Usually seen within one family in which the parents or grandparents were traumatized, and each generation of that family continues to experience trauma in some form ... Direct survivors of these experiences often transmit the trauma to later generations when they don't recognize or have the opportunity to address their issues. Over the course of time these behaviours, often destructive, become normalized within the family and their community, leading to the next generation suffering the same problems" (Crisis & Trauma Resource Institute, n.d.).

Meegwetch: Expression of gratitude (i.e., thank you), Cree spelling.

sq*aw: As a Cree woman, I have reclaimed this word. In spaces beyond the one I have created for my poetry, it is offensive, violent, and pejorative to use.

Wachiye: A greeting (i.e., hello), Cree spelling.

FURTHER READINGS/WEBSITES

Acoose, J. (1995). *Iskwewak—Kah' Ki Yaw Ni Wahkomakanak: Neither Indian princess nor easy squaws*. Toronto, ON: Women's Press.

Crisis and Trauma Resource Institute. (n.d.). Intergenerational trauma, healing, and resiliency. Para. 9. Retrieved on November 25, 2019 from https://ca.ctrinstitute .com/blog/intergenerational-trauma.

264 Decolonizing and Indigenizing Education in Canada

Glesne, C. (1997). That rare feeling: Re-presenting research through poetic transcription. *Qualitative Inquiry, 3*(2), 202–221.

Ralstin-Lewis, D. (2005). The continuing struggle against genocide: Indigenous women's reproductive rights. *Wicazo SA Review, 20,* 1.

Tuck, E., & Yang, K. W. (2012). Decolonization is not a metaphor. *Decolonization: Indigeneity, Education, & Society, 1*(1), 1–40.

Tupper, J. A. (2014). The possibilities for reconciliation through difficult dialogues: Treaty education as peacebuilding. *Curriculum Inquiry, 44*(4), 469–488.

REFERENCES

Anderson, K. (2011). Native women, the body, land, and narratives of contact and arrival. In H. Lessard, R. Johnson, & J. Webber (Eds.), *Storied communities: Narratives of contact and arrival in constituting political community* (pp. 146–167). Vancouver, BC: UBC Press.

Barker-Benfield, C. (1977). *Sexual surgery in late-nineteenth-century America.* New York, NY: Vintage Books.

Cairney, R. (1996). "Democracy was never intended for degenerates": Alberta's flirtation with eugenics comes back to haunt it. *Canadian Medical Association Journal, 155*(6).

Carey, A. (1998). Gender and compulsory sterilization programs in America: 1907–1950. *Journal of Historical Sociology, 11*(1), 74–105.

Caulfield, T., & Robertson, G. (1996). Eugenic policies in Alberta: From the systematic to the systemic? *Alberta Law Review, 34*(1), 59–79.

Cheechoo, K. (2016). I'll (not) be home for Christmas. *The Fulcrum.* University of Ottawa.

Cheechoo, K. (2017a). Agency. *Northern Ontarian Innovative and Indigenous Poetics.* Contemporary Verse 2: The Canadian Journal of Poetry and Critical Writing.

Cheechoo, K. (2017b). Feral. *Northern Ontarian Innovative and Indigenous Poetics.* Contemporary Verse 2: The Canadian Journal of Poetry and Critical Writing.

Cheechoo, K. (2017c). Leave. *Northern Ontarian Innovative and Indigenous Poetics.* Contemporary Verse 2: The Canadian Journal of Poetry and Critical Writing.

Cheechoo, K. (2017d). Systemic squaw. *Northern Ontarian Innovative and Indigenous Poetics.* Contemporary Verse 2: The Canadian Journal of Poetry and Critical Writing.

Corntassel, J., & Holder, C. (2008). Who's sorry now? Government apologies, truth commissions, and Indigenous self-determination in Australia, Canada, Guatemala, and Peru. *Human Rights Review, 9,* p. 466.

Crisis and Trauma Resource Institute. (n.d.). Intergenerational trauma, healing, and resiliency. Para. 9. Retrieved on November 25, 2019 from https://ca.ctrinstitute .com/blog/intergenerational-trauma.

Donald, D. (2009). Forts, curriculum, and Indigenous Métissage: Imagining decolonization of Aboriginal-Canadian relations in educational contexts. *First Nations Perspectives, 2*(1), 1–24.

Gadgil, M., Berkes, F., & Folke, C. (1993). Indigenous knowledge for biodiversity conservation. *Ambio, 22*(2/3), 75–91.

Grossboll, D. (1980). Sterilization abuse: Current state of the law and remedies for abuse. *Golden Gate University Law Review, 10*, 1152–1153.

Indigenous and Northern Affairs Canada. (2016). About the independent inquiry. Retrieved from https://www.rcaanc-cirnac.gc.ca/eng/1470140972428/1534526770441?wbdisable=true#chp2

Kovach, M. (2009). *Indigenous methodologies: Characteristics, conversations, and contexts.* Toronto, ON: University of Toronto Press.

LaDuke, W. (2005). Foreword. In A. Smith, *Conquest: Sexual violence and American Indian genocide* (pp. xv–xviii). Cambridge, MA: South End Press.

Littlewood, T. B. (1977). *The politics of population control.* Notre Dame, IN: University of Notre Dame Press.

Mitchell, H. (2013). *Bush Cree storytelling methodology: Northern stories that teach, heal, and transform.* Vernon, BC: Charlton Publishing.

Radek, G. (2011). Confusion reigns over number of missing, murdered Indigenous women. *CBC News.* Retrieved from http://www.cbc.ca/news/politics/mmiw-4000-hajdu-1.3450237

Ralstin-Lewis, D. (2005). The continuing struggle against genocide: Indigenous women's reproductive rights. *Wicazo SA Review, 20*, 1.

Royal Commission on Aboriginal Peoples (RCAP). (1993). *Ethical guidelines for research.* Ottawa, ON: Author.

Simpson, L. (2000). Anishinaabe ways of knowing. In J. Oakes, R. Riew, S. Koolage, L. Simpson, & N. Schuster (Eds.), *Aboriginal health, identity and resources* (pp. 165–185). Winnipeg, MB: Native Studies Press.

Simpson, L. (2014, March 4). Not murdered and not missing. *Voices Rising.*

Smith, B., Ng-A-Fook, N., Berry, S., & Spence, K. (2011). Deconstructing a curriculum of dominance: Teacher education, colonial frontier logics and residential schooling. *Transnational Curriculum Inquiry, 8*(2).

Tupper, J. (2012). Treaty education for ethically engaged citizenship: Settler identities, historical consciousness and the need for reconciliation. *Citizenship, Teaching & Learning, 7*(2), 143–156.

Truth and Reconciliation Commission of Canada (TRC). (2015). *Truth and Reconciliation Commission of Canada: Calls to Action.* Retrieved from https://nctr.ca/assets/reports/Calls_to_Action_English2.pdf

Wilson, S. (2008). *Research is ceremony: Indigenous research methods.* Black Point, NS: Fernwood Publishing.

CHAPTER 15

The Future for Indigenous Education: How Social Media Is Changing Our Relationships in the Academy

Taima Moeke-Pickering

SITUATING SELF

Kia Ora, greetings. My name is Taima Moeke-Pickering, I am a Māori of the Ngati Pukeko and Tuhoe tribes from **Aotearoa** (New Zealand). I am a Full Professor in the School of Indigenous Relations at Laurentian University, where I teach courses on Indigenous research methodologies, international Indigenous issues, and Indigenous pedagogies. I have lived in Sudbury, Canada, for 12 years. Over the last three years, I have been working with a research team on social media big data analysis and reframing Indigenous and women empowerment activism using social media analytics.

INTRODUCTION

Digital technology is framed as the future for all socio-economic engagement, politics, and education. The powerhouses of digital technology will control educational content, price, data analytics, pace, and power. If left unchecked, the technology sphere will remain colonized and we must, as Indigenous educators, seek to decolonize technology. The good news is, like our Indigenous ancestors, we too can learn to adapt to the world around us. This includes the technology world. Indigenous peoples (including youth) have picked up the use of digital technology very quickly. Many Indigenous peoples must master this technology as a means to communicate, strengthen cultural networks, and seek connections that matter for Indigenous communities and education. I contend that technology powerhouses will control education and academia (if they haven't done so already) and assert that Indigenous educators position their educational agenda to integrate knowledge and skills in the digital world.

Maintaining a decolonization and indigenizing lens in the academy is not easy. Why? Under colonization, Indigenous peoples were viewed (still are) as degenerative savages stuck in a primitive condition (Youngblood Henderson, 2008). Christians, saviours, and overeager helpers found Indigenous peoples as the ideal candidates for fixing (Youngblood Henderson, 2008). They still do. The general framework for colonization is rooted in modernity, science, and progress maintained by legal order. Framing Indigenous as primitive maintains the colonial order. A decolonial and indigenizing lens assists with debunking and disrupting colonial myths. A decolonial and indigenizing lens provides us with answers to what is possible, what is our potential, how we get there, and how we should get there. Therefore, a decolonial and indigenizing lens assists to ensure that digital technology does not leave Indigenous education behind or become further entrenched under the many layers of colonization.

As Indigenous academics, it is our utmost responsibility to write forward as a means to centre a decolonial and indigenizing standpoint. We must keep writing to future Indigenous academics, students, and allies if we want to sustain a decolonial positionality in the academy. They rely on us to provide solutions, to inspire them when they are tired and distraught, and to provide them with a set of tools for thinking outside the colonial box. The aim is to advance a critical scholarship and to show them how to interrogate complexities relevant to decolonization and indigenization. Frantz Fanon infers that colonization is violent (1963), and Freire (1970) says that it is racist and oppressive, so we must be prepared to infect and infiltrate systems creatively while at the same time protesting loudly for change. Sometimes that means kicking the door down when it is locked shut. This requires emotional strength and sources of support. It is no easy feat and there is no romantic version. It is a labour of love if you want to advance Indigenous education. How do we transform the world around us so that we maintain a rightful place for Indigenous peoples in the arena of education? This chapter outlines ideas to sustain Indigenous space, resistance, and reconciliation contextualized in the digital technology environment.

INDIGENOUS FUTURISM THROUGH STORYING

Our ancestors implanted in our traditional teachings a map to frame the future. It is up to us to analyze their teachings and to navigate our way forward (Buck, 1994; Nabigon, 2006; National Indian Brotherhood, 1972; Rangihau, 1981). Indigenizing the academy means reclaiming the way our traditions inform our future. This includes the way we communicate with each other, the way we form relationships and meaning, and the way we write. Indigenous storying empowers Indigenous authors to situate their worldviews, theoretical frameworks, and aspirations for self-determination. Storying embraces the past and provides a map that can be drawn upon for the present and the future. Indigenous storying is both a decolonial and indigenizing strategy that dismantles and weakens hegemonic and racist academic pedagogies, theories, and methodologies (Moeke-Pickering, 2010).

Indigenous storying empowers its descendants to imagine, create, and understand the world around them. Storying situates and connects us to our origins and enables us to transcend our visions (Rangihau, 1981). My ancestor **Irakewa** was a **matakite**/seer. He used the power of his dreams to find a home for his descendants. They traversed the Pacific Ocean, using his dream and directions as a guide. They left **Hawaiki** (an island in the Pacific) over 600 years ago to find their home in Aotearoa, New Zealand. Irakewa told his people of three things he had seen in his vision: There is a land far away that is a good place for you to go to; there is a waterfall at that place and a cave in the hillside for **Muriwai**; and the rock standing in the river is myself. True to Irakewa's vision, his descendants led by Toroa, my great-ancestor, landed the **Mataatua** voyaging canoe in that exact place in the town now known as **Whakatane**. What this story and many Indigenous stories impart to us is that we have the power of imagination and trust; therefore it is up to us to navigate and traverse what is possible.

The digital world too relies on what is imaginable, what is possible, and what will engage people. Technology is moving forward at a fast pace. In the era of technologies, being fast is vital. Concepts, software, and digital tools are moving quickly to secure positionality in the business, political, health, and educational worlds. Companies like Amazon, Facebook, and Apple are designing the trends for education. For example, Apple has been working on transitioning MacBooks and iPads into educational tools for the classroom. Facebook has facilitated the harvesting of data analytics. Amazon sells textbooks and educational materials. Trending among Indigenous peoples is a technological emergence in Indigenous education and politics (Carlson, 2013; Duarte, 2017; Felt, 2016; Moeke-Pickering, Cote-Meek, & Pegoraro, 2018; Molyneaux et al., 2014). Whether it is called data sovereignty, Indigenous big data analysis, or visual arts, Indigenous educators are adapting to futuristic innovation. Futuristic envisioning is a part of our Indigenous DNA and worldview. Our Indigenous worldview allows us to see into the future and adapt the Indigenous education agenda accordingly.

Indigenous peoples have shown the world their ability to adapt, and we are good at it. Indigenous youth are adept at using technology. They use phones, the internet, iPads, Google Docs, and computers at school. The next generation of Indigenous university students will be tech-savvy. The new frontier for Indigenous education is digital technology. We as educators need to ensure that technology assists us with Indigenous education and be open to utilizing technology in our pedagogies, teaching, and research.

INDIGENOUS EDUCATION AND SOCIAL MEDIA

The use of social media has become a medium for Indigenous activism (Carlson, 2013; Carlson, Jones, Harris, Quezada, & Frazer, 2017; Duarte, 2017; Duarte & Vigil-Hayes, 2017; Felt, 2016; Moeke-Pickering et al., 2018; Molyneaux et al., 2014). Social media disrupts the dominant colonial and patriarchy voice, their worldview and control. There is an increase in Indigenous educators engaging social media such as Facebook, Twitter, podcasts, and Instagram (to name a few) to bring awareness and analysis to key Indigenous issues. For example, Indigenous movements use Twitter to amplify their voices, such as those espoused by the most popular hashtags: #trc, #mmiw, #indigenousrising, #idlenomore, #treatyrights, #noDAPL, and #walkingwithoursisters, to name a few. A hashtag (#) is a metadata tag used on social media sites to identify messages on a specific topic. Moeke-Pickering and colleagues (2018) assert that protest hashtags are becoming a norm to assert Indigenous self-determination and to create a rallying space for activism (p. 5). Indigenous educators use their own social media accounts to post messages about their research, their programs, key issues they support, and/or their insights. Likewise they tweet, retweet, or share hot topics they endorse, thereby engaging in educating and facilitating discussions on Indigenous issues.

Many Indigenous educators distrust the academic policies and systems that are supposedly there to represent them. Through social media engagement, they seek support, ideas, and endorsement among their followers

(Carlson, 2013; Carlson et al., 2017; Duarte, 2017; Duarte & Vigil-Hayes, 2017; Felt, 2016; Moeke-Pickering et al., 2018; Molyneaux et al., 2014). Positive reinforcement from likes, retweets, and shares highlights hot topics and key messages and confirms what is meaningful and valued. Those who use social media play a vital role in bringing awareness to Indigenous issues framed from an indigenizing and decolonizing worldview. Informing the political landscape using social media is becoming a key driver for portraying Indigenous issues quickly. Indigenous social media users provide swiftness in disseminating information, strengthen ties among the like-minded, and increase interactions with the world. In this regard, they are teaching beyond the classroom and now reaching out to the world.

Indigenous educators are also using podcasts, Ted Talks, and op-eds to convey their worldviews, reaching beyond the restricted academic borders. While this is a great opportunity to reach wider audiences, for some Indigenous academics, social media activities are not credited within the three promotion criteria consisting of teaching, research, and academic duties. Indigenous educators are advocating that their op-eds, podcasts, and other forms of social media usage be viewed as relevant, peer-reviewed activities. Their readership often reaches thousands of users, often beyond just those who read their articles, journals, or books. Reaching a wider audience through social media activities should be valued as a legitimate way in which academics are accessing readership and potential peers directly. For promotion purposes, digital platforms should be counted as a legitimate scholarly activity.

Social media activism informs indigenizing and decolonizing practices and approaches and strengthens conversations for making a difference (Carlson, 2013; Carlson et al., 2017; Duarte, 2017; Duarte & Vigil-Hayes, 2017; Felt, 2016; Moeke-Pickering et al., 2018; Molyneaux et al., 2014). Digital platforms and technology have the potential to disrupt the stronghold of colonized education.

INDIGENOUS INNOVATION: DISRUPTING EDUCATIONAL BIASES THROUGH SOCIAL MEDIA

Being an innovator is a must when working in the academy. Knowing how budgets and institutional planning work is critical to situate Indigenous programs. Being able to forecast student and faculty numbers, enrollment projections, and possible innovative ideas is a good skill to have. My experience as both a faculty member and Director (Chair) showed that often we are shut out from real decision-making, the real budget (not the one we are asked to give suggestions for), appointments (the ones we really want and need), and promotion. Like many of my Indigenous colleagues, we are sought after to problem solve, teach the culture (really, really fast), and imagine ways to increase Indigenous enrollments (again, really, really fast). For many of us who have held leadership positions in the academy, you really have to imagine, respond, and think quickly, sometimes in a New York minute. There is enormous pressure to situate the Indigenous programs as sustainable and viable. As the Director, defending Indigenous programs was my 100 percent job. Other than it being a labour-intensive job, one in which we all rise to the occasion, I must say that my heart broke on a number of occasions due to academic and inequitable pressures on Indigenous programs. I get that there are fiscal responsibilities in the academy, but the "one-size-fits-all" model is racist and oppressive. I often announced loudly and with a strong tone that the level field is different for oppressed groups, so why are Indigenous programs expected to give up the few resources they were given in the first place? Depleting Indigenous resources is, in my experience, always the first move when in a fiscal hole. Goals of social justice and reconciliation often take a backseat. There is a labour of love associated with sustaining Indigenous programs. This often means working later, looking for funding outside the university, and being innovative to survive. Sadly, this effort can be misconstrued: "they are so innovative that they do not really need that budget anyways." Leadership and being innovative are synonymous with sustainable Indigenous education.

In order to disrupt educational biases, I recommend employing social media activities. To survive in a fiscally constrained academic system, we have to be creative. I am an avid social media user. I use Twitter and Facebook daily to communicate with others, to read up on posts, and/or to advocate where necessary. I encouraged my peers in our program to also use social media, namely Twitter and Facebook, to reach potential students, to market our programs to relevant communities, and ultimately take back control of our stories, experiences, and our adventures. Our School's faculty and staff enrolled in a number of digital workshops to increase our skill sets, as well as encouraged our students and alumni to co-share their stories and experiences with us and to others. We learned that with a laptop and internet connection, we can reach people around the world. Along the way, we became creative at sharing our events, using relevant pictures and cultural aspects in our content, became entrepreneurial about our program and needs, and, indeed,

Chapter 15 | The Future for Indigenous Education **273**

used digital platforms to indigenize our readership. By becoming tech-savvy and mastering digital media, we increased our community and student engagement as well as branded our programs to the world. We increased our networks, allies, and enrollments as a result of digital media outreach.

Here is what I often say when talking forward to academia: I see amazing opportunities for Indigenous programs. We are Indigenous; it is our job to think outside the box. We don't fit in where sometimes—actually, most times—we are not wanted. We ensure that our students find the best opportunities, whether it be in graduate programs, research, jobs, or field placements, by thinking creatively and advocating hard. We can connect through every type of social media there is now; it is free and most of the students are on them now. For example, Moeke-Pickering and colleagues (2018) highlighted the volume of conversations that the #noDAPL hashtag had with its readership. Using SYSOMOS Map, a big data analytical tool, our research found that the #noDAPL hashtag had over 13.3 billion users and 23.5 million users who interacted on social media between August 2010 and June 18, 2017 (Moeke-Pickering et al., 2018, p. 6). #noDAPL is a protest movement against the Dakota Access Pipeline, and activists have been protesting the construction of this pipeline since 2014. This movement was created by a 17-year-old Indigenous girl and a small group of youth who wanted to protect their lands and waterways because they held cultural significance to the Lakota Nation and other communities downstream from the proposed pipeline. Simply, these youth wanted the best for their community. By using social media, they brought their issues and concerns to the attention of the world. We might have many of these youths in Indigenous programs and who might see themselves as part of changing the world. We must, and can, form the united front that makes Indigenous education matter for families and communities. Indigenous faculty and students have the potential to be leaders for their communities.

INDIGENOUS MENTORING IN THE ACADEMY

Mentoring is critical in the digital world. There is a dark side to digital technology and social media usage. That is, it also attracts negative users. So while there is an upside to digital usage, it is important to mentor Indigenous users about how to protect themselves when being cyberbullied, receiving hate, harassment, and hurtful, racist, and traumatic threats (Carlson et al., 2017). The colonization and vilification of Indigenous peoples continue in the digital world, so it is vital that proper training and support are provided to Indigenous colleagues, peers, and students. Carlson and colleagues (2017) share that these experiences can be traumatic and emotionally and psychologically scarring for Indigenous peoples. Felt (2016) reminds us that sustaining a sense of community and creating a space for emotional reflexivity can ensure the necessary solidarity to sustain long-term action. Therefore, Indigenous mentorship in the digital tech world is absolutely vital.

Indigenous mentorship is important because, as Indigenous educators, we work tirelessly to decolonize and indigenize the academy. We need mentors who confirm the importance of our academic research, cultural values and traditions, programs and projects, and leadership. As an Indigenous woman educator and mentor, I choose to live my life in a good way, by learning the language and culture, being respectful to the land and the environment, and ensuring my politics and sense of social justice are in alignment. As Indigenous educators, the mentorship we can offer is support, encouragement, and connections, and to plant seeds in the hope they will grow and flourish.

Indigenous education is political, it is beautiful, and it is our right. We find ourselves constantly expected to fix up the past, make sure colonization does not repeat itself in education, and ensure that our research findings minimize poor health outcomes, as well as align our cultural practices for teaching in the educational context (Cote-Meek, 2014). This is a huge responsibility and commitment. My experience when working with Indigenous educators is that we take our role seriously. We use instinct, we defend when we need to, we are creative, we spend a lot of time on the whys, we use diplomacy and often put our own feelings aside to make sure Indigenous goals are achieved. I have been lucky enough to have elders and senior colleagues who mentored me throughout my career in the academy. My educational style and approach are stronger as a result of being mentored by Indigenous colleagues and being supported by academic mentors. As the digital and social media descend upon us, it is very important to be surrounded by Indigenous mentors.

CONCLUSION

Currently, there are only a few articles on the impacts of digital technology and social media for Indigenous education, showing that this area is still being explored. It is highly likely that digital tech will influence education, and Indigenous educators must be at the forefront early as opposed to trailing innovations in the academy. This chapter is an attempt to inspire Indigenous educators to look at digital technology as a potential tool for teaching, research, and administrative leadership. Why is this important? A decolonial and indigenizing framework helps us to navigate the maze of racism and colonial assaults. Our power to re-imagine what the world should be, and how we connect those imaginations with like-minded others, will help us to sustain Indigenous education and worldviews in the academy. Digital technology and social media usage plays a mobilizing role in Indigenous self-determination, traditional sharing and storying, and collective activism. Indigenous peoples are posting, tweeting, sharing, and interacting with one another online. The future of Indigenous education can benefit from being tech-savvy and incorporating this skill and knowledge as part of planning, envisioning, and teaching. Being digital tech-savvy is one way of slowing down the impact of colonization in academia, as well as providing the necessary mechanisms for reaching our communities and peers, to recruit top-level Indigenous academics, and to ensure Indigenous education flourishes.

DISCUSSION QUESTIONS

1. What digital technology and/or social media training do you have at your university?

2. What are ways that you might indigenize or decolonize digital technology or social media usage?

3. What might be the benefits of digital technology for your Indigenous programs, research, pedagogies, and administrative activities?

4. What safety planning would you recommend for Indigenous peoples who use digital and social media?

5. How can you sustain traditional storying in the digital technology world?

GLOSSARY

Aotearoa: The traditional name of New Zealand.
Hawaiki: The eponymous homelands of the Polynesian peoples (an island in the Pacific Ocean).
Irakewa: The name of a Polynesian ancestor.
Kia Ora: A Māori greeting, meaning to wish you wellness.

Mataatua: The Polynesian voyaging canoe that landed in Aotearoa around 1350 AD.

matakite: A seer/the ability to forsee.

Muriwai: The name of a female chief who came on the Mataatua voyaging canoe.

Whakatane: The name of a beach town in the Bay of Plenty, Aotearoa.

FURTHER READINGS/WEBSITES

Any cyber security training at your university or your place of work.

Any social media policies at your university or place of work.

ASPER School of Business Executive Education, University of Manitoba. Training on social media marketing: Engaging your stakeholders through social media. http://umanitoba.ca/faculties/management/exec_programs/digital-marketing-analytics.html

Indigenous Corporate Training Inc. A blog for those working effectively with Indigenous peoples. Engaging via social media. https://www.ictinc.ca

Professional Development Institute, University of Ottawa. Training on social media and public services—An introduction. https://www.pdinstitute.uottawa.ca

REFERENCES

Buck, P. (1994). *The coming of the Maori*. Wellington: Whitcombe & Tombs.

Carlson, B. (2013). The "new frontier": Emergent Indigenous identities and social media. In M. Harris, M. Nakata, & B. Carlson, (Eds.), *The politics of identity: Emerging indigeneity* (pp. 147–168). Sydney: University of Technology Sydney E-Press.

Carlson, B., Jones, L. V., Harris, M., Quezada, N., & Frazer, R. (2017). Trauma, shared recognition and Indigenous resistance on social media. *Australiasian Journal of Information Systems, 21*, [1570]. doi:10.3127/ajjs.v21i0.1570

Cote-Meek, S. (2014). *Colonized classrooms: Racism, trauma and resistance in post-secondary education*. Halifax, NS: Fernwood Publishing.

Duarte, M. (2017). Connected activism: Indigenous uses of social media for shaping political change. *Australasian Journal of Information Systems, 21*, [1525]. doi:10.3127/ajis.v21i0.1525

Duarte, M. E., & Vigil-Hayes, M. (2017). #Indigenous: A technical and decolonial analysis of activist users of hashtags across social movements. *Media Tropes eJournal, 7*(1), 166–184.

Fanon, F. (1963). *The wretched of the earth*. Broadway, NY: Grove Press.

Felt, M. (2016). Mobilizing affective political networks: The role of affect in calls for a national inquiry to murdered and missing Indigenous women during the 2015 Canadian federal election. Paper presented at SM Society '16, July 11–13, 2016, London, United Kingdom. doi:10.1145/2930971.2930978

Freire, P. (1970). *Pedagogy of the oppressed*. London, UK: Penguin Books.

Moeke-Pickering, T. (2010). Decolonisation as a social change framework and its impact on the development of Indigenous-based curricula for helping professionals in mainstream tertiary education organisations. PhD thesis, University of Waikato, Hamilton, New Zealand. Retrieved January 15, 2018, from https://hdl.handle.net/10289/4148

Moeke-Pickering, T., Cote-Meek, S., & Pegoraro, A. (2018). Understanding the ways missing and murdered Indigenous women are framed and handled by social media users. *MIA Media International Australia*, 1–11. doi:10.1177/1329878XI8803730

Molyneaux, H., O'Donnell, S., Kakekaspan, C., Walmark, B., Budka, P., & Gibson, K. (2014). Research in brief: Social media in remote First Nation communities. *Canadian Journal of Communication, 39*, 275–288.

Nabigon, H. (2006). *The hollow tree: Fighting addiction with traditional Native healing*. Montreal, QC: McGill-Queen's University Press.

National Indian Brotherhood. (1972). *Indian control of Indian education*. Ottawa, ON: Author.

Rangihau, J. (1981). Being Maori. In M. King (Ed.), *Te Ao Hurihuri: The world moves on aspects of Maoritanga* (pp. 171–184). Auckland: Longman Paul.

Youngblood Henderson, J. S. (2008). *Indigenous diplomacy and the rights of peoples: Achieving UN recognition*. Saskatoon, SK: Purich Publishing.

CONTRIBUTOR BIOGRAPHIES

Avril Aitken is a settler scholar working in traditional, unceded Abenaki Territory, at the School of Education of Bishop's University. Through her teaching, she involves future educators in discussions and action related to how their professional practice will promote equity and justice—particularly in the face of the ongoing effects of colonialism.

Dr. Trudy Cardinal is a Cree/Métis educator from northern Alberta. As Associate Professor in the Elementary Education Department of the University of Alberta, she is dedicated to continuing to deepen understanding of the educational experiences of Indigenous children, youth, and families. Of particular interest is the potential of Indigenous and relational pedagogies in the creation of an education system that honours the whole being of the learner.

Dr. Keri Cheechoo is a Cree Iskwew from the community of Long Lake #58 First Nation. Keri seeks to share the missing histories, and the intergenerational and contemporary impacts of colonial violence on Indigenous women's bodies, as a part of her commitment to the educational and reconciliation process toward Indigenizing school curricula.

Dr. Sheila Cote-Meek is Anishinaabe from the Teme-Augama Anishnabai and is the Vice-President, Equity, People and Culture at York University. She is the former Associate Vice-President, Academic and Indigenous Programs at Laurentian University. A leader in Indigenous education, Dr. Cote-Meek has focused on bringing about systemic changes that attend to equity, diversity, and inclusion in post-secondary education.

Dr. Michelle Coupal (Algonquin/French) is Canada Research Chair in Truth, Reconciliation, and Indigenous Literatures, and Associate Professor in the Department of English at the University of Regina.

Mary Ellen Donnan is a Sociology Professor at Bishop's University on Abenaki Territory, specializing in how social and structural inequalities in Canadian society cause homelessness. She is a person of settler identity raised in Treaty 6 Territory in Saskatchewan who has resided, over her life thus far, in five different provinces of Turtle Island.

280 Contributor Biographies

Chantal Fiola is Red River Métis from Manitoba and is the author of *Rekindling the Sacred Fire: Métis Ancestry and Anishinaabe Spirituality*. Dr. Fiola is Assistant Professor in the Urban and Inner-City Studies Department at the University of Winnipeg and is undertaking a SSHRC-funded research study exploring Métis relationships with ceremony in Manitoba Métis communities.

Candace Kaleimamoowahinekapu Galla, Kanaka Maoli from Hawai'i Island, is Associate Professor at the University of British Columbia in the Institute for Critical Indigenous Studies (Faculty of Arts) and the Department of Language and Literacy Education (Faculty of Education). Her research and scholarship focus on Hawaiian language and Indigenous languages at the intersection of education, revitalization, digital technology, well-being, traditional and cultural practices, and policy and planning; and decolonizing and Indigenizing the academy to create pathways for Indigenous thinkers and scholars and scholarship—locally, nationally, and globally.

Emily Grafton (Métis Nation) is the Executive Lead, Indigenization at the University of Regina, Saskatchewan, where she lives with her husband and two children. Her work concerns critical discourse analysis of settler colonialism, as well as the decolonization and Indigenization of colonial structures.

Dr. Marc Higgins is Assistant Professor in the Department of Secondary Education at the University of Alberta and is affiliated with the Faculty of Education's Aboriginal Teacher Education Program (ATEP). As a settler scholar, his work centres the concept of educational response-ability to analyze how Eurocentrism, whiteness, (neo-)coloniality, and modernity come to shape the (in)ability to respond to ways-of-knowing (i.e., epistemology) and ways-of-being (i.e., ontology), such as Indigenous science or ways-of-living-with-Nature.

Amanda Holmes is Kanien'keha:ka (Mohawk) on her mother's side, Highland Scottish on her father's side. She grew up in the Hudson River Valley of New York. She has had her Clan returned to her. She is Turtle Clan. She recently graduated with her Doctorate in Language Reading and Culture at the University of Arizona's College of Education.

Arlo Kempf is a Settler Canadian and Assistant Professor in the Department of Curriculum, Teaching and Learning at the Ontario Institute for Studies in Education of the University of Toronto. He researches race, whiteness, and settlerhood in education.

Dr. Lynn Lavallee is Anishinaabe Métis registered with the Métis Nation of Ontario. She is a full professor in the School of Social Work and Strategic Lead, Indigenous Resurgence in the Faculty of Community Services at Ryerson University.

Shauna MacKinnon is Associate Professor and Chair in the Department of Urban and Inner-City Studies at the University of Winnipeg. Her research interests and pedagogical approach are inspired by a passion for social and economic justice.

Dr. Brooke Madden is Assistant Professor within the Aboriginal Teacher Education Program and the Department of Secondary Education at the University of Alberta. She works to acknowledge both her Indigenous (Wendat, Iroquois, Mi'kmaq) and settler (French, German, Irish, English) ancestries in complex ways that honour her relations, while acknowledging privilege and resisting appropriation of traditional knowledges and experiences that are not her own.

Jean L. Manore is a settler scholar who focuses on the history of Treaty relations in Canada, most particularly Treaty 9. She is also interested in the shaping of technological development by the natural environment and the history of heritage and commemoration.

Dr. Patricia D. McGuire is Anishinaabe Wiisaakadekwe. She is affiliated with Bingwi Neyaashi Anishinaabe, although she has community connections at Kiashke Zaaging Anishinaabe. A consistent theme throughout her work has been the creation of respectful frameworks for the inclusion of Anishinaabe knowledge(s) in broader academic, social, and political contexts.

Jérôme Melançon, a settler on Treaty 4 land, is Associate Professor in the French and Francophone Intercultural Studies program at the University of Regina. His recent work in political philosophy focuses on reconciliation and on Francophone communities, as well as on democracy and anti-colonialism in French and Canadian philosophy.

282 Contributor Biographies

Dr. Taima Moeke-Pickering is a Māori of the Ngati Pukeko and Tuhoe tribes. She is a full professor in the School of Indigenous Relations at Laurentian University where she teaches courses on Indigenous research methodologies, international Indigenous issues, and United Nations and Indigenous social work. She has extensive experience working with international Indigenous communities, evaluative research, big data analysis, and photovoice methodologies.

Brett Pardy is a doctoral candidate at McGill University and an instructor at the University of the Fraser Valley (UFV). He draws on his background in history, cultural studies, and media to explore the affective potential of film's ability, when combined with a setting inductive of transformative learning, to engage non-Indigenous students in discussing difficult issues around decolonization and Canadian racism.

Dr. Linda Pardy is the Associate Dean of Students, College of Arts at the University of the Fraser Valley (UFV) in BC. UFV is actively engaged in Indigenization and is recognized as a leader for their work in this area. Dr. Pardy, along with the university's Senior Advisor on Indigenous Affairs Shirley Hardman, facilitates faculty development workshops—helping faculty and administrators from various BC institutions to embrace decolonization and reshape their approach to curriculum, campus spaces, and teaching and learning.

Celeste Pedri-Spade, PhD, is an Anishinabekwe researcher and artist from Lac des Mille Lacs First Nation and is Associate Professor at Laurentian University. She currently serves as the inaugural Director of the Maamwizing Indigenous Research Institute, and her area of research expertise includes the relationship between Indigenous arts and decolonization.

Fiona Purton is a doctoral candidate at the Ontario Institute of Studies in Education at the University of Toronto. In the last two decades, she has worked as a middle school teacher and research assistant and taught in multiple Bachelor of Education programs across Canada. Her interests include pedagogies that bridge theory and practice in teacher education and foster teacher candidates' awareness of their responsibilities as Treaty partners.

Contributor Biographies **283**

Bryanna Rae Scott is a Métis woman originally from Fort Frances, Ontario. She is employed at Lakehead University as the Indigenous Educations Programs Coordinator in the Faculty of Education and also teaches part-time in the Department of Indigenous Learning. She is a doctoral candidate in Education.

Dr. Evelyn Steinhauer is an agent for change in the advancement of Indigenous Education. Born in Alberta, and a member of the Saddle Lake Cree Nation, Dr. Steinhauer completed her undergraduate degree with Athabasca University, and a Masters of Education and a PhD at the University of Alberta through the Department of Educational Policy Studies, where she specialized in Indigenous Peoples Education. Her enthusiasm for Indigenous education extends into her roles as Associate Professor (Department of Educational Policy Studies) and Director of the Aboriginal Teacher Education Program (ATEP) at the University of Alberta.

Dr. Noella Steinhauer is Plains Cree from the Saddle Lake Cree Nation in northeastern Alberta and Assistant Professor in Educational Administration and Leadership in the Department of Educational Policy Studies at the University of Alberta. Dr. Steinhauer has held various leadership roles, in addition to having more than ten years of experience as a secondary classroom teacher. Throughout her career, she has remained focused on the improvement of Indigenous student success. Her research interests include: leadership, First Nation school leadership, Indigenous ways of knowing, and collaborative leadership. She continues to maintain a high level of interest in policy, First Nation education, and the Cree language.

Dr. Patricia Steinhauer is a member of the Saddle Lake Cree Nation #125 in Treaty 6 Territory. She is Assistant Professor in the Aboriginal Teacher Education Program and the Department of Educational Policy Studies at the University of Alberta. Patsy's research remains focused on Indigenous Intelligences and standards embodied in our Indigenous-language contexts.

Dr. Sandra Styres is a Tier II Canada Research Chair in Iethi'nihsténha Ohwentsia'kékha (Land), Resurgence, Reconciliation and the Politics of Education, and Assistant Professor with the Department of Curriculum, Teaching and Learning at the Ontario Institute of Studies in Education.

284 Contributor Biographies

She has served two terms as Chair of the Dean's Advisory Council on Indigenous Education and is currently Co-Chair of the Deepening Knowledge Project.

Misty Underwood is a non-enrolled descendant of the Muscogee Creek and Choctaw Nations of Oklahoma. Misty is currently a doctoral candidate in Educational Policy Studies at the University of Alberta.

Dr. Angelina Weenie is Associate Professor at First Nations University of Canada, Indigenous Education. She is Plains Cree from Sweetgrass First Nation.

Angela Wolfe (MEd) is a member of the Ermineskin Cree Nation in Maskwacis, Alberta. She is currently the Associate Director of the Aboriginal Teacher Education Program (ATEP) within the Faculty of Education at the University of Alberta. With expertise in teacher education, she works to insure the ATEP experience for pre-service teachers is one that is rich with nurturing mentorship. She advocates healing through education from the historical relationship of education of Aboriginal people of Canada for all students and in all classrooms. As part of the ATEP team, she supports and encourages ATEP students in multiple layers to assist them in their journeys to reaching their dream and goal of being educators.

INDEX

Abenaki, 203, 205

Aboriginal Teacher Education Program
(ATEP), 73–74

academia
attitude towards Indigenous knowledges in, xviii–xix, 61, 123–124,
146–147, 167
colonizing force of, 52
current interest in decolonization and
reconciliation, 117–118
current state of decolonization in,
120–121
developmental gap in ability to decolonize, 229–233
exclusionary practices of, 54–55, 58–59
experience as Indigenous faculty member of, 271–272
and funding for indigenization, xix,
128–129, 166, 271–272
hierarchy of knowledges in, 123–124
hiring of Elders in, 122–123, 143
and identity politics, 124–125
inappropriateness of aim of reconciliation for, 120
increasing Indigenous academic staff,
127–128
and Indigenous faculty, xvii–xviii, xix,
127, 199
IT as possible model of decolonization
for, 63–65
movement towards Indigenization
within, 122–123, 142–145, 160–161
offering mandatory Indigenous courses
as cover for real change, 182–183
partnerships with Indigenous leaders,
203, 204, 205
pitfalls of attempts at decolonization,
145–147, 161–162
and push for more Indigenous students,
143–144

racism in, 120, 121
reconciliation in, 107–108,
117–118, 123
shortfalls of Indigenization in, 143,
145–147
as site of colonization, xv–xvi
soft and radical decolonization in,
195–196
suggestions for indigenizing, 127–129,
147–148
tokenism in, 120–121, 127
and transformational change in, xvii–xx
and UIC's commitment to Indigenization, 162–163, 164–168
See also education

academic aunties, 108–109

advisory circles, 145–146, 163

agency, 260–262

Anishinaabe
ability to survive on the land, 24–25
colonialism towards, 25–27
importance of stories to, 28–29
knowledge of viewed by settler society,
27–28
land-centred concepts, 19
and performance autoethnography, 95
and Robinson-Superior treaty, 23–24
as teacher assessing her job, 92–93
women's responsibilities for land,
22–23
and word for truth in, 215
worldview, 28–29
writing of, 20–22

Antone, Eileen, 126

assimilationist views, 197, 198

Association of Canadian Deans of Education
(ACDE), 160, 179

asterisking of Indigenous Peoples, 105,
110, 161

Australia, 218–219, 223n2

286 Index

Barton, Bradley, 253

Battiste, Marie, 126

Bebonang, Susan, 24

Benjamin, Akua, 123

Bishop's University

    barriers to decolonization reform at,
197–199

    beginning of Indigenization at, 194–195

    research into decolonizing, 196–197

    response to limited decolonization,
200–202

    response to relational decolonization,
202–203

    results of research into decolonization
reform, 204–205

Blackbird, Harry, 10

Boushie, Colten, 255, 259

Burning in This Midnight Dream (Halfe), 216

Campbell, Maria, 44

Canada, Government of, 23, 25–27, 179,
213, 219

Cardinal, Bob, 73–74, 80

ceremonies, 165–166, 167, 203

child welfare, xiv, 26, 119

circlework, 10, 73–74, 84–85, 89

climate change, 14

cluster hiring, 161

cognitive imperialism, 58, 66–67

colonial logics, 199, 206

colonization/colonialism

    of academia, xv–xvi, 55, 120–121

    and academia's response to
reconciliation, 107–108

    decontextualization of, 104–105

    definitions, 129, 137, 149

    and demeaning of Indigenous peoples,
xiv–xv

    effect of on perception of Indigenous
content course, 185–187

    Euro-Canadian students reaction to
learning about, 181–182

    and hierarchy of knowledges in
academia, 123–124

    how it blocks decolonization, 141–142

    Indian Act as, 26

    and Indigenous knowledges, 138

    Indigenous Peoples asked to educate
non-Indigenous on, 240–241

    and injustice, 102–104

    internalized, 158

    its control of decolonization, 162

    its reinscription through
Indigenization, 146

    and land rights, xiv

    and neoliberal funding schemes,
198–199

    relationship of Indigenous epistemology
to, 138

    and structural violence, 101–102

    teaching of, 220

    through religion, 119–120

    toward Anishinaabe, 25–27

    violence from, 93–94, 98–99, 105–107

comfortable diversity, 232–233, 240

Community Education Development
Association (CEDA), 166

conscientization, 161

conservation, 14

cooptation, 146, 149

Cote-Meek, Sheila, 123–124

Cree, 203, 205

critical pedagogy, 158–159, 169

critical race theory, 157, 169

crocus, 5

cultural appropriation, 231, 236, 241

culture camps, 7–11

curricula

    changes to due to TRC, 179, 180

    changes to include Métis history in,
37–39

    Indigenous content v. infusion model
debate, 128

    Métis plea for culturally relevant, 41–43

    ridicule of Indigenous, 257

    UIC's progressive, 164

    as way of addressing reconciliation,
220–221

Dakota Access Pipeline, 273

Daniels v. Canada, 36, 39

decolonization

of assessment, 77, 81–82

barriers to at Bishop's University, 197–199

Bishop's University research into, 196–197, 204–205

as complex process, xvi

control of by colonization, 141–142, 162

current state of in academia, 117–118, 120–121

definitions, 129, 138, 232

described, 135–136

developmental gap in ability for, 229–233

in education, 32

examples of false approaches to, 237–239

experience of running workshops in, 239–240

explaining process of, 141–145

and funding problems, 198–199

and future of digital technology, 267–268

history of at UIC, 163–165

how it can go wrong, 136, 145–146

importance of land rights to, 159, 162

and Indigenous content course given to teacher-trainers, 181–188

IT as possible model for, 63–65

IT methodology for, 52–54

notable work of Indigenous scholars on, 126–127

pitfalls of academia's attempts at, 145–147, 161–162

response at Bishop's University to limited, 200–202

response at Bishop's University to relational, 202–203

role of Euro-Canadian settlers in, 144–145

soft and radical versions of, 195–196

spaces for, 145, 200

through media activism, 271

and transformational learning, 240–242

typology of, 195–196

at UIC, 157, 163–165

in undergraduate class, 233–237

and white fragility, 237

decontextualization, 104–105

Department of Urban and Inner-City Studies (UIC), 156–159, 163–168

digital technology

aim of decolonizing, 267–268

dark side of, 273–274

speed of change in, 269–270

used to advance Indigenous education, 270–271, 272–273, 274–275

Dish with One Spoon, 177, 189

domination, 139, 149

Dumont, Jim, 75, 215

dyscalculia, 251

education

changing the nature of assessment, 76–82

fear in, 82

as focus of TRC's calls to action, xi, 175–176, 179–180, 193, 229

future hope for, 125

and land-based learning, 14

Métis statistics on, 46n1, 46n2

plea for culturally relevant curricula, 41–43

recommendations from TRC on, 37–38, 39

and reconciliation of Métis through, 36–39, 44–45

residential schools compared to higher, 55

and structural violence, 101–102

student self-assessment, 83–86

teaching reconciliation in, 32, 219–222, 257

See also academia; curricula; Indigenous education

288 Index

Elders
    bringing into classrooms, 220
    definition, 130
    as guide for undergraduate class,
      234, 235
    hiring of in academia, 122–123, 143
    and reform at Bishop's University, 203
    relationships with pre-service
      teachers, 82
    at UIC, 159, 166
    used in Indigenous content course, 183
emancipation, 139–140, 141–142, 149, 165
epistemology. *See* Indigenous knowledges
Ermine, Willie, 126
ethical relationality, 258–259, 263
ethical spaces, 258
ethnostress, 251, 255
Euro-Canadian settlers. *See* settler society
Eurocentrism, 195, 206

feeling unsafe, 93
felt knowledge, 137, 216
First Nations University of Canada, 7
Fitznor, Laara, 126
Fontaine, Tina, 255
Ford, Doug, 222n1

gender equilibrium, 23
Gladue, Cindy, 253
Great Law of Peace, 177, 189

Halfe, Louise Bernice, 216
Harper, Stephen, 123
Harper, Vern, 117, 123
heterodox economic theories, 157, 169
Howard, John, 219

ICR (Indigenous Course Requirement),
  162–163, 166–168
identity politics, 124–125
Indian Act, xv, 26, 139
Indigenization
    of academia, 122–123, 142–145,
      160–161

    advisory circles, 145–146, 163
    at Bishop's University, 194–195
    definition, 130, 149
    described, 135–136, 141
    explaining process of, 142–145
    funding for in academia, xix, 128–129,
      166, 271–272
    and hiring Indigenous for faculty posi-
      tions, 166–167
    how it can go wrong, 145–146
    as Indigenous project, 231–232
    possible downside of, 136
    and religion, 160
    and report *Principles on Indigenous Ed-*
      ucation, 193
    shortfalls in academia, 143, 145–147
    as something more than comfortable
      diversity, 232–233
    suggestions for academia on, 127–129,
      147–148
    UIC's commitment to, 162–163,
      164–168
Indigenous activism, 164–165, 270–271, 273
Indigenous Advisory Circle (IAC), 163
Indigenous content course at southern On-
  tario university, 181–188
Indigenous Course Requirement (ICR),
  162–163, 166–168
Indigenous Cultural Alliance (ICA), 195, 206
Indigenous education
    academia's aggressive push for students
      of, 143–144
    adapting classroom techniques for,
      83–86
    effect of teachers on, 183
    experience as literary resource teacher/
      librarian in, 259–260
    experience teaching undergraduate,
      233–237
    making digital technology a part of,
      267–268
    mandatory courses offered in as cover
      for real change, 182–183
    and mentoring, 273–274

and *Principles on Indigenous Education* report, 193, 197
questioning the value of assessment in, 79–81
students response to limited reform at Bishop's University, 200
at UIC, 157, 164–165
use of self assessment in, 83–86
use of social media to advertise, 272–273, 274–275
and UW's implementation of Indigenous Course Requirement, 162–163

Indigenous knowledges
academia's attitude towards, xviii–xix, 61, 123–124, 146–147, 167
Anishinaabe's worldview, 19, 28–29
being coopted, 146
debased, xv, 238
examples of scholarly work done in field of, 126–127
honouring languages as way to acknowledge, 3–4
how Anishinaabe's is viewed by settler society, 27–28
IT's program to promote, 53–54, 61–62
left out of school assessment, 78, 79
level of interest in at Bishop's University, 203
personal experience studying in, 125–126
relationship to colonialism, 138
relationship to Indigenization, 142
stories as, 6, 137
when academia classes as culture, 146–147

Indigenous languages
acknowledging of, 3–4
importance of to speakers, 74, 76
minimizing, 74, 80
presence of on campus, xx
research on, 53
response to at Bishop's University, 201

Indigenous Peoples
ability to adapt to digital world, 270
asked to educate non-Indigenous on colonization, 240–241
asterisking of, 105, 110, 161
definition, xii
effect of school assessment on, 77–79
on faculty of academia, xvii–xviii
how academia has excluded, 54–55
and identity politics, 124–125
importance of own language to, 74, 76
learning disabilities of, 251
making digital technology for them, 267–268
population of, 45n1
racialized constructions of, xiv–xv
right of sovereignty for, 212
seen as victims, 221
understanding of teaching and learning, 74–76
and University of Arizona, 55–56
wariness of claims of decolonization, 162
See also Anishinaabe; colonization/ colonialism; Indigenous knowledges; Métis/Métissage; stories

Indigenous Thinkers (IT)
and Arizona's racist laws, 56
asserting Indigenous epistemologies, 61–62
decolonization methods of, 52–54
development of critical consciousness at UA, 57–59
formed, 52
methods used to achieve goals, 62–63
as possible model for decolonization, 63–65
as safe haven for Indigenous students, 59–61

infusion model, 128
intention, 12
intentional act, xv, 93
interculturalism, 137, 144, 149
intergenerational trauma
at Bishop's University, 199
described, 55, 67, 206–207

290 Index

intergenerational trauma (*continued*)
experience of, 248–249, 252, 255–256
experience of in students, 259
explained, 263
reconciling of, 262–263
See also residential schools
internalized colonization, 158

Kinder Morgan Trans Mountain Pipeline, 213
Kinunwa, Lionel, 74, 75
knowledges. *See* Indigenous knowledges

Lake Superior, 20–21
Lakehead University, 162
land
Anishinaabe women's responsibilities
for, 22–23, 24–25
and Anishinaabe worldview, 19
learning from, 5–7
protocols, 20
tie to Indigenous women's bodies, 253
University of Arizona's use of
Indigenous, 55–56
land rights, xiv, 159, 162, 212–215
land-based learning, 7–9, 11–14
Laroque, Emma, 126
Lavallee, Barry, 121
Lavallee, Bea, 10
Lavalley, Jacquie, 123
layered text, 110
leaders/leadership, xix–xx
learning circles, 10
listening circles, 89
literacy, 79–80
lived experiences, 83

medicine camp, 11–13
mentoring, 143, 183, 201, 241, 273–274
Métis/Métissage
assumptions and judgements made
about students, 40–41
educational statistics for, 46n1, 46n2
history of, 31
identity of, 33–36
plea for culturally relevant curricula,
41–43

population of, 45n1
and reconciliation, 36–39, 44–45
and treaties, 212
mindfulness, 259–260
mining, 25
missing and murdered Indigenous women,
253
Morrisseau, Norval, 20, 21, 28
multiculturalism, 219, 232

Naskapi Nation of Kawawachikamach
(NNK), 203, 205
Native Access Program (NAP), 251
nature deficit disorder, 9
Neil-Kumiga, Theresa, 235
neocolonial state, 121
neoliberalism, 193, 198–199
New Zealand, 223n2
#noDAPL hashtag, 273
non-Indigenous teachers and students
blocks put up to avoid decolonizing by,
237–239
developmental gap in ability to
decolonize, 229–233
experience giving course on
reconciliation to, 257–259
experience teaching Indigenous course
by, 233–237
guilty of tokenism, 236
opposition to Indigenous content from,
xvi, 167–168, 220
reaction to Indigenous content course,
181–188
ridiculing Indigenous curricula, 257
teaching ICRs, 167
transformative learning by,
240–242
unfamiliarity with Indigenous content,
219–220
See also academia; settler society

Ontario, Government of, 26, 44–45, 222n1
oppression, 139, 149
oral exams, 81, 83
oral history, 20–22
other, the, xv, 240

Index **291**

palatable Indian, 124–125
pedagogy of place, 157
pedagogy of resistance, 157
pedagogy of witness, 221–222, 224
performance autoethnography, 94–107, 110
performative response, 236
place, importance of, 4, 5
poems
    Agency, 260–262
    Feral, 256–257
    I'll (Not) Be Home for Christmas,
      249–250
    Leave, 247–248
    prairie lily, 5
    Systemic Squaw, 253–255
poetic inquiry, 248, 252
post-colonialism, 138
prairie lily, 5
Principles on Indigenous Education (report),
  193, 197
Project of Heart, 220

racism
    in academia, 120, 121
    of Arizona's recent legislation, 56–57
    Bishop's University data on, 199
    and culture camps, 11, 13
    experience confronting, xii
    experience growing up with, 251–252
    and negative attributes of Indigenous
      Peoples, xiv
    See also colonization/colonialism
reconciliation
    academia's current interest in, 107–108,
      117–118, 123
    an individual gives up hope on, 255, 257
    and Bishop's University research into
      decolonization, 197
    in the classroom, 32, 219–222, 257
    connection to truth, 217–218
    co-opted by settler society, 217–219
    definitions of, 118, 150
    and ethical witness, 221–222
    experience giving course on to teacher
      trainers, 257–259
    as fluctuating concept, 140–141

    issues which obscure, 211–212
    meanings of, 216–217
    of Métis through education, 36–39,
      44–45
    moves made by Ontario government
      towards, 44–45
    reframing of, 262–263
    religious connection to, 118–120,
      216–217
    and UNDRIP, 213–215
    as viewed by Truth and Reconciliation
      Commission, 160, 250
    See also Truth and Reconciliation
      Commission of Canada (TRC)
Red Pedagogy, 186–187
redress, 213, 222, 224
religion, 118–120, 160, 201, 216–217
residential schools
    and culture camp, 8
    effect of, xv
    experience of, 119
    as genesis of TRC, 179
    higher education compared to, 55
    as part of curriculum, 220–221
    survivors testimony at TRC, 216
    See also intergenerational trauma
resurgence, 140, 142, 150
Reynolds, Margaret, 11
Right to the City, 158, 170
Robinson-Superior treaty, 23
rock paintings, 20, 21–22
Royal Commission on Aboriginal Peoples
  (1996), 117, 179–180, 250

sacred pipe ceremony, 165–166
safe spaces, 145, 200, 258
Saskatchewan Indigenous Student
  Council, 143
settler anxiety, 181
settler society
    and co-opting of reconciliation, 217–219
    and decontextualization of
      colonization, 104–105
    defined, 67, 137, 150
    how Anishinaabe knowledges are
      viewed by, 27–28

292 Index

settler society (*continued*)
 and Indigenization, 146
 responsibility for reconciliation on, 158
 role in decolonization and
  indigenization, 144–145
 their version of truth, 215–216
 and white amnesia, xiii
 and white fragility, 230, 237
 See also academia; non–Indigenous
  teachers and students
Shirt, Pauline, 123
Silver, Jim, 163
Sinclair, Murray, 125
Skead, Alex, 108
smudging, 101, 234, 236, 237
social activism, 164–165, 270–271, 273
social justice, 57, 126, 164–165, 272, 274
social media, 270–275
South Africa, 218, 223n2
sovereignty, 212, 218, 270
speech acts, 182, 214, 216, 217
spirituality, 5, 9, 21–22, 76
sterilization, forced, 252
stories
 Anishinaabe, 20–22, 28–29
 as examples of performance
  autoethnography, 94–95
 as felt knowledge, 137
 as force for empowerment, 269
 knowledge passed on through, 6
 as part of Indigenous pedagogy, 237
 and pedagogy of witness,
  221–222
 and truth, 215
structural transformation, 158
structural violence, 101–102, 111
sweetgrass, 12

tokenism
 in academia, 120–121, 127
 defined, 150
 hiring Elders as, 122
 instead of substantive change, 146
 interculturalism mistaken as, 144
 non-Indigenous teacher guilty of, 236

too bad, so sad syndrome, 221, 224
Traditional Knowledge Holders, 122, 130, 166
 See also Elders
transformational change, xvi–xx, 118, 230
treaties, 33, 38, 212, 220
Trudeau government, 213
truth, xiii, 215–216, 217–218
Truth and Reconciliation Commission of
 Canada (TRC)
 collected truth of, 216
 and current interest in by academia,
  117–118
 described, 207
 effect of its calls to action on education,
  xi, 175–176, 179–180, 193, 229
 findings of, 160
 need of to include UNDRIP, 213, 215
 and performance autoethnography,
  94–98
 and push for mandatory Indigenous
  courses in academia, 182
 quote from that resonates, 257
 recommendations from on education,
  37–38, 39
 response to at Bishop's University, 198
 as spur for creation of Indigenous
  content course, 175, 179
 view of reconciliation in, 250
 and witnesses at, 222

UIC. *See* Department of Urban and
 Inner-City Studies (UIC)
United Nations Declaration on the Rights of
 Indigenous Peoples (UNDRIP), 213–215
Universities Canada (UC), 193, 207
University of Arizona (UA), 55–56, 57
University of Winnipeg (UW), 158–159,
 162–168

*Waniska: An Awakening of Indigenous
 Knowledge* (video), 10–11
Weenie, Archie, 5
white amnesia, xiii
white fragility, 230, 237
willow bundles, 12–13